Advance Praise for
CHILDREN OF A MODEST STAR

"The clarity in this analysis of the world governance system is truly powerful—it's a major contribution to our shared cognitive map of where we are now, and how we got here. Moving beyond diagnosis in a way that one hopes for but doesn't always see, Jonathan S. Blake and Nils Gilman make specific and practical suggestions for action. This fills an urgent need of our time, which is for plans that can be put to use right now. Many books are important—this one is, I think, crucial."

—**KIM STANLEY ROBINSON**, author of *The High Sierra:*
A Love Story and *The Ministry for the Future*

"As intellectually resourceful as it is ambitious, *Children of a Modest Star* cuts cleanly through the obsolete assumptions that stultify much thinking about the present and future. It offers, in our paralyzing moment of polycrisis, a bold and bracing account of what we can still do."

—**PANKAJ MISHRA**, author of *Age of Anger: A History of the Present*

"Jonathan S. Blake and Nils Gilman are willing to face down the challenge of getting specific about planetary governance while avoiding the specter of world government. They offer real ideas for how inhabitants of the planet can govern ourselves at multiple scales, in ways that really could enable us to survive and thrive."

—**ANNE-MARIE SLAUGHTER**, CEO of New America, and author of
Renewal: From Crisis to Transformation in Our Lives, Work, and Politics

"What would governance look like if our planetary condition was central rather than ancillary to our culture and politics? This is the question posed by the thought-provoking *Children of a Modest Star*. Our current systems of governance, premised on sovereign states, are fundamentally misaligned with the scale of the planetary problems we face. The solution, Jonathan S. Blake and Nils Gilman suggest, is to develop a set of content-specific, task-oriented institutions at a variety of levels of governance, and to do this quickly, before it is too late."

—NAOMI ORESKES, co-author of *The Big Myth: How American Business Taught Us to Loathe Government and Love the Free Market*

"As an Earth scientist, I've been frustrated by the world's inability to prevent climate catastrophe. National governments cannot handle threats that transcend their boundaries, and existing international bodies lack the power to compel change. *Children of a Modest Star* defines institutions that can deal with the problems we face that, like climate change, require governance from local to planetary scales. This book is a great conversation starter."

—KATE MARVEL, senior climate scientist at Project Drawdown

"Jonathan S. Blake and Nils Gilman have written an extraordinarily important and much-needed book. The world faces any number of vexing, potentially catastrophic planetary challenges, which our current governing practices and institutions are ill-suited to meet. Deeply researched and sharply argued, *Children of a Modest Star* explains why our current institutional architecture is inadequate, and lays out a bold, forward-thinking, but plausible, agenda to develop a new conceptual lens to generate the governing practices, processes, and policies we desperately need. This book could not be timelier."

—FRANCIS J. GAVIN, author of *Nuclear Statecraft: History and Strategy in America's Atomic Age*

Children
of a
Modest
Star

Children of a Modest Star

Planetary Thinking for an Age of Crises

Jonathan S. Blake AND Nils Gilman

STANFORD UNIVERSITY PRESS

Stanford, California

Stanford University Press
Stanford, California

Printed in the United States of America on acid-free, archival-quality paper

Library of Congress Cataloging-in-Publication Data
Names: Blake, Jonathan S., author. | Gilman, Nils, author.
Title: Children of a modest star : planetary thinking for an age of crises / Jonathan S. Blake and Nils Gilman.
Description: Stanford, California : Stanford University Press, 2024. | Includes bibliographical references and index.
Identifiers: LCCN 2023034594 (print) | LCCN 2023034595 (ebook) | ISBN 9781503637856 (cloth) | ISBN 9781503639072 (ebook)
Subjects: LCSH: Environmental protection—International cooperation. | Environmental policy—International cooperation. | Global environmental change—International cooperation. | International organization. | Subsidiarity. | Nation-state.
Classification: LCC JZ1324 .B53 2024 (print) | LCC JZ1324 (ebook) | DDC 363.7—dc23/eng/20230824
LC record available at https://lccn.loc.gov/2023034594
LC ebook record available at https://lccn.loc.gov/2023034595

Cover design: Lindy Kasler
Cover photograph: Unsplash

For Ari, Ezra, Daphne, Pico, and Io

How hard it is to set aside
Terror, concupiscence and pride,
Learn who and where and how we are,
The children of a modest star,
Frail, backward, clinging to the granite
Skirts of a sensible old planet,
Our placid and suburban nurse
In SITTER's swelling universe,
How hard to stretch imagination
To live according to our station.

—W. H. Auden, "New Year Letter"

Contents

Preface

After nearly a decade of conversations about the inadequacies and outright failures of contemporary governance structures around the world,
we finally picked a date to start writing this book: Monday, January 4,
2021. At the time, we couldn't have known it was going to be such an
inauspicious—or was it auspicious?—week to begin work on the mala-
dies of existing systems of governance. But that week the ramifications
of our crumbling governance institutions hit especially close to home.

Come Monday morning, one of us was ill—thankfully, not too
badly—with COVID-19. The other was trying to work at home while
also watching after his toddler, who was frolicking around the house
after positive COVID tests shut down his daycare. Neither condition
was exactly conducive to writing. Then on Wednesday morning, Pacific
time, armed insurrectionists stormed the United States Capitol in an
attempt to overturn the results of the 2020 presidential election. The
unwelcome distractions notwithstanding, it was incredible—in the
most literal sense—to begin a book about the failures of our institutions
of governance at a precise moment when those failures were so visible
and visceral. The consequences of the inability of those foundering
institutions—nation-states, international organizations, local govern-

ments, and the like—to govern effectively and legitimately had irrupted through our doorposts, was pulsing through one of our bodies, and was erupting in a minor rebellion in the "world's oldest democracy."

This book, while not a direct response to the events of that week, was written in the shadow of these and other institutional bumblings, bunglings, and breakdowns. It reflects our sense that the entire structure for governing the planet is not up to the task, that the broad system is structurally incapable of addressing the most urgent concerns of the present and future. Our institutions are unfit for the scope and scale of problems, and authority is maldistributed. And while resources, political capital, and democratic attention are frequently wasted, the problems we are facing don't wait. In the time it took us to write this book, concentrations of atmospheric carbon dioxide continued to tick up, millions of people worldwide died in a still-evolving pandemic, and some untold number of species went extinct during Earth's ongoing sixth mass extinction event. What is to be done?

The answer that we come to—a reconstructed governance architecture for the planet, or "planetary governance," guided by the principle of planetary subsidiarity—is not meant to provide a quick fix. If realized, it will represent a thorough structural transformation of the means of governance from the largest scale, the planet itself, to hyperspecific, localized scales. Building this system will be no easy task. We don't expect political leaders to embrace our ideas immediately or comprehensively.

At the same time, this book isn't about how many angels can dance on the head of a pin. We have not set out to write some "kind of hopelessly utopian ideal political theory [that] orients us toward an ideal regime that has no likelihood of being brought into being," as the imaginative democratic theorist Hélène Landemore puts it.[1] We do not start from abstract assumptions or presume a blank slate from which we can construct a society of transcendental beauty, one that attains perfect peace, perfect justice, perfect health, and abundance for all.[2] We work with politics and the planet as we see them—warts and all. Yes, we push things further than they are currently willing to go, and critics will likely place us, with Landemore's good company, "in the camp of . . . utopian and hopeless dreamers."[3] So be it. We present here a vision, a new sense of what might be possible and what we believe is needed. *Children of a Modest Star* is our sketch of what planetary governance should be and how it should be institutionalized.

The world today is in desperate need of reform, but offering practical ideas for incremental change, while important and necessary, is not our endeavor. The pages that follow are not a white paper or a policy report, and you won't find nuts-and-bolts recommendations for immediate next steps. Our task is to provide a conceptual lens to reframe the challenges of today and tomorrow and jolt readers' political imaginations. The institutional structures that we advocate are, we believe, good ones, but they are also a provocation, a shot across the bow meant to set off productive, forward-looking debates. There's certainly more to be said and alternative institutional schemas to propose that take seriously humankind's planetary condition. We need as much inspired inventiveness as we can get, for we as a species have a tremendous task ahead: building political and governance institutions befitting the immensely exciting and terrifying new knowledge that we have about the planet and our place in it.

Los Angeles
July 2023

Children
of a
Modest
Star

Introduction

Who and Where and How We Are

The COVID-19 pandemic ranks among the deadliest pandemics in human history, which as of March 2023 had infected hundreds of millions, officially causing nearly seven million human deaths, with estimates of the true total of excess deaths running to more than twice that.[1] What started in Wuhan in the late fall of 2019 became within weeks a major global event. The pandemic was, however, more than just an event in global history—that is, the human history of global connections, in politics, economics, culture, and science. It was also an event in biological history. As an episode in the history of life on Earth, the pandemic had many faces. It marked a significant moment in the coevolution of *Homo sapiens* and viruses and sparked a rash of evolutionary adaptations of SARS-CoV-2 as it branched into more and more variants. This evolutionary perspective places the pandemic in a different light than the perspectives to which we are accustomed—the perspectives offered by the histories of globalization, of modernity, or even of agriculture, the rise of which twelve thousand years ago prompted the emergence of many of humankind's major infectious diseases.[2]

The lens of biology offers synchronic perspectives as well, helping us see the pandemic not just as an episode in biological time but as an event experienced simultaneously by living beings across the planet. SARS-CoV-2 doesn't care about Linnean distinctions between species. As long as the virus's "spike" protein fits with a cell's ACE2 receptor, it eagerly enters and infects the host. Cats, civets, and Caribbean manatees are just three of the many mammals that have ACE2 proteins similar enough to those of humans, and SARS-CoV-2 has charged ahead in all of them.[3] The pandemic manifested, in other words, as a multispecies event.[4]

The virus also touched the biosphere via its impact on human behavior. Responding to fear and government mandates, humans across the globe retreated to their homes, briefly taking up a little less space on the planet. Other species noticed. To the wild goats of Wales and the cougars of Chile, the sign that something was different was the sudden absence of human beings and their loud and lethal technologies of transportation.[5] Skies cleared. Asphalt arteries emptied. Rambunctious urban centers turned quiet, temporarily becoming open spaces for other creatures to explore, stalk through, or flutter by. This momentary human confinement registered as an event in the history of the biosphere.[6]

A larger, longer perspective comes from observing the pandemic through the biogeochemical history of Earth. To the global network of scientific sensors that record and make knowable this history, the sign that something dramatic was underway registered in changes to the planet's atmospheric chemistry. In late February 2020, for instance, satellite imagery revealed an abrupt decline in nitrogen dioxide pollution— caused by cars and industrial production—in the air over China. The pollutant's decline began over Wuhan, the first city locked down, but spread across the country, following the spread of lockdowns.[7] Additional observation showed that the human reactions to the pandemic in the first half of 2020 resulted in a sudden 8.8 percent reduction in global carbon dioxide emissions from the year before. SARS-CoV-2 did what no well-meaning climate policy has yet been able to achieve, causing "the largest ever decline in emissions."[8] It proved to be only a blip on the seemingly inexorably increasing Keeling Curve—a graph displaying the concentration of atmospheric carbon dioxide, measured continuously since 1958—but it was nonetheless a telling episode in Earth history.

To protect human health and human life from a virus that measures no more than 140 billionths of a meter, societies undertook "among history's largest exercises in state power," shutting themselves down and locking in two and a half billion people—acts of social sacrifice and individual quarantine and isolation that added up to have planetary-scale impacts on the Earth's atmosphere.[9] The COVID-19 pandemic revealed both the discordant perspectives and the profound interconnections between three histories distinguished by the eminent scholar Dipesh Chakrabarty: "the history of the planet, the history of life on the planet, and the history of the globe made by the logics of empire, capital, and technology."[10]

A perspective shift reveals our placement in the deep histories of biology and the planet, laying bare our inseparable interconnection with those histories and all that emerges from them. Adopting these perspectives, moreover, has tremendous implications for how we should live together and manage our collective lives—that is, how we should govern ourselves.

The problems posed when events of biological or geological scale pierce the defenses of governance on a human scale were on dazzling display during the COVID-19 pandemic. The existing global governance system turned out to be unable to stop COVID-19's lethal spread. While the scientific capacity to understand the nature of viral infection has improved exponentially since Old World viruses devastated the New World over the long sixteenth century, the capacity of our global political system to control the spread of a pandemic disease has scarcely improved at all. At the same time, the globalization of our economic system has only accelerated the rate at which viruses can proliferate. Whereas the Black Death took eight years to march from Kyrgyzstan to Crimea in the 1330s and 1340s and the 1918 influenza took three months to move from Kansas to Europe, SARS-CoV-2 spread from Wuhan to Europe and North America within three weeks, causing public health system meltdowns and thousands of deaths in Lombardy and New York.[11]

If one looks at the system of global governance for pandemic response, it becomes clear why, despite our vastly improved understanding of the science of viruses, we were collectively unable to respond in a way that could prevent the virus from becoming a planet-wide health catastrophe. The present global system of governance was developed during the twentieth century to facilitate the integration and interaction of national states, especially around economic cooperation and international peace and security. It was and is designed, therefore, to represent the interests of its member national states in international forums. It is fundamentally *not* geared toward addressing planetary challenges like pandemics. Nor does this apply only to pandemic response: for many of the most pressing challenges that we now face, the existing structures of governance are simply not fit for purpose. Our governance institutions are not attuned to the deep murmuration of the planet—nor are they prepared for the inescapable consequences.

What would governance look like if our planetary condition was central rather than ancillary to our political self-conceptions? What issues would become paramount, and how might this change our views?[12] How would we act if we took seriously humanity's profound integration into Earth's planetary systems, demonstrated by the COVID pandemic, from the microbiological scale of the virus to the macrosystemic scale of the planet's atmosphere? What would change as a result of human beings being revealed, not as masters of the planet, but as part of it?[13]

───────

Human beings are essentially and ineluctably embedded within planetary-scale phenomena: we affect and are affected by our Earthly home. Western science, which is the bedrock of modern technology, politics, and worldviews, however, emerged in large measure in denial of this embeddedness. Springing from a secularized distillation of Christian belief ("And God said, Let us make man in our image," according to King James' Genesis, "and let them have dominion . . . over all the earth"), this scientific tradition rested on the precept that humans were inherently different from all of God's other creatures. Unlike the beasts, the "fowl of the air," and "every thing that creepeth upon the earth," humankind was endowed with reason and a capacity, if not moral duty, for technical mastery over the natural world—a unique inheritance that set us humans apart from nature. Yet the scientific method that developed over time from those precepts—a method of inquiry rooted in the scrutiny of evidence and radical skepticism—has, by the early twenty-first century, revealed that there is no separation between human beings and the natural world. In a triumph of the scientific method, the tools of science overturned science's most basic assumptions. This insight has been percolating for about a century, catching the attention of the occasional forward-thinking scientist, but it is now increasingly clear that the idea of humans distinguished from nature is intellectually unsustainable. It is, moreover, ecologically ruinous. The idea of "humanity apart" is, and for a long time has been, encouraging grave harm to the ecosystems in which humans dwell and the biosphere of which humans are a part.

These discoveries have changed the face of science and, in turn, have triggered a rupture in philosophy. But these insights about the state of the world and our place in it have yet to trickle out of the scientific labs, specialist journals, and rarified seminar rooms and into the mainstream consciousness. They certainly have not yet affected how societies *act*. With this book, we hope to change that. Given what we now know—and are likely to still learn—about Earth and the place of humans on it, the question that animates this book is: What should we do about it?

Our answer is that we must transform our modes and systems of *governance*, which is to say the institutionalized social rules that tell us how we are supposed to live in common.[14] Governance is typically understood to happen through law and government—and the government of sovereign national states in particular. But governance operates

at many levels and comes in many forms. Subnational political institutions (like city and state/provincial governments) set rules for their
jurisdictions, as do many nonstate actors (like firms, nongovernmental
organizations, and religious institutions). Global governance institutions, such as the United Nations, the UN Framework Convention on
Climate Change, and the World Health Organization, work to manage
global issues. This system of multilevel governance—with subnational
governments expected to take care of local issues like garbage collection or street cleaning, the national government setting the basic legal
framework for the society as a whole and managing macroeconomic
matters, and multilateral, global governance institutions managing relations between national states and matters that require international
cooperation—has, since the end of World War II, become, more or less,
the model for how governance happens around the world.

The reigning structure of multilevel governance is no longer adequate to the challenges of our current age, an age that some scholars
have come to refer to as *the Planetary*. The concept of the Planetary is
one that has emerged over the last several decades from the work of
scientists, especially Earth system scientists and biologists, as well as
philosophers, particularly philosophers of science. At the heart of the
idea of the Planetary is a holistic vision of the planet as consisting of
an almost infinitely complex interlaced and nested array of dynamically interacting biological, chemical, energetic, and geological systems. This concept, in turn, is informed by new knowledge of the place
and role of human beings within this vast system. At the macrocosmic
scale, we now know that human activity is deeply interconnected with
atmospheric chemistry and Earth's climate and geology; at the micro-
cosmic scale, discoveries about the human microbiome have revealed
our deep entanglement with bacteria and other microorganisms, one
that affects our very mental states, that supposed hallmark of human
distinctiveness and autonomy.[15]

This emerging and rapidly expanding body of knowledge is bringing
forth what we call *planetary sapience*—that is, a technologically enabled
self-understanding of the planet and its deeply systemic interconnect-

edness.[16] Human beings, like all other creatures, have of course always been embedded in this system of systems, existing in a position of codependency with them. Indeed, virtually every traditional religion and indigenous epistemology has emphasized this embeddedness, and the need to respect and sustain our "Mother Earth."[17] What has changed over the last few centuries, and especially over the last few decades, is that a rapidly expanding techno-scientific apparatus of measurement devices and computing has enabled an understanding of the nature of the embeddedness to a degree of detail and precision that before was literally unimaginable. Planetary sapience is the product of the rapidly expanding array of sensors in, on, and over the Earth—continuously monitoring everything from temperature to moisture to chemical compositions to deforestation—as well as the algorithms and supercomputers that organize these data and scrutinize them to detect overarching patterns, abnormalities, and changes in individual ecosystems and the planet as a whole.

An increasingly precise understanding of how the Earth system operates and how its subsystems interoperate is one of the greatest scientific achievements of all time. So vast is the scale of this new knowledge and the new perspective it offers that it has enabled—indeed necessitates—a fundamental rethinking of the human place on the planet. Planetary sapience has already revealed that the unintended consequences of human actions have remade and continue to remake the biogeochemical conditions that have thus far sustained our flourishing here. After such knowledge, we must reckon with our ways of being if we want to keep the planet habitable for ourselves, our descendants, and all the other living beings that call this rocky sphere home.

Unfortunately, growing planetary sapience has so far mainly revealed wreckage rather than redemption. It has made us exquisitely aware of the planetary challenges we face: climate change, pandemic diseases, stratospheric ozone depletion, atmospheric aerosol loading, space junk, growing antibiotic resistance, biodiversity loss, anthropogenic genetic disruptions, declining soil health, upended nitrogen and phosphorus cycles, freshwater depletion, ocean acidification, oceanic plastics—and maybe even emerging technologies with terraforming potential, like bioengineering and artificial intelligence. By one widely respected measure, human activity (or more accurately, *some* humans' activity) has breached six of nine quantified "planetary boundaries," potentially pushing Earth beyond the "safe operating space for humanity."[18] To achieve planetary sapience is to realize that humans can no longer treat the planet as an endless font of resources or a bottomless sink for waste. Above all, planetary sapience uncovers *the condition of planetarity*, the inescapability of our embeddedness in an Earth-spanning biogeochemical system—a system we now know is undergoing severe disruptions from the relative planetary stability of the previous twelve millennia. The condition of planetarity is and always has been an ontological fact—that is, a verifiable, empirical statement about our place inside the planet's biogeochemical feedback systems—even if it has only recently been disclosed by planetary sapience (enabled by an assemblage of planetary-scale technologies of perception). Together, these two concepts mean that humans are capable of understanding the damage that we are doing to ourselves when we damage the planetary systems that we are a part of and that sustain us. Appreciating the condition of planetarity entails an unflinching embrace of the fact that humans cannot thrive unless the ecosystems we inhabit are themselves thriving.

From this condition of planetarity flows the ethical through line of this book: our governance institutions must promote *habitability* in order to enable *multispecies flourishing*. The idea of habitability stands in contrast to the concept of "sustainability" that guides much of global governance today, in particular as embedded in the United Nations' Sustainable Development Goals, which have been at the heart of the international system's economic development and environmental governance strategies over the last decade.[19] Whereas the sustainability concept implicitly if not explicitly suggests that nature be seen and treated as something separate from humans, a standing reserve of resources and "ecosystem services" to be managed and responsibly harvested for human benefit, the idea of habitability begins from the scientific understanding of human embeddedness and inseparability from nature. Its focus, therefore, is on creating the conditions for the continuity of the entire web of life in which humans are inextricably embedded.

The question then becomes: How can humans govern effectively in the name of habitability? Doing this requires, first, that we entirely rethink how to govern. This book presents a foundational critique of the existing architecture of global governance. The problem with the existing system is that none of our current international institutions that are charged with addressing planetary challenges answer to the imperatives of the planet as such; rather, they answer to the member states that they represent. This institutional structure leaves planetary challenges unresolved and creates span of control/responsibility asymmetries and other pathologies that we will discuss. We propose therefore a new architecture for governance of the planet, based on a rethought version of a centuries-old principle known as *subsidiarity*. The principle of subsidiarity states that authority within a pluralistic system of administration should be allocated to the smallest-scale governing institution capable of managing the task effectively. Regional authorities take over only what the local authorities can't do for themselves, national authorities only what the regional authorities can't, and so on. Subsidiarity, in short, aims to maximize local control within an overarching governance framework that retains the capacity to manage shared problems.

Combining the observation about the condition of planetarity and the principle of subsidiarity, we propose a fundamentally new architecture for the governance of the planet, what we call *planetary subsidiarity*, based schematically on three scales of institutions: the planetary (which is to govern and guarantee habitability and multispecies flourishing), the national (which is to govern and guarantee development and redistribution), and the local (which is to ensure that the aforementioned principles are implemented in accordance with local conditions and preferences). A key argument of planetary subsidiarity is that the condition of planetarity makes clear that the smallest scale at which planetary issues can be governed effectively is the planet itself.

The vision of planetary subsidiarity differs radically from previous proposals for and instantiations of global governance, whether the existing United Nations system or the ideas of world federalism that were briefly popular in the years after the Second World War. On the one hand, whereas most older schemes for a "world state" or "global federalism" imagined a single, integrated, general-purpose global-scale government—the classical Weberian image of the state projected to the planetary scale—our proposed architecture of planetary subsidiarity envisions a series of narrowly scoped, functionally oriented governance institutions. Rather than one hegemonic world Leviathan, we propose separate planetary institutions tasked with managing specific planetary problems: one for the climate, one for pandemics, one for biodiversity, and so on. On the other hand, our vision also differs from the existing UN system, where multilateral member-state institutions ultimately answer to the sovereign national states that join them. We instead imagine putting people with expertise in the relevant planetary phenomena at the center of the decision-making process, answering to new forms of democratic publics. Only such a structure of *deliberate multiscalar governance*, one that eschews the fetishization of national sovereignty, can ensure the habitability necessary to enable multispecies (and thus ultimately human) flourishing.

In the end, of course, there is no escape from politics—that is, from the negotiations and power struggles between individuals and groups with differing values, interests, and needs. And so this book, while primarily concerned with planetary governance, also underscores the need for a new form of *planetary politics*. To achieve multispecies flourishing, we must find new ways to include the interests of nonhumans in this planetary politics, and to that end we also make a plea to empower those with the knowledge of how nonhumans operate to represent what those others need, in other words, scientists, as well as those who have the creative capacity of imagining the interior worlds of these others and can serve as their spokespeople. These are some of the bearers of planetary sapience, and to ensure that this knowledge is formed inclusively, it is imperative, finally, that we broaden access to scientific expertise. Where you are born and what identities you embody should not determine your capacity to serve as a planetary knower and spokesperson.

This book aims to join together two conversations that have been taking place in parallel but largely in ignorance of one another: the scientific-philosophical conversation that has been developing the concept of the Planetary and the ongoing political conversation about how best to govern the world. On the one hand, people interested in governance—including scholars of politics, international relations, and law; analysts, activists, and journalists interested in public policy; policymakers in local and national governments and international organizations; and informed citizens throughout the world—are barely if at all aware of the latest scientific and philosophical understanding of the Planetary and what it means for how they need to rethink their missions. On the other hand, the communities of specialists in the Planetary, largely in the Earth sciences and philosophy of science, often wish that governance structures and decisions would respond to their findings but are often also uncomfortable with and professionally disincentivized from promoting normative claims at a level of specificity that would make a difference. As a result, these two communities talk separately if not past each other, missing out on opportunities for mutually beneficial exchanges. Thus we hope to build a bridge between the conversations and introduce these communities to one another using mutually intelligible language to enable productive communication between them. We hope this book will kick off a broad and ongoing dialogue between those who understand the condition of planetarity and those with the tools—and power—to do something about it.

This goal determined our method of inquiry. The knowledge that we draw on to make our case primarily comes from the bodies of thought on science, politics, philosophy, technology, and governance that emerged in the North Atlantic over the last century and a half. For the most part, we have not integrated other traditions of thought, notably indigenous traditions, which have often addressed similar concerns of planetary holism. (Indeed, in many ways, Western thought is just now catching up to well-established indigenous insights about the world.) We chose to focus on this particular intellectual tradition for two reasons: first, because this is the conversation to which our primary audiences are already attuned, and second, because of the strengths gained from the Western scientific tradition's commitment to precision and falsifiability. Western science's unique contribution to long-standing intuitions held by other knowledge systems about the holistic integration of humans into our natural habitat is a level of exactitude that enables the rigorous testing and identification of the nature of planetary embeddedness. After a long detour (mis)guided by a belief in human exceptionalism, Western science has in recent decades returned to the ideas of holism and systems.

Some forms of knowledge based in Western science have undoubtedly justified and materially enabled the rapacious and cruel treatments of other human beings, living beings, and the Earth, but the solution to the rapacity and cruelty enabled by science is not less science but better science. Above all, solutions to the problems that Western science has created require better governance systems, ones that can act on the precise and useful knowledge produced by such science. Enhancing planetary sapience through education, technological development, and scientific study is the only way forward.

This is not a book with "ten simple fixes to save the planet!" It's not even a guide to policies that should be pursued to effectively manage problems like climate change and pandemics. Rather, it is a book about *institutions*. Specifically, it's about how to design institutions that can pursue policies to effectively manage planetary issues. Yet we do not go into the details of administrative practice, much less about the black-letter law that will be necessary to codify the institutions we have in mind. Our purpose is not to describe the juridical details of the necessary new planetary institutions, only to make the case for their necessity and to describe the functional capacities they will need to have in order to be effective in addressing planetary challenges.

We recognize that our proposals to build planetary institutions are unlikely to be implemented any time soon—what they represent, rather, is a vision for the future. Meanwhile, ongoing efforts to address planetary challenges within the current institutional matrix must continue, and indeed multiply, even as we build toward more effective structures of planetary governance. We must pursue both our long-term vision and the short- and medium-term tactics aimed at decarbonization, disease control, and so on. Let's be clear: there are real and powerful antiplanetary forces in governments and corporations around the world. They are the adversaries of all who seek the long-term habitability of Earth and the flourishing of all its inhabitants. By contrast, those who believe in those goals but work within the existing governance system—people, organizations, governments, and global institutions working toward a habitable planet—are our allies, even if we disagree (sometimes forcefully) with their strategies. In those cases, our criticism is intended as constructive and as a spur for creative, even radical thinking.

———

Chapters 1 and 2 describe the world's current governance architecture and its functional strengths and weaknesses as well as narrate how it came to be. We show (in chapter 1) that the hegemony of the sovereign national state as the privileged container of governance is a recent phenomenon, one that solidified globally only in the 1960s. Then (in chapter 2) we describe the multilevel global governance system that has grown up around the sovereign national state, explaining how various governance functions have relocated "above" the state, to the multilateral global governance system, and "below" the state, to subnational authorities and nonstate actors.

Chapter 3 offers a genealogy of the concept of the Planetary, a key term in contemporary Earth system and biological science as well as the philosophy of science. Chapter 4 presents our original interpretation of the principle of subsidiarity, an old idea for how to allocate authority within a multilevel governance architecture. Building on the insights of the previous chapter, we argue that we should rethink the principle of subsidiarity in light of our condition of planetarity. These two chapters provide the core conceptual and theoretical innovations of the book.

Chapters 5 and 6, finally, outline how we could redesign governance institutions for a planetary age. The first of these chapters proposes new roles for local institutions and suggests that they will be best able to serve their residents by networking with one another to share ideas and resources. The second sketches a general architectural model for planetary governance, including what planetary institutions for managing climate change and pandemics might look like in practice. As we illustrate these possibilities, we do not intend to offer a full blueprint for new institutions, but rather simply to outline what their key features ought to be.

The vision we put forth will no doubt be dismissed by some as madly ambitious, if not unhinged and perilous—thoughts we have at times shared. But what of alternatives? Is our vision less realistic than the escapist fantasy of building off-world colonies for a few (billionaires) while the world burns? Is it more foolishly optimistic than the belief that the market, aided by no centralized coordination mechanism, will deliver messianic technologies to redeem us? Is it more despotic than the possibility of eco-authoritarianism? Compared to these (alarmingly plausible) alternatives, the proposals in this book, we dare say, seem realistic, just, inclusive, and modest. We are, as the poet W. H. Auden recognized, "children of a modest star"—and we must live on Earth with modesty rather than by mastery.[20]

One

How the National State Became Hegemonic

In late 1955, the United Nations had a problem: it had run out of seats. The fledgling body, then only ten years old, had moved into its permanent headquarters on the east side of Manhattan just three years earlier, but its membership had already exceeded all expectations. It wasn't that the building's architects—a committee comprising some of the mid-twentieth century's greatest, including Le Corbusier and Oscar Niemeyer—had not anticipated that the international organization would grow; on the contrary. "The United Nations is a young and dynamic organization," the committee reported in its design plan of 1947. "Its potentialities for growth and change are unlimited." The team of idealistic builders in fact made this political belief and prognostication a principle of their design. "Though its structures will be of steel and concrete, they must be planned on so flexible a pattern that their interior areas may be easily and economically rearranged to suit changing needs."[1]

This flexibility would turn out to be crucial because the architects' anticipations of the world's political future were way off. "There are at present [July 1947] fifty-five Member States of the Organization; it is well to plan for a possible membership of at least seventy."[2] Talk of the organization's youth, dynamism, and potentially unlimited growth translated into a concrete (and steel) plan for only fifteen new members. By the time the UN moved into its new headquarters in 1952 it had already grown to sixty members. Then, on December 14, 1955, the Security Council passed Resolution 109, recommending sixteen countries for admission to the General Assembly, bringing its total membership to seventy-six—six more than had been planned for less than a decade prior.[3]

UN facilities managers were able to accommodate the necessary additional chairs and desks in the Plenary Hall, "where fortunately sufficient space was available to permit the modifications without complete rearrangement of the rooms." But by 1958, five more new members had joined the UN, and they were running out of space. The organization's rapid growth had pushed membership "far beyond initial expectations," and at "the present time there is room at the tables in the Plenary Hall and Conference Rooms for only one more Member nation." UN secretary-general Dag Hammarskjöld considered it "necessary to plan for the possibility of further expansion of the membership of the Organization," so his 1958 budget request included $50,000 for an engineering and architectural survey for the required "structural change and major alterations to the existing facilities" (a steal compared to the $463,000 requested to replace the carpets).[4] Buried in this dry request for capital improvement funds was an acknowledgment that something profound was happening in world politics.

This wasn't the last time UN work crews needed to add in more desks and chairs to General Assembly Hall. There were 99 members in 1960; 154 in 1980; 189 in 2000; and today there are 193 total members, with South Sudan the most recent to join, in 2011.[5] There remains very little of the earth's surface or human population that is not partitioned and assigned to a national state.[6]

In the immediate aftermath of the Second World War this coming efflorescence of independent, sovereign national states was not at all obvious.[7] Even a cursory glance at a globe in 1945 shows that national states were closer to the exception than the rule: India was a British colony; Palestine was a British mandate; Algeria was not a French over-seas colony but four *départements* of France; Alaska, Hawaii, Puerto Rico, and even the Philippines (on the verge of independence) remained US territories. In 1938, shortly before the war, 42 percent of the world's land and 32 percent of the population was colonized by the United King-dom, France, the Netherlands, Portugal, Belgium, Italy, the United States, and Japan.[8] The war ended with the clear defeat of the German and Japanese empires, but not of imperialism and other forms of non-national rule. The victorious powers, empires in fact if not in name, saw no reason for this arrangement to change.

When the UN's architects came up with their design, they did not imagine the rapid and total proliferation of national states. From the perspective of the mid-1940s, this outcome was entirely unexpected. This was true not only of the colonial powers who planned to hold on to their widespread territories, but also of many of the anticolonial activ-ists, demanding power in their homelands. Like nationalists and other opponents of empire since the nineteenth century, midcentury activists wanted self-determination, but they were not always convinced that it had to, or even should, take the form of a sovereign national state. Yet over the course of the next three decades, the expectation and desire for a national state would become the universal ambition for seekers of self-determination.

Since about 1965, the place of the national state has become hegemonic—meaning that national states became and remain the only political form recognized as legitimate holders of sovereignty and eli-gible for full membership in international society.[9] The unrecognized state of Somaliland may deliver more services to its population than does the national state of Somalia, but only the latter has the trappings of sovereign statehood, in the sense of having formal diplomatic rela-tions with other countries and the right to seats at various international tables.[10] Conversely, corporations like Apple, AliBaba, and Saudi-Aramco are all more powerful than many national states, but none of these can use violence legitimately, issue a functional passport, get a loan from the IMF, or join the UN. This stands in contrast to earlier periods, when other forms of institutions, including corporations, could legitimately exercise functions that are today the exclusive privileges of sovereign national states. The British East India Company, for example, a "company-state" that asserted de facto dominion over India on behalf of the British crown from 1757 to 1857, wielded violence legitimately (at least from the callous viewpoint of the European state system) on behalf of its own interests.[11]

Indeed, the position of the national state is "so dominant," observed the sociologist Charles Tilly in 1990, "that anyone who dreams of a stateless world seems a heedless visionary."[12] Yet the rise and dominance of the national state as the sole legitimate container of sovereignty and the premier governing unit in world politics was not foreordained. In fact, the national state only recently became the baseline assumption about the "proper" vehicle for governance delivery, with other forms rendered presumptively suspect. The universality of the national state, which today seems inevitable, irreversible, even natural, is none of that.

This chapter charts the history of the national state from its origins as one of many institutional formations of rule in early modern Europe to its position of absolute dominance today. The historical record reveals that at every critical juncture in the development and global spread of the national state, plausible alternatives were proposed, desired, or even implemented. Not until the decades after World War II, with the enshrinement of economic development as the preeminent political project for the world, did the national state become the undisputed institutional manifestation of sovereign political communities. Starting in chapter 3, we will argue that the world has a new overarching political project—managing the condition of planetarity—and so we need different political institutions to respond to the challenge.

The National State Emerges

States, understood broadly as centralized political organizations that create and enforce rules over a population within a given territory, have existed since about 3,100 BCE, when city-states began to emerge on the verdant floodplains of the Tigris and Euphrates.[13] But this deep history of collective rule is not necessary for understanding how one particular type of state, the national state, came to be the dominant vehicle for organizing political life and providing governance today.

The national state emerged in Europe, particularly in England and France, around 1500. European governance in that late-feudal era was marked by institutional diversity, and it was by no means clear that national states would become the dominant institutional form in a landscape already replete with empires, principalities, duchies, bishoprics, urban federations, trade confederations, city-states, free cities, and many other political structures.[14] Beginning in the fifteenth century, the national state began to display advantages over its institutional competitors, particularly in the intertwined processes of fighting wars and collecting revenue. In this context, the concept of the state as an institution distinct from the person of the monarch began to emerge in European thought.[15] Yet in these early modern years, the state was still but one legitimate political form among many. Hugo Grotius, the seventeenth-century Dutch jurist considered the founder of international law, judged many agents to be subject to the law of nations and members of international society, including states, corporations, and individuals.[16]

These diverse forms of states in early modern Europe, however, shared a common purpose: they existed to advance the glory of God and of the ruling dynasty. Whether national states or empires, power was wielded in the name of and for the purposes of the monarch. Louis XIV of France was not so much boasting as stating accepted fact when he famously pronounced, "L'etat, c'est moi": I am the state. The state in the sixteenth and seventeenth centuries did not yet aim to govern society or promote the economy—indeed, the modern concepts of "society" and "the economy" had not yet been invented. The welfare of a state's subjects was not conceived of as something that could be affected by state policy; rather, it was understood to be the result of human nature or divine providence.[17] Likewise, there was no sense of a people in whose name the state governed or claimed legitimacy.

This began to change in the eighteenth and nineteenth centuries as a result of the massive social, economic, and political upheavals ushered in by two world-changing episodes: the industrial revolution, heralded by the invention of the steam engine, and the French Revolution of 1789. The twin challenges that arose—namely, how to manage the social impact of the rise of industrial capitalism and how to respond to the demand for popular sovereignty—pushed European states into forms that begin to become recognizable to contemporary eyes. At the same time, novel technologies that allowed new forms of rule and emerging ideas about the role of states in society, in particular the ideas of "improvement" and "progress," opened up new opportunities for what the state could and should do. Revolutionary France's experiment with direct rule at the national scale, for instance, was the first attempt by any European state to govern in such a way.[18]

During this transatlantic Age of Revolution, ideas of sovereignty and independence churned through Paris, Philadelphia, and Port-au-Prince, but the institutional structure that would house these principles was still being developed. The American Declaration of Independence may have "dissolve[d] the political bands which have connected" the colonies to Britain so that they could "be Free and Independent States," but the form that this would take—independent countries, confederation, or federation—was an open question and hotly debated.[19]

Throughout the Americas, in fact, the dissolution of European empires in the late eighteenth through early nineteenth centuries was not a straightforward march from empire to independent, sovereign statehood. As the Spanish Empire collapsed, the transition to statehood was bumpy and contested.[20] Political demands evolved over time, from calls for American representation within the Spanish Empire to desires for local autonomy to, as a last option, separation from Spain.[21] In the French Caribbean, too, calls for independence emerged only gradually. Saint-Domingue (today Haiti), which, along with other French colonies, the revolutionary French constitution of 1795 declared an "integral part" of France proper, began its struggle for freedom as a movement claiming the rights of revolutionary French citizenship. It was only in response to Napoleon's attempt to reimpose slavery and colonial status on the island that this effort would transform into a fight for secession.[22] Even in the United States, the political form of self-government was not entirely settled after the ratification of the Constitution in 1788 (which itself replaced the earlier form created by the Articles of Confederation). For several decades, prominent political leaders sought to craft an "American System" that would bind together all of the independent states in the Western hemisphere through a series of treaties and alliances.[23] Indeed, it was not until the end of the Civil War in 1865 that the ultimate sovereign form of the United States was finally settled.

As the nineteenth century progressed, two key developments bolstered the case for the national state. First, independence became, in the words of one historian, "a defining political value." The language and principles of the American Revolution spread widely, and the most important aspect of self-government came to be independence, rather than control over territory and people or the ability to govern.[24] "National liberty is independence," declared a Chilean newspaper in 1813, "that is, that the nation does not depend upon Spain, England, Turkey, etc., but governs itself."[25] Here an essential element that distinguished the national state from other forms of statehood emerged: a politically important distinction between insiders and outsiders rooted not just in geographic colocation but in political identity.

Second, states started taking a more active role in society. Over the course of the nineteenth century, novel technologies and administrative techniques converged with new ideas proposing that states should do more. The invention of the railroad, the steam-powered boat, and the telegraph compressed time and space, conveying the sense that the capital and the periphery were one unit (at least among people thinking about it in the capital), that the writ of the state extended uniformly all the way up to the borders delineated on the map, and that, at least in principle, this writ applied uniformly to all members of the national community.[26] At the same time, transformations in scientific, social, and political thought introduced the modern idea of progress and the notion that the state could intervene in society to promote progress.[27]

The goal of the emerging modern state was no longer simply to protect the power of the sovereign but increasingly to improve the life conditions of the people themselves. Starting in the nineteenth century states got much more involved in a wide range of activities, including regulating economic life and population movement; providing social and welfare services, such as public health measures, health insurance, and pensions; policing crime; and collecting social statistics.[28] In a self-reinforcing cycle, the state demanded more of its population and the population demanded more of their state (this era also gave rise to the modern social movement, a form of sustained political mobilization aimed at making claims on the state). As a result, the state become much more of a presence in the lives of its people. This, in other words, is when states began to "govern" in the sense that we understand the term today.

Despite these political and administrative transformations, demand for and attainment of independent national states remained limited in the nineteenth century. While sovereign national statehood had been achieved in much of the Americas by the 1830s, large, multinational empires prevailed throughout Europe for the rest of the century—to say nothing of the overseas empires that Europeans were in the process of building by force. By the mid-nineteenth century, nationalist movements were gaining strength across the continent, with some seeking to unify disparate, independent principalities and statelets into a single state, others seeking autonomy within their empire, and a few seeking to break away from empires altogether. National identity became a culturally congenial way to bind people's loyalty to the state, with shared (if sometimes fictionalized) stories of the past implicitly binding "the people" together in a shared future from which non-national outsiders were explicitly excluded.

Thus national self-determination was on the lips of many Europeans, but it could take multiple forms, and the national state was not necessarily the most popular one. In central Europe, during the Springtime of Peoples—the nationalist and liberal-democratic uprisings of 1848—most of the revolutionaries were *not* trying to overthrow the

Habsburgs or secede from the Austrian Empire (the Hungarians were an exception). Rather, Czechs, Slavs, Poles, and other nationalities rose up to gain the right to restructure and reform the empire, so that their nation could exercise local autonomy while remaining part of it.[29] National self-determination, for many nineteenth-century nationalists, was entirely consistent with imperial loyalties. As one Czech nationalist expressed in 1848, "Had the Austrian state not existed for ages, it would [assuredly] have been in the interests of Europe, and indeed of humanity to endeavor to create it as soon as possible."[30]

What's more, nationalist sentiment—which by midcentury was widespread and deeply felt among intellectuals, students, and elites—was not shared by the great mass of rural peasants. Building on a Romantic tradition that exalted the spirit of a people, self-consciously nationalist movements emerged among the educated classes across Europe in the 1830s. The elite view of "the nation," which initially hewed to a limited notion focused on the nobility, expanded with time. By 1848, a nation represented a cultural idea that encompassed the masses. But the masses were in most cases not yet on board with the nationalist political project, and nationalist movements lacked popular support, which was how many contemporaries explained the failure of most of the uprisings of that year.[31]

"Self-Determination" after World War I

The idea of an independent, sovereign state that could and should govern in the name of and for the benefit of a distinct people thus developed over the course of the nineteenth century. Yet implementing this idea required a drastic break with Europe's imperial status quo. The opportunity for restructuring the European political landscape came with the defeat and collapse of the multinational empires of central and eastern Europe and the Middle East at the end of the Great War, in 1918. The confluence of imperial frailty, nationalist demand, and the verdict of the victorious powers led to the defeated empires being broken apart. As peace talks got underway, however, the types of the political communities and governance institutions that would replace the defeated empires remained uncertain. In February 1918, US president Woodrow Wilson had declared that "national aspirations must be respected; people may now be dominated and governed only by their own consent. 'Self-determination' is not a mere phrase; it is an imperative principle of action, which statesmen will henceforth ignore at their peril."[32] But the principle of self-determination contained great ambiguities, among them: What political form should exercise it? Only one month earlier, in his famous Fourteen Points speech, Wilson had advocated giving the peoples of the Habsburg Empire autonomy rather than independent statehood.[33] Unsurprisingly, the application of the principle during the Paris Peace Conference in 1919 turned out to be quite tricky. Even Wilson's own secretary of state was unsure of what Wilson meant: "When the president talks of 'self-determination' what unit has he in mind? Does he mean a race, a territorial area, or a community?"[34]

In the end, the signatories of the Treaty of Versailles settled on the independent national state as the best administrative channel to realize "national aspirations" within, in Wilson's words, "a new international order based upon broad and universal principles of right and justice."[35] Dismantling the empires of the Triple Alliance seemed to ensure that these countries would no longer be able to wage effective war against the still-intact French and British empires, while also adhering to Wilson's vision that every "civilized" people should enjoy self-rule. New borders were drawn in general accordance to the ethnic majority in the area (with favor shown to nationalities whose leaders had supported the winning side).[36] In ethnically mixed areas, such as Schleswig, Carinthia, and Upper Silesia, plebiscites were held to determine where the lines should be drawn.[37] In practice, however, kaleidoscopic ethnic geographies meant that while sixty million people in eastern and central Europe were granted a state where they belonged to the titular national majority, twenty-five million were left living as national minorities.[38]

These practical difficulties notwithstanding, the signing of the Treaty of Versailles in June 1919 marked the moment when the national state became the hegemonic organizing unit in European law and politics.[39] After Versailles, the national state was the predominant institution for governing people and territory on the Continent.[40]

Outside of Europe it was another story altogether. The years after the Great War marked the high-water mark of European overseas imperialism. The British Empire reached its greatest extent in the years after World War I, at which point it had varying degrees of control over nearly a quarter of the Earth's surface. The British, French, and Dutch colonial powers had no intention of voluntarily relinquishing their wide-ranging rule. Before the war, anticolonial movements in most colonies had surprisingly thin support, partly because of the gulf between the ambitions of local elites and the relative indifference of the vast majority of the population.[41] Yet even anticolonial activists in this era typically did not seek secession from empire. An Egyptian uprising in 1882 did not demand independence, and neither did most mainstream late nineteenth- and early twentieth-century Indian nationalists.[42] But the barbaric and catastrophic course of the Great War fatally damaged the sense of both European cultural superiority and imperial inevitability.

While Wilson himself had never intended his principle of self-determination to apply to nonwhite colonial subjects, after 1919 anticolonial activists increasingly quoted his rhetoric as the basis for their political demands.[43] In 1905, the president of the Indian National Congress (INC) had explained the organization's political program: "India should be governed in the interests of the Indians themselves, and . . . over the course of time, a form of Government should be attained in this country similar to what exists in the Self-Governing Colonies of the British Empire."[44] Two decades later, this gradualism and compromising stance with empire was gone. In 1929, INC president Jawaharlal Nehru announced the organization's new goal: "India must sever the British connection and attain *Purna Swaraj*, or complete independence."[45]

Nationalism's Internationalism

The European and American diplomats gathered in Paris in 1919 did not limit their scope to a nationalist future; they envisioned an internationalist one as well. Alongside the establishment of new national states in eastern and central Europe, the Treaty of Versailles also created an international body unlike anything that had come before it: the League of Nations. Though not as far-reaching and all-powerful as some at the time hoped, the League was invented as a permanent forum "to promote international co-operation and to achieve international peace and security."[46] At the inaugural meeting of the League Council—the organization's upper house—the moment was hailed as "the date of the birth of the new world."[47]

Yet at the same time, the very design of the League's structures and procedures reinforced and presaged the expansion of the national state form. In its initial membership, the League recognized the universal applicability of the national state. The forty-two inaugural members were overwhelmingly European and American but also included Liberia, Persia, and Siam. Though these members differed enormously in terms of their international power, their common membership indicated a formal recognition of sovereign equality. But among the League's founding members were also nonsovereign entities: most glaringly, colonial India had a seat, as did the self-governing dominions of the British Empire (Australia, Canada, New Zealand, and South Africa). In this period, recognized sovereignty was not yet a prerequisite for legitimate membership in international society.

What's more, the League itself became a forum for the public, international recognition of independent statehood and created formal procedures for achieving this recognition.[48] The Mandate system, through which Britain and France administered territories ceded by the German and Ottoman empires under the oversight of the League, provided one such procedure. In the League's view, these lands were "inhabited by peoples not yet able to stand by themselves under the strenuous conditions of the modern world," but the purpose of the Mandate was to develop them under the "tutelage" of the "advanced nations" so that they could "stand alone." Mandatory officials believed it would take decades or even centuries for this to happen, but establishing the system tacitly acknowledged that independence was the ultimate and legitimate objective that all peoples, including non-Europeans, could and should aspire to.[49]

The Contest to Organize the Postwar World

Then came the global shock of the Second World War. The war affected the incentives and political imaginations of both the colonizers and the colonized in profound ways. These sea changes marked the beginning of the end of the vast European overseas empires and set the stage for national states to become the predominant political form in their wake. First of all, the war set the stage for imperial collapse in the metropoles and the colonies. The war severely weakened the European powers and their grasp on their overseas territories. By 1945, the European empires were socially and economically exhausted at home, and the image of the lasting strength of their authority decisively dissipated during Japan's wartime occupation of their Asian colonies. The only reason why the empires did not collapse in the 1940s was an infusion of American financial support to Europe.[50] Moreover, the war ended with two remaining superpowers of unparalleled political and military strength—the United States and the Soviet Union—that perceived themselves as anti-imperialists, even if they often didn't act that way. Yet during the war and in its immediate aftermath, it was by no means clear that the end was near for Europe's overseas empires. Indeed for many Europeans, the imminent end of their empires was not only undesirable but unimaginable. Giving independence to the African colonies, the British foreign secretary said in 1951, was like "giving a child of ten a latch-key, a bank account and a shotgun."[51] So when the end of empire came, it came swiftly, taking many Europeans by surprise.

Adding to the shock, as Europe's overseas empires were breaking

apart, it was not known what form of political organization would replace them. The future role of the national state was still being debated.
For the two decades after World War II, statesmen, revolutionaries, and
intellectuals in the colonies and metropoles considered several ideas for
how to organize the postwar, postimperial world. Out of this political
maelstrom, the national state eventually triumphed as the postcolonial
heir, but it was by accident—a result, not a goal, of decolonization, one
that emerged as leaders realized that their prime imperative was economic and political modernization.

World Government

Assessing the wreckage after the war, one thing was clear: European
national states—the oldest and, to many contemporary observers, most
advanced—had just led the world through two bloodbaths in three
decades, unleashing the exuberant brutality of mechanized warfare,
featuring industrial death camps, firebombing of cities, and nuclear
weapons. The cataclysmic implications of the atomic bomb, in particular, shook many people to their core. Given these dangers, it is unsur-
prising that so many came to believe that "World Government is the
only alternative to world destruction."[52]

   In these first, frenzied postwar years, many people concluded that
national states were not the solution but the problem. As the University of Chicago's Committee to Frame a World Constitution declared in
1948: "Iniquity and war inseparably spring from the competitive anarchy of the national states." The only solution, the committee decided,
was that "the age of nations must end, and the era of humanity begin."
To that end, they drafted a constitution for "the Federal Republic of the
World" in which all states would pool "their separate sovereignties in
one government of justice to which they surrender their arms."[53]

   The movement for world government was no fringe idea in the 1940s:
Albert Camus, Winston Churchill, Mohandas Gandhi, Martin Luther
King Jr., Jawaharlal Nehru, Rosika Schwimmer, H. G. Wells, and Wendell Willkie were all at one time or another proponents of the idea.[54] "I
advocate world government," Albert Einstein wrote in 1948, "because

I am convinced that there is no other possible way of eliminating the most terrible danger in which man has ever found himself."[55] Einstein and other prominent physicists, who truly understood the potential for annihilation that the new atomic weapons represented, believed in the need for a "supranational organization" with binding authority "supported by a military power that is exclusively under its control."[56]

Nor was world government just the dream of rarified intellectuals. The idea of world government found widespread mainstream support, including in the United States, the newly preeminent power. The United World Federalists, a US-based advocacy organization founded in 1947, had mass appeal and membership. A 1947 poll found that 56 percent of the Americans surveyed agreed that "the UN should be strengthened to make it a world government."[57] In 1949, the House Committee on Foreign Affairs even held two days of hearings on a resolution, cosponsored by 105 members of Congress (including then-Representatives John F. Kennedy and Gerald Ford), proclaiming that "it should be a fundamental objective of the foreign policy of the United States to support and strengthen the United Nations and to seek its development into a world federation open to all nations with defined and limited powers adequate to preserve peace and prevent aggression through the enactment, interpretation, and enforcement of world law."[58]

The resolution, like the broader movement, did not prevail. The world political institution that was founded in the postwar era—the United Nations—enshrined rather than dethroned the principle of state sovereignty. The UN Charter emphasized "the sovereign equality of all its Members" and stated plainly that the UN was not authorized "to intervene in matters which are essentially within the domestic jurisdiction of any state."[59] The founding of the UN in 1945, in fact, was a step toward the foreclosure of alternative options to the national state, both as a cause and as a reflection of underlying currents. While multiethnic empires remained intact and cherished in imperial capitals from London to Moscow, the very structure of the United Nations presided over by these same imperial powers implied that postcolonial governance would eventually take the form of national states. But in the late

1940s, many people took seriously the idea that world government represented an alternative—perhaps the only alternative—to a world order based on rivalrous national states and empires that kept producing mass death.[60]

Non-national Self-Determination

After centuries of imperial rule, which demolished indigenous governance institutions and forcibly imposed colonial state structures, anticolonial elites were open to numerous possibilities for what would come next. World War II and the early postwar years set the stage for the ultimate and overwhelming triumph of the national state in every part of the world; but before the national state solidified its grasp on the political imagination, anticolonial activists put forward a range of collective futures.

Multinational federations were of particular interest to anticolonial elites around the world. Throughout the colonial and postcolonial world, leaders proposed and even implemented federations of various flavors. Anticolonial activists of very different political stripes were well aware that formally independent national states that were small, poor, and at the mercy of international economic forces would be sovereign in name only. Thus achieving independence as a national state did not amount to true self-determination—it was "merely being free to fly our own flag and to play our own national anthem," in the words of Ghana's first prime minister, Kwame Nkrumah.[61] True self-determination meant freedom from economic dependence and political domination, which, these activists concluded, could be achieved only in a larger political federation of diverse peoples. As Mamadou Dia, later the first prime minister of Senegal, argued in 1955: "It is necessary that the imperialist concept of the nation-state give way definitively to the modern concept of the multinational state."[62]

Such a multinational federal state was envisioned in multiple ways. Leopold Senghor, who became Senegal's first president in 1960, proposed a federal structure for the future of the French Empire composed of three levels: the individual African territories with local autonomy;

a federation of French West Africa with significant political authority; and, at top, a French confederation, where the West African federation, metropolitan France, and any other units from the French Empire who wished to join could associate as equal members. Félix Houphouët-Boigny, who became the first president of Cote d'Ivoire, also in 1960, wanted to cut out the middle layer, so that the individual African territories could directly enter into a federation of equals with European France.[63] Ghana's Nkrumah sought to construct a Union of African States with sovereign powers. He even ensured that the 1960 Ghanaian constitution included the power of the parliament "to provide for the surrender of the whole or any part of the sovereignty of Ghana" to the Union once it was formed.[64] In the British Caribbean, anticolonial elites collaborated with the British Colonial Office to create the West Indian Federation in 1958. This federation sought to unite ten "weak and small" islands in order to gain the strength needed to secure political and economic self-determination.[65] Jamaica's opposition to the power of the federal unit over the individual members' economic autonomy tanked the federation in 1962, and the island decided to enter international society not as a member of a large regional federation but as a small, independent national state.

Yet for other newly independent postcolonies, achieving independence as a national state did not end their experimentation with multinational federations. Egyptian president Gamal Abdel Nasser, seeking to erase the boundaries among Arabs that had been artificially imposed by the European empires, merged Egypt with Syria in 1958 to form the United Arab Republic, which then entered into a confederation with North Yemen known as the United Arab States. Both unions fell apart in 1961. Likewise, the Union of African States linked the West African states of Ghana and Guinea in 1958 before including Mali in 1960, only to disband in 1963. In 1961, the mainland Federation of Malaysia, independent since 1957, combined with North Borneo, Sarawak, and Singapore to reconstitute itself as Malaysia, only to separate from Singapore in 1965, at which point Kuala Lumpur would consolidate its authority over the remaining portions of insular East Malaysia.[66]

While each of these episodes had distinct dynamics, together they demonstrate that even for postcolonial leaders, the national state was hardly the only form of governing institution considered though the early 1960s.[67]

The Quest for National Economic Development

These visions of non-national governance all failed or never got off the ground. While many colonial and anticolonial leaders experimented with alternative political forms from the 1940s through 1960s, the national state's position got stronger and stronger. In fact, even as World War II seemed to open the doors to new political possibilities for postcolonial regions, the terms of the postwar settlement also laid the groundwork for the rapid consolidation of the perception that the national state was the only available option. "We are on the cusp of a new era in human history," David Ben-Gurion, soon to be Israel's first prime minister, observed presciently in a 1945 speech titled "We Don't Have a Future without a State."[68]

The question then is: Why did the national state, rather than any other form of political organization, became *the* political form for this "new era in human history"? Nationalism, at least on its own, is not the answer. Anticolonial elites sought to create political institutions that would end their status as humiliated, second-class citizens and liberate, in the words of Martiniquan poet and politician Aimé Césaire, the minds of the "millions of men in whom fear has been cunningly instilled, who have been taught to have an inferiority complex, to tremble, kneel, despair, and behave like flunkeys."[69] But this desire for self-respect, even when coupled with an emotional attachment to one's nation, does not necessarily demand the national state. Like his fellow pan-Africanist Leopold Senghor, Césaire envisioned self-determination without independent national states: his dream was to remake the French Empire into a democratic, transcontinental federation where metropolitan France and its former colonies would be equal members.[70] Thus there were other vehicles for self-respect, and strong emotional ties were not inherent to any particular administrative unit. As the great scholar of nationalism Benedict Anderson observed, administrative units *"in themselves,* . . . do not create attachments"; it takes cultural and emotional labor for them to "come to be conceived as fatherlands." And as we saw, some mid-twentieth-century anticolonial activists, like their nineteenth-century predecessors, put their hopes and efforts for self-determination in structures besides the national state. These other institutional formations could provide self-determination, sovereignty, even emotional resonance—they appeared, in Anderson's phrasing, "emotionally plausible and politically viable."[71] What they had trouble providing was a basis for economic development.

This turned out to be decisive because, in the aftermath of World War II, economic development was enshrined as *the* defining political project of the age. As national economic development cemented its place as the paramount vision for the future, the national state increasing looked like the most natural form for achieving the dream of modernization. Thus it was the elevation of economic development as the ultimate purpose of collective political life that guided postwar decolonization in Asia, Africa, and the Caribbean toward the national state rather than other forms of political organization.

In the postwar period, the national state came to be seen—by both communist and capitalist elites in both the Global North and the Global South—as the best if not only vehicle for realizing economic modernization, which at the time was tellingly synonymous with "nation building."[72] Rooted in a sense of reciprocity and mutual obligation among those participating in the process, economic development entailed collective sacrifice and collective reward, and as such was both an expression of and a means to achieve a collective identity. Where postcolonial leaders considered other objectives (such as regional security) paramount, they often experimented with other forms of statehood discussed earlier. But as the postwar period progressed, and leaders increasingly treated national economic development as the state's prime directive, the national state became seen as the most functionally effective political form.

The ideological role of economic development as a defining national project had been building since at least the 1930s, though its roots go back even earlier. Over the course of the nineteenth and early twentieth centuries, the nascent social science disciplines invented new forms of knowledge that allowed for the world to be understood as a series of discrete social objects such as society, culture, classes, labor, and, most crucially for this part of our story, the economy. As these concepts circulated and caught on, they presented a vision of social objects that expert knowledge could manipulate to promote progress.[73] It was in this context that the concept of the "the economy," and in particular "the national economy," as a self-contained whole of production and consumption, distinct from all the rest of life, emerged in the years between the 1880s and 1940s.[74]

Conceptualizing the economy as a discrete social object with manipulable inputs leading to divergent outcomes allowed for the reorientation of government policy toward economic development in both metropolitan European states and their colonial holdings. By the interwar period, European governments, colonial administrators, and anticolonial elites began to envision the use of scientific expertise to promote economic progress for their citizens and subjects. But the colonial development project—which purported to produce both material improvements in the lives of colonial subjects and economic benefits for the European metropoles via disjunctive infrastructural and economic projects—was increasingly not what anticolonial elites had in mind.[75]

The vision of anticolonial activists, which began to crystallize after World War I, was that independence—beyond a matter of political justice and rights—would enable them to do a better job than their imperial rulers at solving the problems in their societies, chief among them the problem of economic backwardness. Economic development was reconceptualized from being "an archipelago of schemes" (a factory here, a dam there) to instead being about the integral development of the nation itself.[76] In colonial India, for example, the Congress Party began to develop plans for economic development by the 1930s, with Nehru, later India's first prime minister, as head of the party's National

Planning Committee.[77] Crucially, the plans they drafted were for the colonial territory of India, not the broader region or subnational units (hence *National* Planning Committee). The Bay of Bengal, encompassing what is today India, Bangladesh, Burma, Sri Lanka, Thailand, and Malaysia, had long been understood to be a single integrated economic region, but when Congress planned for the economic future, they discounted the region and planned a national economic future for India alone.[78] The target, as Nehru later wrote, was "national self-sufficiency"—not "local," not "regional," but "national."[79]

After World War II, the place of economic development in the anticolonial imagination rose, as the quest for it held great appeal for anticolonial and newly postcolonial elites.[80] The promise of economic progress helped justify the struggle for decolonization. And once independence was attained, working to lift their populations up out of crushing rural poverty and social backwardness gave the new states purpose. It was their blueprint "to create a new world out of the dregs of the old," as Nehru aspired.[81] What, after all, was a better use of self-government? "We cannot tell our peoples that material benefits and growth and modern progress are not for them," Nkrumah proclaimed in 1958, one year after he led the first successful sub-Saharan African independence movement. "Therefore we have no choice. Africa has no choice. We have to modernize."[82]

Postcolonial leaders, moreover, understood that maintaining political independence required economic independence. Economic development was thus not merely an opportunity but a necessity in order to ensure the survival of the newly independent states in the cold, at times violent, world of international politics. Postcolonial states needed development and they needed it fast—it had to be, as Nkrumah put it (both metaphorically and literally), "jet-propelled."[83] Achieving economic autonomy with such rapidity, they concluded, required state intervention. Anticolonial elites wanted to harness the power of the state to overcome underdevelopment, poverty, and lack of industry in the same way that Germany, the United States, and Soviet Union had for wartime production and that western Europe was now doing for social welfare. To anticolonial elites interested in charting their own national paths outside of empire, the apparent successes of economic planning by strong national states held great appeal. They saw the interventionist state as a mighty instrument of social and economic change.

The quest for national economic development was certainly not the only driver toward national statehood during decolonization. Importantly, the European colonizing powers as well as the United States also came to prefer the national state as the institutional form to succeed empire. Once direct colonial rule became too costly to maintain—politically, economically, and morally—the world's powerful states realized that it would be more advantageous to cultivate unequal relationships with politically and economically weak, nominally independent postcolonial national states. Recognizing the sovereignty of new national states, in other words, did not require relinquishing a hierarchical international politics. Imperialism, as Nkrumah grasped, "quickly adopted its outlook to [this] loss of direct political control [and] retained and extended its economic grip" over erstwhile colonies.[84] Many anticolonial leaders held similarly clear-eyed understandings of the motivations of their former colonizers, which is why so many of them opposed national statehood and sought alternatives.

Moreover, promoting national states that could work toward economic development preempted claims for economic redistribution on a global scale. The United Nations and other international organizations also favored the national state and promoted it as the only legitimate political form and as the best way to achieve economic development.[85] From the perspective of anticolonial elites, finally, the national state form offered an additional advantage: it was already there in nascent form. When colonial administrators returned to Europe, they left behind colonial governance institutions that the newly independent leaders could walk right into (often quite literally: the last British chief secretary of Palestine, when asked whom he would be giving his office keys to, quipped, "I shall put them under the mat").[86]

These other factors cannot be dismissed, but the intertwined and mutually reliant goals of political self-determination and economic development were what sealed the deal in favor of the national state form. Economic independence, both as a means toward political independence and as an end in itself, required economic development efforts so massive and so rapid that only a state-led process would suffice. The national state, too, became a means for delivering development and also an end in itself, as a symbol of national sovereignty.[87] The political and economic imperatives pointed, by the early 1960s, to a lone viable vehicle for the legitimate governance of territory and populations: the national state.

The Sole Legitimate Container of Sovereignty

The national state's hegemony was firm by 1965. After that point, there were no more new experiments in non-national state arrangements; self-determination meant having a national state.[88] Colonial rule didn't disappear overnight (Portugal fought bloody wars to maintain their empire for another decade), but it was increasingly seen as illegitimate, and national states came to be seen as their only legitimate replacement. Alternatively governed spaces like the Tangier International Zone, Aden Protectorate, Free Territory of Trieste, and Anglo-Egyptian Sudan either were absorbed by national states or became national states of their own. While some multinational federations survived for a time, no one after 1965 attempted to develop new ones, and even those that remained, such as the Soviet Union and Yugoslavia, were living on borrowed time.

The primacy of sovereign national states had profound ramifications for the conduct of international politics. Before 1945, for instance, it was common for states to try to expand their borders militarily. But since 1945, wars of territorial conquest have nearly disappeared.[89] More generally, state borders lost much of their earlier fluidity, becoming more rigid and absolute in the second half of the twentieth century.[90] Even boundaries created arbitrarily by colonizing powers became sacrosanct.[91] One indicator of this trend is the construction of border walls. Two fortified barriers were erected in the 1950s and only one was built in the 1960s. But, coinciding with the entrenchment of the national state after 1965, five barriers went up in the 1970s, eleven in the 1980s, seven in the 1990s, seventeen in the 2000s, and thirty-four in the 2010s.[92]

Over the course of two decades, then, the international political arena homogenized and the political imagination contracted. The UN's 1960 Declaration on Decolonization equated the "right to self-determination" with the "right to complete independence."[93] This logic took on a life of its own, foreclosing the possibility that some political communities might choose to exercise self-determination without independence. As it happened, the Cook Islanders voted in 1965 to have a constitution with domestic self-government but to place foreign relations and defense in the hands of New Zealand. The UN General Assembly balked, protesting that they had merely "attained full internal self-government," not true self-determination, and committed "to assist the people of the Cook Islands in the eventual achievement of full independence."[94] Self-determination begat self-determination, and smaller and smaller jurisdictions struck out on their own. By the end of the 1960s, the UN had some fifteen members with populations less than one million. In 1969, a UN commission studied the impact of admitting sixty-five potential members with populations under three hundred thousand.[95]

The door was now closed to alternatives to the national state. By the time of the next imperial dissolution, the fragmentation of the Soviet Union, there remained only one legitimate postimperial political form. In March 1990, the Lithuanian parliament voted 124 to 0 to secede from the Soviet Union. Estonia and Latvia soon followed. Then in June, the Russian Republic declared itself sovereign, and similar declarations cascaded through the Soviet Empire. Mikhail Gorbachev, trying desperately to salvage the Soviet Union, proposed adopting a new Union Treaty to reform the federation, but the rejection from the independent-minded republics was decisive.[96] They had one vision for the future: sovereign national states. Even the Soviet republics that did *not* want to dissolve the Union—Belarus, Uzbekistan, Turkmenistan—ended up declaring independence by October 1991.[97] There was no alternative.

As recently as the mid-twentieth century, there were a range of forms of governance on the table. Some of them were brutally coercive, others sublimely egalitarian. Some were tried and abandoned, others were found widely inspiring but never made it past a proposal, still others likely never even made it onto paper—utopian ideas, declared with a flash of excitement, in cafés and classrooms around the world. Not all were viable or even fleshed out, but some of them were; regardless, there were people willing to give them a shot.[98] By the 1960s, these alternative political forms vanished. This is not to say that people have stopped dreaming of a different world—thankfully, they have not. For the past fifty years, though, these dreams have not appeared plausible.

It is worth remembering that when it was first invented, the national state didn't appear plausible either. The ideological and technological trends of the last several centuries just turned out in such a way that it prevailed. The national state is neither inevitable nor natural; it is the product of historical happenstance. Yet it is so ingrained in how we think about the world—organized by lines on a map into discrete national societies, each with its own seat in the UN General Assembly Hall—that it can be difficult to envision a future outside the national state. Indeed, it can be difficult to think of a *history* outside the national state. France, which is generally held up as the oldest and prototypical national state, didn't become "France" as we now think of it—the hexagonal territory in western Europe—until the 1960s. Before Algerian independence, in 1962, over 50 percent of French territory was outside Europe, and the country extended from Dunkirk, on the English Channel, to In Guezzam, on the border with Niger.[99] Even today, France actually extends far beyond its European territory, including French Guiana, Martinique, Réunion, and the rest of *France d'outre-mer*, or Overseas France.[100]

Given all the other ways that people and territory have been governed until quite recent history, why do national states today seem so natural, so permanent? One big reason is that nationalist historians have long portrayed their rise as inescapable.[101] "It is the magic of nationalism to turn chance into destiny," as Anderson writes.[102] This

magic has clouded our thinking and even some of our most basic assumptions. National states are not destiny; they are chance administrative units for territorial governance.

Despite the absolute victory of the national state as an ideological model, as a theory for organizing the political space of the world,
it has never accurately described conditions on the ground. The picture we hold of a system of mutually exclusive, cumulatively exhaustive, and nominally equal sovereign national states covering the globe
that govern everything within their neatly drawn borders is a fiction.
How governance institutions developed to work with and around that
fiction, to manage issues too big or too small for national states, is the
topic of our next chapter.

Two

Governing beyond the National State

Shortly before submitting his latest scientific paper for publication, in August 1956, the oceanographer Roger Revelle realized he had made a mistake. In a study on the circulation of carbon dioxide (CO_2), Revelle—director of the Scripps Institution of Oceanography in La Jolla, California—and the chemist Hans Suess had assumed, like many scientists at the time, that the ocean absorbed most of the CO_2 produced by humankind's burning of fossil fuels. Then one day, he remembered something he'd learned earlier in his career about seawater chemistry. It dawned on Revelle that the assumption that oceans could easily take in excess carbon from the atmosphere failed to account for a "peculiar" mechanism produced by seawater's complex chemical makeup. Yes, a lot of human-produced CO_2 would end up in the ocean, but rather than get absorbed, it would quickly evaporate back into the atmosphere. Over time, this chemical process would lead to increasing amounts of atmospheric CO_2.

A typewritten draft of the study was ready to send to *Tellus*, the scientific journal of the Swedish Geophysical Society. Revelle typed a new paragraph noting this observation on a clean piece of paper and Scotch-taped it to the manuscript. Though even he didn't comprehend it at the time (the rest of the 1957 publication still relied on the old assumption), Revelle's finding would soon upend the prevailing understanding of the effects of human activity on the atmosphere. Human activity, scientists began to realize, could affect the global climate.[1]

Thirty-five years later, at the Riocentro Convention and Event Center, about an hour west of Rio de Janeiro's iconic beaches, diplomats from around the world met to discuss their concern "that human activities have been substantially increasing the atmospheric concentrations of greenhouse gases."[2] On June 12, 1992, 154 countries attending the Rio Earth Summit—officially the UN Conference on Environment and Development—signed the United Nations Framework Convention on Climate Change (UNFCCC), agreeing to the "stabilization of greenhouse gas concentrations in the atmosphere at a level that would prevent dangerous anthropogenic interference with the climate system."[3] The UNFCCC was the first international legal treaty to specifically act on Revelle's last-minute discovery about the behavior of carbon.

Stabilizing Earth's climate has become an explicit goal of global governance. Yet there is nothing in the scientific literature that dictates how the climate should be managed. The form that climate governance took in Rio and that has developed since reflects the hegemony of the sovereign national state that we discussed in the last chapter. On the one hand, the treaty acknowledges "that change in the Earth's climate and its adverse effects are a common concern of humankind" and that, as a result, "the global nature of climate change calls for the widest possible cooperation by all countries and their participation in an effective and appropriate international response." But the treaty is explicit that national states have "the sovereign right to exploit their own resources," and it reaffirms "the principle of sovereignty of States in international cooperation to address climate change."[4] The tension between these two positions remains central to how the climate is—and isn't—governed.

The governance architecture that has developed "to protect the climate system for present and future generations," in the words of the UNFCCC, is firmly multilevel. Policy decisions are made by UN bodies and other multilateral institutions, like the World Bank; by the European Union, the primary supranational governor in existence; by the executives, legislatures, and judiciaries of national governments; by subnational authorities at the provincial and municipal levels (sometimes, as we'll explore in chapter 5, working across international borders in collaborative translocal networks); and by nonstate actors, like corporations and NGOs. The Twenty-First Conference of the Parties (COP 21) of the UNFCCC, which produced the 2015 Paris Agreement—the apotheosis of international climate diplomacy thus far—explicitly endorsed this multilevel governance environment, recognizing the importance of "non-Party stakeholders, including civil society, the private sector, financial institutions, cities and other subnational authorities, local communities and indigenous peoples."[5] All of these institutions have a role to play in the multilevel system, but only one of them—the national state—is sovereign. As a result, the national state is the immovable, structural foundation of the architecture of global governance.

Yet the governance superstructure that sits above, below, and beside the national state is still important. That's because the sovereign national state's ideological triumph by 1965 was never fully reflected in actual governance practice. The sovereign national state achieved its global hegemony because it was seen as the best political form for addressing what felt to many like the most pressing governance challenge of the second half of the twentieth century—delivering national economic growth. But economic development was never the only problem in need of governance. In particular, concentrating governance functions and responsibilities at the national level left two broad classes of problems unaddressed: challenges that transcended national boundaries, like climate change, and challenges at the local level.

In response to the hegemony of the national state, an array of actors developed institutions to tackle the outstanding challenges that national states were ill equipped to handle. In the 1960s, at the very moment of the national state's global triumph, there was simultaneously an efflorescence of non-national forms of governance at all levels.[6] Above the national state, the number of international treaties took off: from 8,776 signed by 1960 to 63,419 by 2010 (and for international treaties countersigned by the UN, which signifies a treaty's importance, the number grew from 942 by 1960 to 6,154 by 2010).[7] Fully 90 percent of international nongovernmental organizations—groups like Médecins Sans Frontières and the World Anti-Doping Agency—were formed after 1969.[8] By the mid-1970s, mass publics and policy elites alike recognized that the tangled web of economic and political relationships among national states had led to a new condition of international relations, a "complex interdependence" that required some sort of international coordination and management.[9] Indeed, the Rio Earth Summit's precursor, the UN Conference on the Human Environment—the event that put global environmental problems on the global governance agenda—was held in Stockholm in 1972. Meanwhile, below the national state, a global trend toward decentralization and privatization of state authority began in the 1970s and 1980s, respectively.[10]

In the past half century, even as national states solidified their place as the only legitimate form of sovereignty, these same national states shared, delegated, and outsourced more and more governance functions to subnational and international institutions. At the same time, subnational, international, and national institutions' "spans of control" (that is, what decisions these institutions have the formal or informal authority to make) continued to fail to match their "spans of responsibility" (that is, the results they were held accountable for).[11] Mismatches between the two led to persistent perceptions of governmental underperformance, as institutions and the leaders were held accountable for results over which they did not have effective control.

Today, international organizations do more than ever before, but many of the most important global challenges remain not just ungoverned but *ungovernable* within the current institutional architecture. Likewise, local governments do more than they did decades ago, yet their capacity is often hampered by national governments' sovereign prerogatives. Governance today is produced by the operational capacity of a wide range of institutions at diverse scales, but sovereignty remains stubbornly national. In other words, while operational responsibilities have migrated, sovereignty has not. Despite all that has changed since 1965, the keystones of governance are the nominally equal sovereign national states that blanket the globe. This chapter will explain what has changed, what has not, and what it all means for governance around—and of—the planet.

Multilateralism

For as long as there have been national states, there have been challenges that exceed them. Wars and rivers, for example, have always crossed national boundaries. As a result, the development of nationalism went hand in hand with the development of internationalism as leaders, activists, and intellectuals tried to devise ways to govern problems without borders. Indeed, the term *international* was coined at the dawn of the national era, in 1780, by the English philosopher Jeremy Bentham to describe "the mutual transactions between sovereigns, as such." The concept clearly resonated with the times since in 1823 Bentham could notice that the word had "taken root in the language. Witness reviews and newspapers."[12]

Bentham could have noted further that his idea had taken root in the design of political institutions, including ones implemented and imagined. As far back as 1795, while France was still in the throes of revolution, the German philosopher Immanuel Kant sketched out the idea of a federal "world republic" that would bring "perpetual peace" to the pugnacious peoples of Europe.[13] Twenty years later, after Napoleon's defeat at Waterloo, the five major European powers met in Vienna to form a new international order secured by cooperation and regular meetings among them—"a principle of general union, uniting all the states collectively with a federative bond," as one Austrian official described it in 1818.[14] Beyond the marquee international institutions aimed at bringing peace to Europe, there have been lower-profile, yet often more successful, transnational collaborations since the early days of the modern statehood. France and the Holy Roman Empire established an international Rhine Commission in 1804 to govern the river's navigation and upkeep.[15] International public health institutions arose in Europe in the mid-nineteenth century to share information about epidemics, particularly cholera, and to coordinate quarantine practices among countries.[16]

Today, the primary political mechanism for addressing challenges that transcend individual national states is multilateralism, in which international organizations representing multiple member states pursue shared goals on an *intergovernmental* basis. Multilateralism manifests in the "alphabet soup" of international agencies: the ICC, WTO, WIPO, IMF, and so on. The central premise of multilateral institutions is bringing together multiple sovereign national states to promote coordination and cooperation among themselves. So while collaboration is the goal of multilateralism, national state sovereignty is its bedrock. This means that when tensions arise between collaboration and sovereignty, collaboration blinks first.

There are hundreds of intergovernmental organizations and agencies, but the preeminent multilateral body today—and indeed since its founding—is the United Nations. Unique among international organizations, the UN is both universal and general-purpose: it is open to every national state, and its remit is not limited to a specific region or set of issues. It has also created or adopted a number of specialized, subject-specific multilateral bodies—the World Health Organization (WHO), the International Atomic Energy Agency (IAEA), the International Labour Organization (ILO), the United Nations High Commissioner for Refugees (UNHCR), the Food and Agriculture Organization (FAO), the United Nations Children's Fund (UNICEF), the United Nations Framework Convention on Climate Change (UNFCCC), and so on—that together make up the UN system. This is not the place to revisit in detail the UN's well-known inadequacies and outright failures, or its grand successes.[17] But in order to understand the particular role that it plays we must touch on the deep tensions that are foundational to the UN's structure and systems.

Established just two months after the end of World War II, the UN was beset from birth with contradictions. It is "based on the principle of the sovereign equality of all its Members," but five permanent members of the Security Council were blessed with a veto that gives them unequaled powers.[18] The preamble of the UN Charter invokes the authority of "we the peoples" and speaks of "the dignity and worth of the human person" but was written by the architect of South African apartheid, who saw the new organization as a vehicle for maintaining European empires.[19] The organization promised to foster a world where states "live together in peace with one another as good neighbours" but was intended by the American diplomats who planned and promoted it to be an instrument for the legitimation of US power and military supremacy.[20] Above all, the UN's lofty goals amount to the ambition of making the *world* a better place for *humanity*, yet it represents neither the world nor humanity but instead national states.[21] Rhetoric aside, the UN is an association of sovereign states: it answers to states and for states, particularly the most powerful ones.

The UN's structure centered on the sovereign national state, which it inherited from the League of Nations, affects everything about the institution, from the design of its headquarters—as we discussed in the previous chapter—to its approach to solving global problems. This approach relies primarily on encouraging, goading, even pleading with states to coordinate their national policies or to cooperate with each other to provide collective solutions. While this "organized volunteerism" is born of the UN's congenital inability to compel member-states to coordinate or cooperate, it nonetheless provides workable solutions for many international issues.[22] It is particularly viable for a class of issues that game theorists call "coordination problems," in which players (in this case national states) care more about adopting the same course of action as other players than they do about which particular course of action they adopt.[23]

For instance, the UN specialized agency that focuses on information and communication technologies—the International Telecommunication Union (ITU), which is, in fact, one of the oldest international organizations, dating to 1865—successfully coordinates states' use of the radio spectrum and satellite orbits.[24] National states are generally indifferent to which specific radio frequencies they use or on which specific orbits their satellites travel; they primarily want to ensure that other states do not use the same ones to prevent radios from jamming or satellites from crashing. For issues like this, the UN and other multilateral institutions can be invaluable facilitators of international coordination.

Despite the UN's many successes in resolving international coordination problems, its sanctification of national state sovereignty has left the nature of the international system intact. The essential characteristic of the contemporary international system is what international relations scholars describe as "anarchy." In international relations jargon, anarchy does not mean chaos but rather an absence of central political authority that can make and enforce decisions because every state is sovereign. The opposite of anarchy is thus hierarchy, like what exists (or is imagined to exist) in national political systems, where the domestic central government can (at least in theory) make and enforce decisions. Under conditions of anarchy, national states can and do cooperate with each other and often form international organizations to formalize and institutionalize their cooperation. But, significantly, each state remains and retains the ultimate authority within its borders, including the authority to cooperate, or not, with others. As a result, multilateral institutions work for their member states, not for the general good, and only when the leaders of the member states allow them to.

National state sovereignty might produce satisfactory outcomes if each state was completely independent and could achieve its goals regardless of what other states did. But they are not independent; the international system—and the planet it exists on—are defined by interdependence. National states—even the most sovereign among them—must be concerned with the actions of other states.[25] In multilateral institutions, the logic of anarchy trumps the logic of interdependence: despite their effects on others, each state can plot its own course. Privileging state sovereignty is a core feature of multilateral governance, but one that hobbles its own effectiveness.

Supranationalism

To get around the problems that national state sovereignty poses for multinational cooperation, the idea of supranationalism recommends favoring the whole over the parts, diluting state sovereignty and enhancing the authority of supranational institutions. In practice, this means that supranational institutions can make legally binding decisions that apply to each member state without them having to adopt the policy in national law. Supranational institutions do not supplement national policymaking and governance, they are a substitute—what the supranational body says goes.

The most ambitious recent attempt to move in this direction has been the European Union. In its quest for "ever-closer union among the peoples of Europe," the EU has taken on key powers that typically accrue to national governments.[26] In day-to-day governance, the EU has assumed enormous authority to make policy that affects the lives of its 450 million citizens and many others outside its jurisdiction.[27] Its power notwithstanding, the EU remains something less than a sovereign state. At the same time, it is something more than a multilateral institution. It is institutionally sui generis—"un objet politique non-identifié," in the words of former European Commission president Jacques Delors: an unidentified political object.[28] Whether the EU is truly a supranational political institution remains contested, but for the present discussion we follow the lead of many close observers and classify it as supranational.[29] What matters most for us is that it often governs as if it were a supranational institution.[30]

European integration has profoundly affected how and where policy issues in Europe are governed, but the present-day EU is a limited political entity compared to the original plans bruited in the mid-1950s. Jean Monnet and other early architects of "the European project" envisaged an even more robust set of institutions, including a European Defense Community, with a unified military command, and the European Political Community, which together would have completely recast the nature of state sovereignty.[31] As Robert Schuman, then the foreign

minister of France and a key proponent of European unity, wrote in
1951: "From now on the treaties must create not just obligations but institutions, which is to say supranational organs with their own independent authority.... These organs are at the service of a supranational
community with objectives and interests that are distinct from those
of each of the participating nations. The individual interests of those
nations merge into the common interest."[32] These postwar considerations in Europe in many ways paralleled similar thinking, explored in
chapter 1, among anticolonial and postcolonial leaders at the exact same
moment. In fact, just like many African, Asian, and Caribbean elites,
proponents of a united Europe often described their aim as "federation"
until the late 1940s. The term *integration* took hold only after being
popularized by Americans.[33] Out of this era of open political experimentation, a number of pan-European institutions were proposed or
created. For its first decades, the European Community (EC; the EU's
predecessor) competed with these other institutions for dominance on
the Continent. It was not until the mid-1980s that the EC achieved primacy as the principal institution for European political cooperation and
economic integration.[34]

The EU's appeal comes from the fact that the member states delegated real, binding powers and functions to it. Thus the EU can govern
in ways that multilateral institutions cannot. The EU, for example,
issues a common currency and common debt. Its high court has the
supremacy to overturn most national laws. It can require its member
states to enforce identical standards and regulations on a wide range
of issues, from pollution and product safety to transportation. Unlike
multilateral governance, these decisions are not optional in any meaningful sense. Consequently, the EU achieves policy breadth and depth
that eludes other international organizations.[35]

The EU has succeeded in practicing supranational governance by
transforming the nature of European statehood in ways that multilateral institutions have not. States that join the UN and other multilateral institutions remain sovereign national states. They commit
to following the basic rules of the organization, but the organization

likewise commits not to interfere in the states' internal affairs. States that join the EU, by contrast, become a new, different type of state: one that voluntarily abrogates its own sovereignty in order to limit national power via binding commitments to the EU. This transformation from national state to EU "member state" places constraints on national governments, breaking (or at least loosening) the link between national politics and policymaking. In the view of some critics, the primary political relationship should now be seen as the horizontal ties between and among national governments and EU institutions, not the vertical ties between national government and national society.[36]

This transformation of statehood was not the result of hidden structural forces or an insurmountable logic of integration. The individual member states, and more specifically their political leaderships, made decisions at every step to pursue closer union. They willingly remade the nature of the states they led, limiting their own national governments, constricting their own freedom to act, and moving the level at which consequential governance decisions were made.[37] In practice, decision-making authority was almost always moved "up" from national governments to the EU. Despite the emphasis in the 1992 Maastricht Treaty, the EU's founding document, on the principle of subsidiarity—the idea that decisions should be made as close to the affected communities as possible for an adequate resolution of an issue—governance decisions were rarely moved "down" either from the European level to the national level or from the national level to the regional and local level, a problem we will explore in chapter 4.[38]

The EU's defining feature, however, and arguably its most consequential flaw, is not its institutional structure but its primary functional domain, namely economic integration. The EU's paramount goal has been the establishment of a common market based on "freedom of movement for persons, services and capital" among members states and a common trade policy with outside countries.[39] The European Community's and then European Union's focus on economic integration has led to an ever-expanding remit. Since the economy can plausibly be argued to touch on nearly every aspect of collective life, the EC and EU pushed to take on more governance functions in more areas: from its traditional purview of monetary, trade, and agriculture policies and market integration to labor regulations, public health, education, traffic safety, food safety, and internet privacy. European integration could have taken many paths, but the one it did take has been defined by a market logic that has agitated for the centralization of powers in Brussels (and Frankfurt, Luxembourg City, and, less so, Strasbourg).

The problem with the EU is that, at heart, integration through the EC and EU has been a neoliberal (or, more accurately, ordoliberal) economic project, that is, one bent on curbing redistributional politics, which (as argued in chapter 1) is a properly national function. By taking over economic governance from national states but refusing to engage in democratically determined distributional politics, the EU has gradually revealed itself as little more than a high-minded rationalization for commerce and the domination of societies by markets, all enforced from Brussels. The consequences of this position came into full snarling view in the aftermath of the global financial crisis of 2007–8. When Greece and other southern Eurozone members suffered severe economic emergencies, the EU had the opportunity to govern in many possible ways. Its supranational architecture didn't dictate any particular position—if anything, the founding spirit of the structure would suggest a move toward pan-European solidarity. Yet the path it chose was the domineering imposition of neoliberal reforms and austerity measures.[40] The problem in this case was not the delegation of powers "upward" above the national state but the ends toward which those powers were used. The EU's economically focused design, combined with a refusal to engage in cross-national distributional politics, effectively narrowed the scope of democratic debate over the topic that more than anything else the modern national state was established to govern.[41]

Whatever the flaws of taking distributional debates out of the politics of economic governance, the EU's power to impose its policies on member states nevertheless demonstrates how supranationalism avoids the inherent weakness in multilateralism. If multilateral governance's effectiveness is hampered by state sovereignty, Europe's experiment with supranationalism reveals the possibilities that are opened when that sovereignty is subordinate. While the EU to date has used the subordination of state sovereignty to pursue neoliberal economic commitments, there remains the possibility that a reimagined European project could serve as a model for supranational governance at a planetary scale. For political philosopher and activist Lorenzo Marsili, the European Political Community—a forum founded in 2022, in the wake of Russia's invasion of Ukraine, that includes far more members than the EU—contains the seeds for such a project: it "may become the first democratic laboratory for a 'planetary' politics that goes beyond the nation state and bestows tangible benefits and rights on the citizens of participating states."[42] The Community is still new, so we'll have to wait and see.

Decentralization, Privatization, and Nonstate Governance

At the same time that national states began to delegate some responsibilities "up" to international organizations, they also started to delegate certain other responsibilities "down" to subnational units, reflecting a strong trend toward decentralizing authority around the world. By this we mean that there has been a meaningful movement of political, fiscal, and administrative powers, as well as resources, from national governments to lower tiers of government. This decentralization has made subnational governments, such as municipal and provincial governments, increasingly significant interfaces between the state and its citizens.[43]

Starting around 1970, national states in both the Global North and South began to devolve governance powers to subnational tiers of government, such as regions, provinces, states, and municipalities.[44] By one measure, countries on average undergo a reform that reconfigures the loci of governmental authority (from the national to regional level, for example) every thirteen years—in large countries it's every eleven.[45] The institutional architecture of governance within national states is marked by fluidity rather than rigidity. (For American readers this might be surprising, but the United States' inflexible institutional design is one site of relative American exceptionalism.) These transfers of authority mean that, in general, subnational governments now have greater fiscal autonomy and more power to set goals and implement policies to achieve them within their territory. There has also been a growth in subnational democracy, with more lower tiers of government holding elections and having elected assemblies.[46] Even China has held elections for village leaders since 1988.[47] Subnational governments are thus more powerful and more representative than they were in the mid-twentieth century.

There were several impetuses for national states to shift decisions and resources to lower-level component parts beginning in the 1970s. National states around the world sought to relax the centralizing drives of nationalism, authoritarianism, and war that characterized much of the twentieth century. States made concessions to ethnic minorities' demands for self-rule and crafted strategies to position cities to compete for international capital in the globalized economy.[48] Moreover, in the rich countries of the Global North, stagflation and perceptions of national governments' mismanagement of economic matters drove elites away from the impulse for centralized decision-making. In the United States, the rollback of federal power in favor of states began under Richard Nixon, accelerated under Jimmy Carter's deregulation initiatives, and consolidated under Ronald Reagan's New Federalism in the 1980s. And in the Global South, the evident failure of postcolonial national states to achieve economic development, their chief objective since birth, eroded the mystique of the centralized state. Centrally planned development projects came to be seen by national elites, foreign creditors, and international organizations as wasteful, corrupt, and incapable of producing either domestic economic growth or the resources to repay lenders.

By the 1980s, international institutions, especially the IMF and World Bank, urged countries to decentralize their governance, arguing that this would improve responsiveness and performance, minimize central state corruption, and improve democratic accountability.[49] When recommendations did not spur desired action, multilateral lenders turned to more coercive means, conditioning loans, which Third World governments needed in order to remain solvent, on "structural adjustment," including reducing the size of national governments by decentralizing and privatizing (discussed shortly) state functions. These prescribed reforms remade the structures of governance across Latin America and Africa, in particular.[50] The EU likewise made decentralization a prerequisite for membership for the ten postcommunist states that joined in 2004.[51] These reforms, while often originating from outside the national state, were sometimes taken up happily by domestic elites, eager to shift blame for a lack of resources and poor performance onto others. Decentralization, for national elites, meant that many persistent challenges now became someone else's problem.

The trend toward decentralization was often accompanied by a proliferation of subnational governance units. India, for example, has doubled the number of states in its federation since independence; Nigeria went from three regions at the time of independence in 1960 to twelve states in 1967, to nineteen in 1976, to thirty-six in 1996, with these latter further divided into 774 "local government areas"; after apartheid, South Africa doubled its number of provinces and quintupled the number of municipalities; and Czechoslovakia, Hungary, and Brazil each increased their municipalities by about 50 percent during periods of democratic reforms.[52]

This decentralization and devolution of authority has restructured the nature of governance within the national state.[53] Yet with sovereignty still held exclusively by national governments, the power of subnational governments to govern themselves remains constrained, as meta-authority—the authority to decide which authorities are vested in which institutions—and the ability to overrule locally made decisions continue to sit at the level of the national state. We will return to this problem in chapter 4, arguing that further delegation of authority to smaller-scale institutions, when principled and careful, is a key aspect of a reimagined governance architecture for the planet.

In addition to decentralization's rearrangement of the positions of power within the state, since the 1980s there has been a trend toward delegating governance functions outside the state altogether. In fact, the rise of the concept of "governance," as opposed to "government," emerged in the context of prevalent antistatism of the 1980s and 1990s.[54] The increasing privatization of governance took place in both the Global North and South, but it took on a different guise in each. In the Global North, voters elected leaders, epitomized by Ronald Reagan in the US and Margaret Thatcher in the UK, who were ideologically opposed to state governance. In the Global South, international lenders and donors, like the World Bank, pushed economically weak and indebted national states to cut spending, including by decentralizing some state functions, as just discussed, and eliminating or outsourcing others to the private sector or nongovernmental organizations (NGOs). The result of these processes is that in much of the world overall governance is provided by what political scientists call a "hybrid" system, involving contributions by both state and nonstate actors.[55]

Nonstate governance providers run the gamut: from local to international, formal organizations to informal networks, for-profit to nonprofit, socially inclusive to exclusive.[56] Oxfam, the Islamic State, the International Chamber of Commerce, and ExxonMobil, to name just four very different sorts of organizations, each in its own way governs populations and territory, providing order, settling disputes, regulating transactions, producing public goods, delivering social services, and more. These actors' interactions with the state likewise vary widely. In some circumstances, the state dominates provision of a governance function, and nonstate actors might only fill in limited gaps in the geographic or social peripheries. In other cases, the state provides a function so poorly that nonstate providers take on a larger role. In still other situations, the state plays little to no role in the provision of governance, and nonstate actors serve as a substitute.[57] Any of these hybrid arrangements can be by design, stemming from an explicit or implicit agreement between the state and nonstate providers, or can emerge from nonstate providers backfilling (or crowding out) a state that is failing to furnish governance services that the population demands. Except in the most extreme circumstances, however, governance is rarely a case of *either* only the state *or* only nonstate providers; much more often it is a case of "both/and"—the sum total of governance is the result of contributions by state and nonstate actors.

The scale and diversity of private governance institutions are apparent even in the most characteristic state function: order and security. When the state can't (or doesn't) secure a monopoly of violence in a territory, private actors often emerge to supplement or replace the state.[58] Under such circumstances, nonstate security providers—including rebel militias, criminal gangs, vigilante groups, private security firms, and neighborhood watch organizations—take it upon themselves to provide order, however brutal. The experience of order and security by many populations, rich and poor, all throughout the world, is not the sole product of state action but the result of nonstate security providers working alongside, at the behest of, in place of, or even against the state.

Take the example of Dudus Coke, Jamaica's most powerful "don," or community leader-cum-crime boss, until he was extradited to the United States in 2010 for trafficking drugs and arms. In his Kingston neighborhood, Coke's organization *was* the government—everyone called him "president." The state police could enter only with his approval; Coke's men provided security, order, and justice, using their own judges, jail, and executioners. His methods were rough, but some preferred them to the ineffective state. Inform the Jamaican police of a robbery and "you never heard from them [the police] again," according to a local pastor. Tell Coke's men about it, however, and "in a few hours, maybe a day, you get back your thing. . . . They get it done." Many residents left their doors unlocked. But it was more than security: "the system," as it was known, collected taxes, provided free food, lent money to businesses, subsidized electricity, and disbursed financial aid for school tuition, legal fees, and medical bills. After sustained international pressure, Jamaica's prime minister ordered Coke's arrest. Eventually, the military and police raided his neighborhood and reasserted state control, but only after killing dozens of residents.[59]

Hybrid governance doesn't just take the form of strongman-run, government no-go zones, however. Take another example: collaborative efforts on environmental protection between the Liberian government, the UN Development Program, Liberian NGOs, and a host of other local, national, and international actors. This jointly provided environmental governance is the product of multiple institutions working together: funding local civil society organizations, training young people, offering scientific exchanges, building climate-resilient infrastructure, and promoting green energy sources. Neither the Liberian government nor community NGOs could afford many of these initiatives; and neither the UN nor foreign national governments could implement these policies directly without clear violations of Liberia's sovereignty. But through collaboration among the institutions at various scales, the totality of on-the-ground governance is produced.[60]

Coke's private statelet in Jamaica's capital and Liberian environmental actions are only two of countless examples of public and private governance providers clashing, coexisting, or collaborating. From urban slums to suburban gated communities, periurban settlements to remote villages, governance arrangements in most of the planet's inhabited territories are heterogeneous and lumpy rather than uniform and smooth. The idea of a homogeneous national state that totally controls its sovereign territory and consistently governs all its residents is a fiction.[61]

Actually Existing Multilevel Governance

Since the 1970s, many of the governing functions and capabilities that once sat, at least in theory, in centralized state institutions have moved to international organizations, subnational governments, or a wide array of international and subnational nonstate actors. Despite this dislocation, relocation, and sometimes dismemberment of the loci of power in territories throughout the world, we still tend to see the world as atlases portray it: every inch of land designated by color code as belonging to a single particular state. This manner of representing the world presents and sustains two ideas as natural: first, that each of these states exerts its power uniformly over the entire uniformly colored territory the map designates it as possessing, just as every other state does; and, second, that national states are *the* salient mechanism through which the planet is (and should be) governed. As this chapter has argued, neither is accurate. Governance today is provided by multiple actors working at multiple scales and on multiple levels. Put another way, world maps display claims to sovereignty, not actually existing governance.

The trends in rescaling governing institutions up (multilateralism and supranationalism) and down (decentralization and privatization) along with the continued power of the national state have led to the emergence of the world's actually existing multilevel governance system.[62] Outcomes depend on decisions made and actions taken at all levels. Through a mix of delegation, cooperation, and usurpation, the various institutions above, below, beside, and of the national state have forged countless *modi operandi* for dealing with challenges at all scales. But these institutions do not operate on a level playing field. While all of them govern, only the national state is sovereign. And sovereignty gives the national state the legitimate authority to interfere in the work of the others. The resulting multilevel governance architecture is ad hoc: it emerged when and where sovereign national states allowed it to. The scale of a problem may be a better fit for supranational or subnational management, but the sovereign national state gets to decide whether non-national action is warranted.

Two challenges that manifest at scales incompatible with the national state are climate change and infectious diseases. Neither carbon nor microbes care about human jurisdictions, and each exposes the interdependences, rather than independence, of all political communities. These characteristics, we will argue in the next chapter, distinguish them as *planetary* challenges. In other words, they are challenges that emanate, not from the international arena or global flows and competition over human concerns such as goods, services, people, and money, but rather from the dynamic biogeochemical ferment of the planet itself. Yet the governance architecture for addressing each of these planetary challenges remains firmly anchored in national states: they are the institutional form with the right of first refusal and the right to authorize action at other levels. The actually existing ad hoc multilevel governance structures that address these problems spring from this national foundation.

Climate change is a quintessential planetary problem, a phenomenon on the scale of the Earth itself. Efforts to mitigate its worst outcomes have naturally focused on achieving global action. But achieving global action requires multilateral cooperation; and, unfortunately, the failures to achieve global action exemplify the problem inherent in multilateralism. In three decades of international climate negotiations, the two most important agreements were reached in Kyoto in 1997 and Paris in 2015.[63] These two agreements illustrate the barrier to resolving a planetary problem like climate change in a world of sovereign national states—even when countries agree on a multilateral solution. In Kyoto, negotiators reached an agreement with strict and binding limits on greenhouse gas emissions for countries to meet. These emission limits, however, applied only to wealthy countries; poorer countries, which included China, did not have to meet them. Moreover, the United States, the largest emitter at the time, refused to ratify the agreement.[64] The Kyoto Protocol's effort tackle the root causes of climate change by aggressively reducing greenhouse gas emissions therefore failed to gain the participation of the two largest emitters.

In contrast to Kyoto, the Paris Agreement included nearly every country: the signatories account for 97 percent of global emissions. The diplomats negotiating the Paris Agreement understood that there was a trade-off between binding limits on emissions and comprehensive participation and opted for wider membership at the expense of binding limits. They gained near-universal participation by making countries' pledges to limit their national emissions under the agreement voluntary.[65] These voluntary commitments are not without meaning or power—the very act of making public commitments emphasizes the importance of the issue to the public and sets targets for domestic political mobilization to aim for—but they lack teeth at two crucial points. First, national states that are party to the Paris Agreement set their own domestic emission reduction goals, which means that their goals are not necessarily ambitious enough to keep global temperature increases within the agreed-upon limits.[66] Second, there is no mechanism for ensuring that national states meet their commitments for emissions reductions. Each state is on the honor system. "Parties shall pursue domestic mitigation measures," the Paris Agreement states, "with *the aim of* achieving the objectives of such contributions."[67]

Kyoto and Paris each failed to reduce emissions in their own way. Kyoto failed to get major emitters inside the strong and binding multilateral framework; Paris got them inside a multilateral framework, but it is weak and unenforceable. Either way, multilateral climate agreements have not reduced or even stabilized global carbon emissions. But neither have the efforts of individual national states, subnational governments, or nonstate actors. The problem is too big to be solved absent a planetary-scale collective solution. Subglobal institutions can (and should) take important efforts to not make the situation worse, but they cannot make things substantially better on their own. Their good work can be undone by emissions elsewhere, or, in the case of subnational governments, can be countermanded by their national government.

In sum: actually existing multilevel climate governance is a stark failure. In 1997, when Kyoto was signed, the global average atmospheric carbon dioxide was 363 parts per million (ppm). In 2016, when Paris entered into force, it was 403 ppm. In 2022, the latest year for which we have annual data, it was 417 ppm.[68] Moreover, the most recent national commitments under the Paris Agreement are not sufficient to meet the agreement's goals.[69] This means that even if every national state party to the agreement meets its own stated targets—which most are *not* doing anyway—global average temperatures will surpass the 2°C increase that Paris is committed to averting.[70]

The existing multilevel architecture for public health governance similarly breaks down in the face of state sovereignty, though for a different reason. The primary international public health body, the World

Health Organization, has great breadth, with 194 member states.[71] But it gained such extensive membership at the cost of depth, or its ability to act independently of its members, especially the most powerful members. In the case of public health surveillance, the continuous collection and analysis of health data, the WHO is able to monitor and warn of possible disease outbreaks only when the country experiencing the disease permits it. If the national government finds the WHO overly intrusive or worries that its public health surveillance might reveal something that the government would not want public, it can forbid or curtail the WHO's work. The WHO of course understands this dynamic and therefore often opts to not push members states too hard for fear of losing access.

The problem underlying WHO access to sovereign states sits atop another structural issue: the primary responsibility for public health surveillance lies with national health authorities. Diseases are not national, yet the structure of the international system means that the main institutions for monitoring and reacting to diseases are. Making matters still more difficult, many national authorities lack the capacity to monitor outbreaks or react in much of their territory. Nevertheless, the national government retains the authority to allow outsiders to monitor or assist with this work.

These structural deficiencies were on full display during the emergence of the COVID-19 pandemic. First, China's national public health surveillance system, the Contagious Disease National Direct Reporting System, failed to detect the growing outbreak in Wuhan in December 2019 because local health officials did not want to be the bearers of bad news to the central government.[72] This lack of knowledge delayed a national response in China. While this particular cause of the breakdown was specific to China's system of governance, it was not unique: such a national failure could happen in almost any country. (In the mid-1960s, scientists estimated that 95 percent of all smallpox cases worldwide went unreported to national and international authorities, in part because local officials feared the consequences of informing their superiors about an outbreak in their district.)[73] Second, Beijing was willing to notify the WHO of an outbreak of the novel coronavirus but was unwilling to let the multilateral public health agency conduct a full response. In order to receive the necessary permission from China to send an international team of experts to the country to investigate the origins of the COVID-19 outbreak, the WHO agreed to not question Beijing's early actions or to visit key locations in Wuhan where the outbreak might have originated. As one of its former officials explained, the WHO "prioritizes access to the country" over other goals.[74] A second WHO fact-finding trip included more but not complete access to requested sites and data, and was allowed to happen only after the WHO gave China control over central parts of the research. National, subnational, and nonstate public health and health care providers around the world had their work impaired by one national state's sovereign prerogatives.[75]

Other national governments also made missteps that hastened the spread of the virus. For instance, national states have the sovereign ability to stop international travel in and out of their borders, which could have dramatically slowed the pandemic's progress, but few acted in time; social distancing guidelines could have been implemented more stringently but in many cases weren't; and vaccine rollouts could have taken place more effectively but often didn't. These governance failures in the face of the pandemic provoked a series of national political crises. In fact, to a very large extent, blaming national leaders was unfair, since national leaders were presiding over governance institutions that simply did not have the scale and capacity to successfully address a pandemic that was, by definition, planetary in scope. The lack of a supranational authority capable of acting autonomously and securing compliance meant that national states were left alone to fight a battle that they could not win on their own.

No Easy Victories

The existing ad hoc multilevel governance system is not without successes. In the domains of both the environment and public health, existing institutions have generated significant achievements, including repairing the ozone layer and eradicating smallpox, and it is important to understand why these institutions succeeded in these cases.

In the 1970s, scientists—including James Lovelock and Paul Crutzen, whom we will hear from in chapter 3—discovered that certain chemicals in common industrial processes and consumer products, including refrigerators, air conditioners, and aerosols, were degrading the ozone layer, which protects living beings from ultraviolent radiation. Public fears of a cancerous future due to excess UV radiation led a desire for action. In the early 1980s, the UN Environmental Program convened diplomatic talks that bore fruit in 1985 with the Vienna Convention for the Protection of the Ozone Layer and, more consequentially, in 1987 with the Montreal Protocol on Substances That Deplete the Ozone Layer. The Montreal Protocol set the signatories' "ultimate objective" as eliminating ozone-depleting substances "on the basis of developments in scientific knowledge, taking into account technical and economic considerations."[76] Yet the mere fact that parties reached an agreement in the form of these two treaties is not why the ozone regime is hailed the great triumph of global environmental governance—or even, in the estimation of former UN secretary-general Kofi Annan, "perhaps the single most successful international agreement to date."[77]

The Montreal Protocol's success in halting and reversing damage to the ozone layer results from the "underlying logic and institutions of governance" that it established, particularly what climate policy scholars Charles F. Sabel and David G. Victor call its "experimentalist regime that drew firms and governments into collaboration in solving concrete pollution problems."[78] The institutionalization of multilevel, practical problem-solving produced rapid and pronounced innovations that allowed the regime to phase out and prohibit most ozone-depleting substances. Montreal's governing institutions thus took advantage of the multiple types of actors involved in the problem (especially governments and firms that produce or use ozone-damaging chemicals) to place scientific knowledge (from government, industry, and academia) at the center of a process that evaluates and tightens controls on the use of chemicals that harm the ozone layer. Thus, while national states reached an important agreement in Montreal in 1987, the success of the regime lay in the multiscalar regime that they established. The diplomats sketched a blueprint, but the real work took place on the basis of technical assessments, collaborations among different scales of governance (public and private, global and local, etc.), and experiments in applied and basic science as well as in institutional design and administration.

Even more impressive than the multilateral effort to repair the ozone layer is the WHO's world-historic success in eradicating smallpox. Fully launched in 1967—a time when the disease was taking two million lives each year, contributing to an estimated three hundred million deaths over the twentieth century—the UN global health body's Smallpox Eradication Program (SEP) was able to eliminate the devastating virus in just twelve years. The task was daunting, and the WHO, having just failed in its effort to eradicate malaria, was by no means destined to triumph. What, then, explains why in May 1980 the World Health Assembly could declare "that the world and all its peoples have won freedom from smallpox"? How did the WHO achieve this "unprecedented achievement," demonstrating "how nations working together in a common cause may further human progress"?[79]

The global SEP's accomplishment resulted from innovations in science and technology and administrative methods as well as fortuitous international politics. Politically, both the US and Soviet Union took an interest in ending smallpox worldwide in the mid-1960s, but then left the work to technical experts who operated below the radar of Cold War high politics, meaning that the turbulence of East-West relations were generally removed from the picture. With the geopolitical stage set, these technocrats and the over 150,000 field staff, mainly local health workers from the countries of operation, could focus on the immediate politics and cultural diplomacy of the vaccination campaign: "delicate jockeying in international forums in Geneva, negotiation of 'country agreements' with all participating governments, and the coordination of vaccination campaigns with a host of local actors, from Hausa emirs in northern Nigeria to village heads in rural Uttar Pradesh."[80] Put another way, the SEP operated nimbly in a multiscalar environment, adapting its standardized, scientific practices to fit the international, national, and local social, cultural, and political institutions—in some cases even negotiating with local priests who led their communities in the veneration of smallpox deities.[81] With this cultural and administrative flexibility, SEP staff could take advantage of advances in vaccine distribution and injection to vaccinate billions of people across three continents.

It is instructive to compare the smallpox campaign to the WHO's unsuccessful Malaria Eradication Program (MEP; 1955–69). Three factors stand out. First, unlike the SEP, a product of US-Soviet collaboration, the MEP was a US-led project, as the USSR and its allies boycotted the WHO in those years. As a result, its priorities mirrored US strategic priorities—a focus on Southeast Asia, for example—rather than being comprehensively global in scope. Second, the nature of transmission and the nature of prevention of the two diseases were hugely influential. Malaria is caused by a parasite transmitted to humans by mosquitoes, while smallpox was caused by a virus transmitted directly between humans. Moreover, an effective smallpox vaccine was discovered in the late eighteenth century, while a malaria vaccine was unavailable during the MEP—the first one was approved only in 2022. This led to a crucial difference in the two campaigns. The SEP's primary method was inoculating individual human bodies against the virus. The MEP's main method, by contrast, was attacking the nonhuman carriers of the disease: mosquitoes. To disrupt mosquito-to-human transmission, the MEP used massive quantities of synthetic insecticides, principally DDT. This approach had two problems, one political, one biological.

Politically, during the years of the campaign, DDT came to be targeted for its ruinous ecological consequences—*Silent Spring*, Rachel Carson's influential exposé and attack on the "chemical barrage [that] has been hurled against the fabric of life," was published in the middle of the campaign, in 1962. Biologically, mosquitoes demonstrated what Carson called life's capability of "striking back in unexpected ways."[82] The widespread, global spraying of DDT to control malaria since World War II led to the emergence of DDT-resistant mosquitoes. Thus the MEP's "cure" became politically toxic and practically ineffective. Facing resistance from worried publics and mosquitoes alike, the WHO shuttered the MEP, its first-ever global program, nowhere close to reaching its goal of eradicating malaria from the world.[83]

The Montreal Protocol and the Smallpox Eradication Program were victories for the multilateral system and were by no means easy cases where success was assured. At the same time, they reveal the limits of that system. Montreal worked because it upended the UN system's usual way of doing business. Where multilateralism typically focuses on rigid and constrained international diplomatic processes that produce fixed, top-down targets or mandates, the negotiators in Montreal eschewed the conventional approach and created flexible, open processes with thin initial agreement and room for national, subnational, and sectoral experimentation focused on problem-solving. The SEP worked because the political stars were aligned—uncommon luck, even for problems with a common desire for solutions—and because the disease was susceptible to eradication. Smallpox is a strictly human disease; there were no zoonotic hosts to address. But most infectious diseases are zoonotic, so the SEP approach won't work. It's concerning, therefore, that multilateral health initiatives, which tend to remain rooted in the "global health" paradigm that became prominent in the late twentieth century, often fail to recognize that the interventions they undertake with the aim of improving human life have too often been, like the use of chemical insecticides in the malaria campaign, ecologically catastrophic, counterproductively leading to severe harm to human health itself.[84] We'll consider emerging alternative paradigms that place human health firmly in the context of planetary health in chapter 6.

———

National states today operate in and through a complex network of governance institutions consisting of many types of actors—some of which challenge or subvert the state, others of which complement or strengthen it. For any given territory or policy area, a national state is often, though not always, the most powerful actor, but it is rarely the only actor. Actually existing governance today is hybrid and multilevel. Most populations are governed not by one entity—the national state— but by an institutional matrix or multiplex that includes state and nonstate actors operating at multiple levels.[85] From the neighborhood level through the village, city, provincial, national, and regional levels and up to the planetary level, a riot of institutions collide, cooperate, or ignore each other to produce the variegated totality that is experienced as governance. This general description deliberately leaves room for enormous differences on what this looks like on the ground. There are vast divergences between the lives of, say, an American who relies on private, for-profit health care, sends her children to private, non-profit schools, and drives on public roads monitored by a local police force, and an Afghan who relies on an international NGO for health care, went to state school (subsidized by German aid), and drives on US-funded roads policed by the Taliban. But there is a commonality too: the kaleidoscopic, fragmented, multiscalar nature of governance delivery that shapes their routine affairs and the overall trajectory of their lives.

Beyond the national state, at the regional and global levels, this diversity is just as apparent. The issues that span state boundaries are governed by various institutional forms. Transnational challenges are addressed, with varying degrees of success, by the UN system, bilateral and multilateral treaties, international NGOs, the American hegemon and its global military footprint, and more. And to a certain extent, the scope and level of international cooperation are remarkable. Global governance institutions directly manage territories and populations, such as refugees, that fall outside the authority of national states; resemble a partial regulatory regime for some aspects of the world economy; operate a rough sketch of a global welfare state, facilitating the (immorally inadequate) redistribution of money, food, and medicine from the rich to the poor, delivering or subsidizing a large number of social services in the Global South; and focus the attention of divergent actors, at all the levels of governance, on shared priorities.[86] It's not the utopia that some hopeful, broken souls envisioned for the world after the Somme and Verdun, after Auschwitz and Hiroshima, or after Srebrenica and Rwanda, but for a number of transnational and global challenges, the existing architecture of global governance is sufficient and sometimes even superb. Some things fall through the cracks, but overall the system performs.

For other challenges, though, the existing system does not work at all. For challenges that we call planetary, a system premised on sovereign national states buttressed by subnational governments, nonstate actors, and multilateral institutions *cannot* work. There is a fundamental misalignment between the scale of the problems and the scope of the institutions tasked with dealing with the problems: the problems are world-scale, the institutions are not. This lack of planetary institutions also means there is no political accountability for addressing planetary challenges.

The result of our current system of governance is most charitably characterized as uneven. Some geographic spaces and issue areas are well governed, some are adequately governed, and some are poorly governed. This is true, to a greater or lesser degree, at almost any conceivable scale of collective life, but it is starkest when we consider the whole Earth. From this perspective, we already have a world state—but it's a failed state.[87] People, goods, capital, culture, data, and ideas crisscross national boundaries with ease. Pollutants, animals, bacteria, viruses, and CO_2 cycling through the atmosphere and oceans, as once studied by Revelle, are not aware that national boundaries exist. And yet, the global governance institutions that are tasked with managing these planetary flows lack the authority to act independently of the sovereign national states that make them up. We are stuck in a model that was designed for different problems in mind. Politics, as international relations scholar and diplomat Thomas Weiss laments, "remain imprisoned behind national borders."[88]

Three

The Planetary

In *The World Is Flat*, his best-selling paean to globalization from 2005, *New York Times* columnist Thomas Friedman argued that the fall of the Berlin Wall in 1989 triggered a rupture in consciousness, transforming how we think about the world. The collapse of the East-West divide cleared our vista, he said, and the world was revealed as "a seamless whole." It unlocked "our ability to think about the world as a single market, a single ecosystem, and a single community." Spurred by political change, this reimagination of the world accelerated through technological innovations and corporate strategies: globalization was "flattening the earth," Friedman observed, "and there's nothing people can do but bow down . . . and join the parade."[1]

By Friedman's telling, in this new flat world, this "seamless whole" that enabled unfettered flows, only certain flows mattered. The world was made flat by and for the easy movement of human desires: of people, ideas, goods, money. Everything else was treated as a sideshow or barrier to the real business of global integration. Pandemics, for instance, were relegated to one and one-half pages—of the roughly six-hundred-page book—in the chapter on the "unflat world," the forces that impede the flattening process of globalization.[2] In other words, the world of *The*

World Is Flat was an emphatically anthropocentric one: what mattered most were human intentions, beliefs, power, and agency.[3]

After the dark years of the early 2020s, as a deadly virus spread rapidly from Wuhan to everywhere else, can we still believe that is true? After watching the levels of atmospheric carbon rise to record heights year after year, can we still think human desires matter most? After witnessing epic floods (just in 2020) in Jakarta, Rio de Janeiro, Kyushu, Hyderabad, and the Myagdi District of Nepal? After wildfire seasons in Australia and California that keep growing longer and more destructive? After the HIV pandemic? As we approach the postantibiotic era? Do we still believe we can tame nature and subdue the Earth? Do we still believe we can flatten the planet with no consequences?

Try as we might, our lives as individuals and as a species are not always in our hands. Our ability to live and to thrive is constrained by phenomena that we do not control and with which we must instead learn (or relearn) how to coexist. Our ancestors certainly knew about these constraints—and many people, particularly in the Global South, still do. Infectious diseases, droughts, floods—the elements; acts of God—were and are reality. But today, too many of us act as if we can live apart from nature: ensconced in homes that protect us from wind and rain and heat and cold; in cities that keep wild beasts and factory farms at a comfortable distance; in bodies immunized from many diseases. From this position atop the commanding heights of economic and technological modernity, it was perhaps possible, for a while, to ignore or amend that which we could not control. But then sea levels started inching ever higher and a novel coronavirus crashed the party. The bravado of inexorable globalization simply doesn't ring true anymore, if it ever did.

To understand and address these new challenges, analysts and observers took up the familiar language of the global: global climate change, global pandemic, global biodiversity, global risks of all sorts. The familiar language, however, masks an unfamiliar distinction. For the *global* of globalization, as the historian Dipesh Chakrabarty has pointed out, is not the same as the *global* of global climate change.[4] The *global* of globalization is a conceptual category that frames the Earth in human terms. Hence globalization's human-centric understanding of the worldwide integration of the last few decades—the accelerating flow of people, their goods, their ideas, their money, their data, and so on.

The *global* of global climate change, by contrast, frames Earth without specific reference to humans. This globe references a vast, unified system fueled by solar rays, whose most salient features are physical and biogeochemical processes: fluxes of gases, liquids, solids, and energy on and around the third celestial object from the Sun.[5] This vision of the globe makes plain that Earth is not humanity's alone. We share it with other living beings, nonliving matter, and forms of energy. The *global* of global climate change affects humans and is affected by humans, but it was here before humans evolved and will be here long after humans have gone. This version of the global is a different concept, a different frame of reference than the *global* of globalization, which humans manufactured into being with low-cost maritime shipping, undersea communications cables, and worldwide banking networks. The incongruity between the two global ideas requires distinguishing between them. The human-centric *global* of globalization can remain the *globe* or *global*; the Earth-centric *global* of global climate change is better understood as the *planet* or the *Planetary*.

Seen this way, the planet is an interdependent whole, but this condition of interdependence did not emerge from the intentional work of humans. Dependent on other living beings and embedded in Earth's biogeochemistry and thermodynamics, humans are part of an interconnected planetary system, what scientists call the "Earth system."[6] We stand inside and among, not outside, the flows of life, of matter, of energy that circulate over time and through space in the Earth system.

Begin with the largest scale: it is now evident that fossil fuel–based industrialization is responsible for raising atmospheric carbon dioxide to levels not seen since the Pliocene, some three million years ago, which in turn is forcing profound changes to the biochemistry of the planet. Instead of the fiction that humans stand apart from nature (or perhaps above it, in a position of mastery and control), anthropogenic climate change underscores that we are instead but one (very recent) component in the biogeochemical ferment of the Earth, caught up in feedback loops of the carbon cycle and microbial and multispecies codependency. Though some scientists hypothesized that this might be the case over a century ago, they were largely ignored for decades: their suggestion that humans could affect the Earth entailed too radical a reframing of our understanding of what it meant to be human. But as global sensor networks document in dizzying detail the accidental terraforming effects of human activity, while computer models present terrifying forecasts of where unmitigated climate change will lead us, the sharp distinction between humans and the natural world, between human history and Earth history, dissolves.[7]

At the other end of the scale, microscopic discoveries of the past few decades have also revised our understanding of what humans are. Contrary to the idea that we are each separate individuals, imbued with autonomy and agency, we now know that, like all animals, humans are "symbiotic complexes of many species living together," relying on the presence of hundreds of species of microorganisms in our bodies to function.[8] For example, our abilities to digest food and fight off disease rest on the labor of bacteria that live on and within us. We are able to be human only thanks to the three hundred to five hundred species of bacteria that bloom in our guts.[9] Other living species and nonliving matter and processes permit human life. These sorts of complex dependencies and interdependencies are widely recognized among other species, but many humans continue to imagine ourselves "as autonomously self-maintaining" because, as anthropologist Anna Tsing argues, "Human exceptionalism blinds us."[10]

In this chapter, we explore an interdisciplinary archive of Western science and philosophy to track the emergence of the concept of the Planetary.[11] The result of developments in what have rightly been called "the humbling sciences," the Planetary as a scientific and philosophical category comes from a place of ontological and epistemic humility, acknowledging that we are not so fundamentally different from other creatures and that we are only barely beginning to understand (much less control) the complexities of our interdependencies with planetary systems.[12] If Copernicus's heliocentrism represented the First Great Decentering, displacing the Earth from the center of the heavens, and Darwin's theory of evolution by natural selection the Second Great Decentering, this time of God as the intentional maker of all creatures, then the emergence of the concept of the Planetary as described in this chapter represents the Third Great Decentering, and the one that hits closest to home, supplanting the figure of the human as the measure and master of all things.

The Rise of Planetary Thinking

From the late nineteenth century, a series of concepts were developed—ecology, ecosystem, biosphere, Gaia, and the Anthropocene, among others—that built on each other in a register of holistic systems thinking, eventually culminating in the category of the Planetary as a postanthropocentric understanding of the Earth. This intellectual genealogy unfolded in parallel to two additional, crucial developments: first, the material intensification of anthropogenic effects on the planet through the simultaneous growth of the number of humans and our resource usage; and second, the growth of planetary instrumentation, that is, technologies of perception—sensors, satellites, cameras, computers, and more—that have helped reveal and make sense of the effects that this intensification is having on the planet as a whole. The emergence of these three phenomena—the intellectual development of the concept of the Planetary, the intensification of anthropogenic effects on the planet, and the development of a technosphere capable of sensing those effects—reveals our *condition of planetarity*, representing at once an ontological transformation and an epistemic break with previous understandings of humans' position on the planet.

Ecology, Biosphere, and Noösphere

At the close of *On the Origin of Species*, Charles Darwin evoked an Arcadian scene: "It is interesting to contemplate a tangled bank," he wrote in 1859, "clothed with many plants of many kinds, with birds singing on the bushes, with various insects flitting about, and with worms crawling through the damp earth, and to reflect that these elaborately constructed forms, so different from each other, and dependent upon each other in so complex a manner, have all been produced by laws acting around us."[13] The idea contained in this final phrase—evolution by natural selection—set off an intellectual and cultural cataclysm. After centuries of thinking otherwise, people (especially in the West) were confronted with the thought that we humans were just another beast. We bring up Darwin's passage here, however, because of his description of the "tangled bank" itself: its plants, birds, insects, worms, and damp earth. Though he understood that they were "dependent upon each other in so complex a manner," there was not yet a conceptual language to capture these webs of relations. But over the next century and a half of Western science, a language to describe interconnected, whole systems emerged.

The work of knitting it all together—of rigorously conceptualizing and modeling planetary interconnectedness—began with the English naturalist's foremost champion, the German biologist Ernst Haeckel. Other biologists, Haeckel wrote in 1866, ignored "the relations of the organism to the environment, the place each organism takes in the household of nature, in the economy of all nature."[14] From Darwin, Haeckel understood that organisms are shaped by their whole environment, including both its organic and inorganic elements. He expressed this insight in the idea of "ecology," a term he coined to describe "the entire science of the relationships of the organism to its surrounding external world."[15]

Yet the "surrounding external world" remained in the background for most nineteenth-century researchers. An organism's environment was still considered important only insofar as it affected a scientist's main interest, their organism of study. The view that organisms and their environment fit together as part of an integrated whole took decades to catch on, and ecology did not develop as an independent scientific field until the early twentieth century.[16] Yet as ecological thought spread and was put into practice, the most important organism of all was human beings. Well into the mid-twentieth century, ecology—especially as practiced in and exported by the North Atlantic—remained dominated by a view of the environment as a set of services, a standing reserve for man—specifically, for wealthy white men.

In the 1920s, however, voices that questioned this environmental exploitation–centered stance started to appear. The most important of them was Vladimir I. Vernadsky, a Russian, then Soviet, trailblazing multidisciplinary scientist. He was a mineralogist and biogeologist, as well as a leader and elected representative of the liberal Constitutional Democratic Party (during the tsarist constitutional monarchy of 1905 to 1917), and is considered a father of the Soviet nuclear program. Although his ideas seeped into Western scientific theory and practice, the Iron Curtain and Stalinist repression were for decades a barrier to his renown outside Russia. Among his numerous pathbreaking scientific discoveries, Vernadsky had three insights that were crucial to the development of planetary thinking.[17]

First, he rejected the distinction between living beings and inert matter, bringing them both under the same scientific roof: the field of research called biogeochemistry, which he established in 1923. Unifying previously disconnected fields of study, he made the case for the inescapable interrelation of life and planet. For Vernadsky, this perspective was not a spiritual or ethical statement but rather an empirical observation: life (or "living matter," as Vernadsky preferred to call it) was part and parcel of the geochemistry of the Earth; living and inert matter were intertwined via the exchange of energy and gases. "All organisms," he observed, "are connected indissolubly and uninterruptedly, first of all through nutrition and respiration, with the circumambient material and energetic medium." Human beings, no different from any other life forms, were "geologically connected with [Earth's] material and energetic structure." From this interconnectedness, he concluded, "no living organism exists on earth in a state of freedom."[18]

Vernadsky's discovery, second, was not just that life on Earth depended on the planet but that it *transformed* the planet. He was among the first to understand that living matter—"the totality of all organisms present on the earth at any one time"—was itself a geological force.[19] The "envelope of life" covering the Earth's surface was a "a source of transformation of the planet," he wrote. It "plays an extraordinary planetary role." As he pointed out in the opening line of *The Biosphere*, his masterwork of 1926, "The face of the Earth viewed from celestial space presents a unique appearance, different from all other heavenly bodies." Decades before extraplanetary satellites would visually confirm that view, Vernadsky identified that the biosphere—the worldwide sum of all ecosystems—made for a striking image, coating the surface of the Earth as a single "living film."[20]

Third, Vernadsky argued, the geological, planetary role of life had intensified with time—it had a progressive history. Developments in biological evolution, in other words, had planetary repercussions. The emergence of central nervous systems, for instance, "increased the geological role of living matter." For Vernadsky the key planetary force in the present was humankind, and more specifically the human mind. Beginning at least with the discovery of fire, human beings had used their brains to change the planet, and in so doing for "the first time man becomes a *large-scale geological force*," as Vernadsky put it. In the past few centuries, those changes had become more and more profound, and the human mind was now a "mighty and ever-growing geological force." Adopting the Greek word for "mind," *noos*, Vernadsky labeled this "new geological phenomenon" the noösphere (pronounced *no-oh-sphere*).[21]

Vernadsky developed the concept of the noösphere in dialogue with the heterodox French Jesuit priest and paleontologist Pierre Teilhard de Chardin while both were living in Paris in the 1920s.[22] For the two men, the concept served as a scientific framework for understanding the planetary significance of humankind. They shared a view that the emergence of the noösphere represented the latest historical stage of the biosphere. Teilhard emphasized that the noösphere was "the thinking layer of earth," and Vernadsky agreed that the primary driver of change on the planet now "derived not from its [humanity's] matter, but from its brain."[23] For both men, moreover, the collective planetary brain was more than just the sum of its individual organic human parts, and its planetary force was comprehensible only when understood in terms of its impact on the systemic planetary totality.

From here, however, the two scholars' interpretations diverged. For Vernadsky, the noösphere, like the biosphere that it emerged from, was fundamentally a biogeochemical phenomenon. Energy from the sun was transformed by photosynthesis and was transferred via consumption to humans, where it became "the energy of human culture or cultural biogeochemical energy."[24] This energy, which produced both scientific research and industrial production, was what had enabled the human mind to become a planetary phenomenon: it "knew and embraced the whole biosphere, completed the geographic map of the planet Earth, and colonized its whole surface."[25] By contrast, for Teilhard, whose interpretation is better known in the West today, the noösphere represented an evolutionary stage ("noögenesis") that reconciled his scientific commitments, his mystical experiences, and his Catholic theological ideas.[26] Teilhard's noösphere was both a physical phenomenon constituted by "this irresistible tide of fields and factories, this immense and growing edifice of matter and ideas," and a metaphysical one—the place where the planet "finds its soul."[27] For Teilhard, the noösphere represented an emergent collective consciousness on a planetary scale that would eventually lead to the "Omega Point," his term for the spiritual revelation of God.

Despite these metaphysical differences, Vernadsky and Teilhard shared a view of humankind as a planetary phenomenon: that humans emerged from the planet, remain inseparable from it, and, through the power of thought, transform it. "To a Martian," ventured Teilhard, "the first characteristic of our planet would be, not the blue of the seas or the green of the forests, but the phosphorescence of thought."[28] Humankind had conquered Earth: we lived all over it, drilled beneath it, flew above it, and were changing the physical, chemical, and biological composition of its face. At the same time, humankind was inextricable from the Earth's biogeochemistry. That humans were now *conscious* of the planetary changes they had wrought, and that they could envision it holistically *as a planet*, was a central distinguishing feature of the noösphere. The noösphere was the vehicle through which our condition of planetarity (humans' inescapable embeddedness in the Earth system) revealed itself to us, a threshold point for the emergence of *planetary sapience*—a key term that we will return to later in this chapter.

Ecosystems

Around the same time that Vernadsky and Teilhard were developing their ideas, an unrelated debate in the field of ecology was coming to parallel conclusions. In the early twentieth century, ecologists were working out their understanding of ecological communities in nature. Into this debate, the British botanist Arthur Tansley introduced the concept of *ecosystems*.[29] In a 1935 paper, Tansley rejected prevailing conceptions of ecological communities that focused only on the biological elements, such as "biome" and "biotic community."[30] Rather, he argued, the focus of study should be "the whole *system* (in the sense of physics), including not only the organism-complex, but also the whole complex of physical factors forming what we call the environment of the biome." His proposed concept extended the "basic units of nature" to include both organisms and their inorganic surroundings and placed both components on the same plane. Tansley argued that we must eschew "our natural human prejudices" in favor of living organisms and recognize that the organic and inorganic are both elements of the "one physical system"— indeed, "there could be no systems without [the inorganic elements]."[31]

The term took some time to catch on, but over the next several decades "ecosystem" became a dominant concept in ecology—and outside it too. Thinking in terms of ecosystems continued the process of seeing the deep and multidirectional causal linkages between different elements of the environment, encouraging conceptual holism and de-centering any single element. Moreover, the concept allowed ecological thinking to become scalable, with its principles applied to communities "of the most various kinds and sizes," from an insect's gut to a single pond to a watershed to the planet as a whole.[32] Tansley's intervention also made the case for understanding the role of humans in ecosystems of all scales. "We cannot confine ourselves to the so-called 'natural' entities and ignore the processes and expressions of vegetation now so abundantly provided us by the activities of man," he argued. "Ecology must be applied to conditions brought about by human activity. The 'natural' entities and the anthropogenic derivates alike must be analysed in terms of the most appropriate concepts we can find."[33] Ecosystems, as Tansley introduced them, are an integrated whole, with the climate, soils, plants, and animals, including humans, all connected in interlocking relationships with each other.

Tansley's conceptual innovations notwithstanding, the dominant thinking in the West through the first half of the twentieth century remained rooted in the precept that humans (or, in the language of that time, Man) stood both apart from nature and to benefit from it. While some conservationists, such as US president Theodore Roosevelt or the naturalist John Muir, promoted limitations on such exploitation so that the natural world would retain its instrumental and/or intrinsic value, the prevailing ethos was one of extraction. Most in the West would have agreed with the 1930 statement by 1923 Nobel laureate physicist Robert Millikan that "man is powerless to do to it [the Earth] . . . any titanic physical damage."[34] The planet was still seen as a near-limitless resource, there for humans to exploit.

Hints of a new way of thinking continued to slowly emerge in the wake of the catastrophes of the Second World War, and in particular the nuclear weapons that had ended it. The thought of worldwide nuclear annihilation—a manifestation of interconnectedness if there ever was one—was no longer inconceivable but plainly possible. The same intellectual and political ferment that spawned the United Nations as the first truly global political institution and excited the movement for world government also produced books like *Road to Survival* (1948) by the American ecologist William Vogt and *Our Plundered Planet* (1948) by the American conservationist Henry Fairfield Osborn Jr., which put forward a vision of the planet as a whole. Global modernity, as they saw it, materialized not just in economic growth, rapid technological change, or the ideological division between the capitalist and communist blocs but in the Earth itself. As Vogt put it in his international best-seller, "An eroding hillside in Mexico or Yugoslavia affects the living standard and probability of survival of the American people. . . . We form an earth-company, and the lot of the Indian farmer can no longer be isolated from that of the Bantu."[35] Or as Osborn penned, "Nature . . . is an active, purposeful, co-ordinated machine. Each part is dependent upon another, all are related to the movement of the whole." And if even one part, one element disappears, "the earth will die."[36] This nascent environmental awareness also displays a budding planetary awareness.

Gaia and the Whole Earth

In the late 1960s and 1970s several lines of thought began to merge into a more cohesive and explicit view of our planetary condition. Advances in scientific thought and accomplishment, the dawn of space flight, countercultural trends, and the birth of the modern environmental and other social movements converged to produce a new vision of the planet. Against a backdrop of growing outrage over proliferating environmental crises, new approaches and technologies, including methodological holism, systems theory, proliferating environmental sensor systems, and computer modeling, would come together to synthesize a new scientific and philosophical understanding of the planetary condition.

One afternoon in 1966, while sitting on the roof of his apartment looking out at San Francisco, the American polymath Stewart Brand "had an LSD-laced vision where I asked myself, 'What am I going to do for humanity?'" The answer he arrived at was that "it would change everything" if people "saw a plausible photograph of Earth from outer space, ideally in color and ideally of the whole globe." It was nearly a decade into the Space Age, but no such photo had been made publicly available. Brand started to campaign to see one, distributing buttons that asked, "Why haven't we seen a photograph of the whole Earth yet?"[37] When the US government finally released the picture in 1967, Brand became an evangelist for the icon. He placed a photograph of the whole planet, swirled with white clouds against the black emptiness of space, on the first cover (and many subsequent covers) of his counter-cultural almanac, aptly named the *Whole Earth Catalog*. On one of the first pages of that first issue, from autumn 1968, readers could find instructions on how order a poster of the whole Earth photograph from the catalog ($2.00) or a book of NASA photographs of Earth from above from the US Government Printing Office ($7.00). The *Catalog* itself adopted a cybernetic perspective on the world, exhorting readers to "understand whole systems" and take the earth as a single, interconnected information complex. This holistic perspective was helped by the ability to see the whole planet from space, to take it in from above "as gods."[38]

Around this same time, James Lovelock, a British scientist with wide-ranging interests, was designing instruments for NASA to detect life on Mars when he started to think broadly about life on Earth. By 1972, he determined that Earth had maintained conditions that were "uniquely favorable to life"—the chemical composition of its atmosphere, in particular, but also its surface acidity and climate—for billions of years, despite changing external factors such as the long-term increase in energy from the sun.[39] "The only feasible explanation of the Earth's highly improbable atmosphere," he concluded, "was that it was being manipulated on a day-to-day basis from the surface, and that the manipulator was life itself."[40] In other words, "The entire range of living matter on Earth, from whales to viruses, and from oaks to algae, could be regarded as constituting a single living entity, capable of manipulating the Earth's atmosphere to suit its overall needs and endowed with faculties and powers far beyond those of its constituent parts."[41] On the advice of his neighbor, *Lord of the Flies* author William Golding, Lovelock named this "single living entity" after the ancient Greek female personification of Earth, Gaia.

Lovelock, often in collaboration with the visionary American biologist Lynn Margulis, published a series of scientific papers and popular accounts to promote the idea that Gaia regulates the conditions of Earth via feedback loops to keep "the environment constant and close to a state comfortable for life."[42] His 1979 book *Gaia: A New Look at Life on Earth* brought the idea both public renown and scientific condemnation.[43] In particular, the hypothesis provoked new holistic and comparative approaches to thinking about planet Earth. The hypothesis urged us to look at Earth's atmosphere, biosphere, climate, and so on as a whole and suggested that the properties of "the entire ensemble" were greater than the sum of its parts.[44] As Lovelock recalled, his formulation began with "the view of the earth from space, reviewing the planet as a whole but not in detail."[45] Studying Earth from an interplanetary perspective offered "a fresh standpoint from which to consider life on Earth," suggesting, so far at least, that our planet was a "strange and beautiful anomaly in our solar system."[46]

This 1970s moment was not just one of environmental celebration and appreciating beautiful anomalies, however. Environmental degradation and depletion had grown into international political concerns, and the question of how to square those problems with economic growth was becoming inescapable.[47] There was a growing sense, as UN secretary-general U Thant put it in 1968, that "a new quality of planetary imagination" was needed—one that took "account of the nature of interdependence and the imperative need to change."[48] In response, the UN General Assembly organized the world's first international conference on the environment, which brought over one hundred governments and seven hundred NGO observers to Stockholm in June 1972 for the United Nations Conference on the Human Environment. In the runup to the conference, development economist Barbara Ward, who in 1966 had published *Spaceship Earth*, was commissioned to draft a report—published, with microbiologist René Dubos, as the landmark book *Only One Earth* (1972)—that would provide "a conceptual framework" for the conference.[49] "Today our experts know something new," she declared in her keynote address. "They know that air, soil and water form a totally interdependent worldwide system or biosphere sustaining all life." For Ward, the central question was, "How do we ensure that the need to check pollution does not become an inhibition on the desperate need of two thirds of humanity for development?"[50] National states, she argued, were inevitably and rightly focused on economic development, but how was that to be squared with the emerging understanding of "planetary limits"?

Another opening keynote to the Stockholm Conference was delivered by Aurelio Peccei, an Italian industrialist who spoke about humanity's responsibility as the "governor of 'Spaceship Earth.'"[51] Four years earlier, Peccei had founded the Club of Rome, which had sponsored a team of experts led by biophysicist and environmental scientist Donella Meadows to develop a computer simulation of "long-term, global problems . . . as dynamically interacting elements" in one world system.[52] Delivered on the eve of the Stockholm Conference, the Club's final report *The Limits to Growth* (1972) highlighted the interdependence of all societies, which had no choice but to share "our finite planet."[53] If the economic and social status quo "continue unchanged," the report declared, "the limits to growth on this planet will be reached sometime within the next one hundred years."[54]

Their prediction of "sudden and uncontrollable decline" generated a shockwave among those accustomed to the seemingly limitless growth of the postwar boom.[55] The report helped to define a set of world-scale problems and problems of the world itself: it turned attention to "the carrying capacity of this planet" and whether human behavior at a global scale could "overshoot" it.[56] But behind the environmental anxieties that *Limits to Growth* unleashed was an innovative perspective on the world. The report's findings presented "the alternatives confronting not one nation or people but all nations and all peoples." That is, they imagined the "planet as a whole."[57] And by doing so, they opened the possibility for, in the words of an endorsement on the book's back cover, "planetary planning."[58]

One year after the Stockholm Conference and the Club of Rome report, in 1973, the Norwegian philosopher Arne Naess introduced the concept of "deep ecology" to contrast against the then-predominant "shallow" forms of ecology, which he criticized for their utilitarian and anthropocentric attitude toward nature. Shallow ecology's "central objective," he claimed, was to advance "the health and affluence of people in the developed countries."[59] Deep ecology instead advanced the idea that all living beings have "the equal right to live and blossom," regardless of their instrumental value for affluent human beings. Restricting this right was "an anthropocentrism with detrimental effect upon the life quality of humans themselves."[60] The image of "man-in-environment" must be rejected, Naess argued, "in favor of *the relational, total-field image*." Organisms, including humans, could not be conceptualized in isolation from one another: they were "knots in the biospherical net or field of intrinsic relations."[61]

This embrace of ecological diversity, complexity, and holism led to the conclusion that "the so-called struggle of life, and survival of the fittest, should be interpreted in the sense of the ability to coexist and cooperate in complex relationships, rather than the ability to kill, exploit, and suppress."[62] Deep ecology conceived of humans both as embedded in a dense network of planetary systems and as a destructive force within those systems, one whose full impact was only just beginning to heave into view, not least with respect to the matter of global warming, a term introduced into the scientific lexicon by a 1975 article in *Science* magazine.[63]

The idea of Gaia and "whole earth thinking" thus continued its steady march from the realm of intellectuals into popular culture and political action. Feminist theorists and activists, for example, drew on the ideas of environmentalism and holism to create a new political movement and intellectual critique, known as ecofeminism, to understand and criticize the domination of women and nature.[64] More institutionally, the modern environmentalist movement, heralded by the first Earth Day on April 22, 1970, began to receive official approbation: a number of national states established environmental protection agencies or ministries in the early 1970s (including Sweden in 1967; the United States, United Kingdom, and Malaysia in 1970; Canada, Switzerland, and Japan in 1971; and West Germany in 1974) and the establishment of the United Nations Environment Programme in 1972 in the wake of the Stockholm Conference.[65]

Yet at the same time, this pivotal 1970s moment could eventually be seen as something of a missed opportunity: while concern with "protecting" the environment marked an institutional step forward, it continued to rest on an idea of human stewardship of "ecosystem services" (a term first introduced in *Science* magazine in 1976) rather than on the rejection of anthropocentrism as the basis for understanding ecology.[66]

The Anthropocene and Its Critics

In 2000, Paul Crutzen, an atmospheric chemist, and Eugene Stoermer, a paleoecologist, made a portentous announcement in the pages of a professional newsletter: because of the "major and still growing impacts of human activities on earth and atmosphere," the planet had exited the Holocene, the geological epoch that had begun with the end of the last ice age 11,700 years ago. Since the invention of the steam engine in the eighteenth century and the subsequent mass adoption of fossil fuels for energy, they argued, "it seems to us more than appropriate to emphasize the central role of mankind in geology and ecology by proposing to use the term 'anthropocene' for the current geological epoch."[67] Two years later, Crutzen, a Nobel laureate in chemistry, published a short paper in *Nature* titled "Geology of Mankind," introducing the idea of a "human-dominated" era of the Earth's geologic history to a wider scientific audience.[68]

Crutzen and Stoermer were not the first to argue that human beings were changing the geology of the planet. Vernadsky and Teilhard, as we've seen, had argued in the 1920s that humankind was a geological force. Even earlier, the geologist and Catholic priest Antonio Stoppani had claimed in 1873 that the Earth had entered the "anthropozoic era," calling humans a "new telluric force which in power and universality may be compared to the greater forces of the earth." The geologist Thomas Chamberlain had argued in 1883 that since the invention of agriculture in the Neolithic era, humans had been "an efficient *geologic* agent." Throughout this "Psychozoic age," as he named it, "the entire land life is being revolutionized through man's agency."[69] But the Anthropocene as a concept was an argument for humankind's irrevocable changes to the planet. This, for its proponents, suggested a "radical rupture" with everything that had come before.[70] It proposed nothing less than a new geological epoch.

In 2009, the International Commission on Stratigraphy, the organization of geologists that formally demarcates the geological epochs of Earth's history, formed the Anthropocene Working Group of the Subcommission on Quaternary Stratigraphy to investigate whether human activity did end the Holocene. Ten years later, by a vote of 29 to 4, the working group adopted as their official stance that "the Anthropocene [should] be treated as a formal chrono-stratigraphic unit" that began in the mid-twentieth century.[71] The recommendation is now making its way through more layers of scrutiny by international scientific bodies before becoming official, but in the meantime the term *Anthropocene* has taken on a popular intellectual life of its own.[72]

Beyond technical stratigraphic questions, two related debates have arisen about the Anthropocene as a concept. The first is whether the Anthropocene is the "fault" of *all* humans or just *some* humans. Critics take issue with the *anthropo-* in the term, which suggests that all of humanity is forcing the planet to change. They argue that the name should reflect the fact that humans' geological force results from the activities of a privileged minority of the population. Instead of Anthropocene, some suggest naming the era the Capitalocene, to highlight the role of industrial capitalism, or Plantationocene, to highlight the importance of imperially driven plantation economies.[73] Climate activist Greta Thunberg sketched the political and moral problem with crediting a generic humanity for changing the climate: "Some people say that the climate crisis is something that we will have created, but that is not true," she told the World Economic Forum in Davos in 2019. "Because if everyone is guilty then no one is to blame. And someone is to blame."[74]

The second debate concerns when the Anthropocene began. Most proponents of the concept date the start to the birth of fossil-fueled

industrialization around 1800 or to the "Great Acceleration" of population and industrial output that began around 1950.[75] A problem with
either date is that it imports a kind of Eurocentrism through the back
door.[76] By dating the breakpoint from the Holocene to an event in European economic history, it ignores the myriad other ways that humans
have been reshaping planetary processes for tens if not hundreds of
thousands of years. For example, the arrival of humans in Australia, the
Americas, and islands such as Madagascar, New Zealand, and Hawaii
invariably led within a few hundred years to the loss of many megafauna
species—also a common index of transition between geological eras and
epochs.[77] The advent of agriculture—separately invented at least six
times starting about ten thousand years ago in the Middle East, China,
the Indus Valley, Mesoamerica, South America, and New Guinea—
has also massively altered ecosystems everywhere it has taken place.[78]
Going back even further, hominid control of fire, and specifically the
use of fire in landscape management, has been altering ecosystems for
at least a million years. This suggests that the human tendency to per-
turb the planet has deep roots and is not an artifact merely of modernity or capitalism, which the later dating of the Anthropocene to 1800
or 1950 instead implies.[79]

No matter when it started, there is no doubt that the biogeochemistry of the planet has been remade as the human population has increased
by an order of magnitude over the last three centuries. "It's more than
climate change," averred the philosopher and biologist Donna Haraway
in 2016: "it's also extraordinary burdens of toxic chemistry, mining, depletion of lakes and rivers under and above ground, ecosystem simplifi-
cation, vast genocides of people and other critters," and more. Because
of human activity, she continued, "most of the reserves of the earth
have been drained, burned, depleted, poisoned, exterminated, and
otherwise exhausted." Perhaps she is right that the Anthropocene is
best understood less as a new epoch than as a boundary event, a point of
rupture where "what comes after will not be like what came before."[80]

An additional problem with the concept of the Anthropocene is
that it relies on an unreconstructed concept of human exceptionalism,

albeit this time as condemnation rather than celebration. For in fact, while the concept of the Anthropocene is meant to raise an alarm about the effects of humans on the earth, embedded in the very prefix *Anthropo-* is the idea that humans are unique in their power and agency.[81] From this perspective, the concept of the Anthropocene merely inverts the high modernist narrative over "human triumph over nature," indeed affirming this supposed conquest, but now reframing it as a rapacious, speciesist, colonialist project. As a concept, it does not take on the deeper and more radical insights of Vernadsky's view of humans as (merely) an organic part of the planet's biogeochemistry, or the deep ecologists' insights about the inextricable embeddedness of the human in planetary systems.

This critique of the Anthropocene as implicitly if prejudicially anthropocentric can be best found in a trio of thinkers often associated with postmodern philosophy: the aforementioned Donna Haraway, Indian literary theorist Gayatri Chakravorty Spivak, and French philosopher Bruno Latour. Questions of the Planetary had been in Haraway's mind from the early 1970s, when she spent a spent a year studying at the Teilhard de Chardin Foundation in Paris. In her "Cyborg Manifesto" from 1985, Haraway observed that "late twentieth-century machines have made thoroughly ambiguous the difference between natural and artificial, mind and body, self-developing and externally designed." The lines between humans and animals, between organisms and machines, and between physical and nonphysical were all collapsing, Haraway observed, producing "a cyborg world" that was ultimately "about the final imposition of a grid of total control on the planet."[82]

A decade later, writing in the heyday of the era of globalization that Friedman was at the time celebrating, Spivak embraced "planetarity" as a contrast to the "global." Planetarity, she argued, offered a way to refuse "the sense of custodianship of our planet" implied by globalization, which she saw as a direct continuation of imperialist logics that had long silenced voices of the poor and marginalized. Whereas "the 'global' notion allows us to think that we can aim to control globality," she argued, the concept of planetarity conceives the Earth as "belonging to another system" that humans merely "inhabit" as if "on loan."[83]

For Latour, the concept of the Planetary had an even deeper implication: nothing less than the collapse of "the notion of the arrow of time implied so far by traditional philosophies of history." Unlike Teilhard, who believed that the concept of the Planetary implied progress (toward the "Omega Point"), Latour argued that the Planetary instead suggested the "simultaneity" of emergent "planetary regimes." Latour's view of the permanency of the planetary condition challenged the progressive narratives of high modernism, including modernization and globalization.[84] In other words, for all three of these thinkers, the philosophical realization of the collapsing modernist categories forced into view the question of planetary control.

This last trio of thinkers have largely developed and deployed the idea of planetarity as a way to critique contemporary scientific practice, but we want to take the idea of planetarity seriously as a scientific concept. Specifically, we want to take the concept of the planet, and planetarity, as a spur to think differently about how we are to *govern* the issues associated with the Planetary—specifically, to begin to broker a conversation between, on the one hand, the science of the planetary and, on the other, the theorists and keepers of the institutional order that has so far been put in place to deal with challenges that exceed the national boundaries. For us, the Planetary is thus not just a critique of the existing order but an inspiration to a new one.

The Limits of Globalization

Why have so many strands of thought converged now on the concept of the Planetary?[85] Planetary thinking is a conceptual response both to the rapid acceleration of anthropogenic effects upon ecosystems and to technological developments that revealed and made comprehensible these effects. In other words, the epistemological break entailed by the move from the global to the Planetary is predicated on the production of a vast infrastructure of global sensors and models that make sense of the data coming out of those sensors.

What philosopher of technology Benjamin Bratton calls "the Stack" of sensors, communications systems, algorithms, and machine learning technologies has enabled an unprecedented awareness of the condition of planetarity.[86] For example, the scale of groundwater depletion has become visible through the precise measurement of changes in Earth's gravitational field from space.[87] Remote light sensing technology (light detection and ranging, LIDAR) discloses biomass loss in new and older forest edges, enabling scientists to calculate how much Amazon rainforest deforestation is contributing to carbon emissions.[88] And since 1958 the Mauna Loa Atmospheric Baseline Observatory has been tracking the CO_2 levels in the atmosphere, which, combined with ice core data and other sources, reveal that greenhouse gases are now reaching levels not seen in millions of years. All of these and more data are then put together by algorithms running on supercomputers, for example at the German Climate Computing Center in Hamburg, to disclose the systemic totality of planetary-scale climate change.

The key point is that without all that apparatus it would be difficult to know that massive or distributed phenomena like climate change are systemic and planetary rather than merely a series of unconnected local events. Without a planetary array of instruments, algorithms, and integrated computing stacks to sense and make the patterns visible, it is doubtful that anyone could by themselves notice the Earth's 1.1 degrees Celsius of warming over the last few decades—spiking to 1.5 degrees in the summer of 2023. In some regions where the local change has been more dramatic, like the Arctic, people—particularly members of indigenous communities—have been able to personally experience the change, but only in their local settings, not for the planet as a whole. More broadly, many would no doubt have observed that their local weather has been extreme in recent years and without precedent in living memory. But that direct and personal experience doesn't suggest anything about an Earth-scale phenomenon. It is only the data produced by Earth's technological "distributed sensory organ" of orbiting satellites, mountaintop observatories, airborne instruments, seaborne gauges, and ice-core drills (as interpreted by computer models and simulations) that has enabled us to begin systematically perceiving the scope, the interconnected causal mechanisms, and the cumulative significance of the changes taking place.[89]

It's not just climate change: the emergent technological planetary sensorium now enables increasing awareness of biodiversity loss, the distribution and spread of pandemic disease, the garbage patches in the oceans, and every other planetary phenomenon.[90] So powerful is this "planetary self-awareness" that Bratton describes it as "planetary sapience."[91] Indeed, the concept of *planetary sapience*—the growing scientific knowledge about the planet and our embeddedness in it—is a good approximation, now more fully realized through technology, of Vernadsky's secular conception of the noösphere.[92]

Beyond this technologically enabled planetary self-awareness, there is also a more narrowly political driver of the recent growing concern for the Planetary. Indeed, what gives the concept of the Planetary urgency today are the conceptual and practical failures of globalization. For all the wealth it has created for some, extraction-based globalization has also unleashed a planetary destabilization. As discussed in the last chapter, four decades into the era of neoliberal capitalism as the world's dominant political-economic system and ideology, it has become all too apparent that our existing institutional matrix is incapable of addressing the crises of the planetary condition. What this system of international interconnectedness has achieved is the acceleration of the integration of anthropocentric flows; it has created and promoted global networks, both wide and deep, for the exchange of commerce, capital, information, and ideas.

The focus on human flows, however, has proved too myopic. It is now clear that many other things flow around the world, outside of human intentions or control. SARS-CoV-2 remains on a viral joy ride around the world; ever-growing numbers of carbon compounds circulate unimpeded through the atmosphere; space junk orbits and ocean plastics whirl—all blithely unconcerned with human desires or intentions. While the intellectual trends underpinning the concept of the Planetary were incubating for over a century, it is the abject failures of globalization to contain these harmful flows that have propelled the concept into the limelight today.

Globalization—perhaps in the form of Davos Man—might defend itself by saying, "These things are not in my ambit. I sought to connect the world for good and for profit, not for nasty pandemics or climate change." But it is precisely this inability for globalization as a paradigm to take charge of nonhuman flows that necessitates a new way of thinking. What's more, the ascendency of the Planetary is in part rooted, counterintuitively, in the very successes of globalization. Global commercial integration exacerbated planetary problems. Turbocharged carbon-fueled economies increased greenhouse gas emissions. Easy and cheap transportation facilitated the transmission of diseases—and emitted more greenhouse gases. The rapacious demand for new land to house and feed our growing lot pushed us to demolish biodiverse habitats—which exposed humans to new zoonotic diseases.[93] Thus the successful global interconnectivity and economic growth prompted by globalization unleashed, or at least uncovered, planetary processes beyond human will and control.

If there was a victory of anthropocentric globalization over the planet, it was pyrrhic at best. The contribution of globalization to remaking the planet's biosphere, hydrosphere, lithosphere, and more is now evident. The planet was always there but largely ignored (at least by everyday politics) in the tacit high modernist faith that it could be controlled or mastered.[94] The evidence that has emerged over the past few decades has shaken us from the stupor of globalization and made clear that a new conceptual framework is needed. In fact, the planet cannot be tamed, much less shrugged off. Rather, humans must learn a fundamental humility with respect to its calculability and shed our vanity with respect to its controllability. As a scientific and philosophical category that does this sort of work, the Planetary provides a plausible framework for life, including political life, moving forward.

Planetary Issues

What does adopting the intellectual category of the Planetary do for us? It provides, above all, a way of approaching the world: a clear-eyed empirical and ethical assessment of Earth as it is and our place on it. As a practical matter, the concept illuminates and distinguishes a new category for politics and policy: *planetary issues*. Planetary issues differ from global issues, even if some of them until now have been misdiagnosed as global. In coming chapters, we will argue that what planetary issues have in common is that they are yet to be effectively governed because existing governance institutions are national and global. Planetary issues, by contrast, require institutions that are as unbound by national territories as the issues themselves.

What defines a "planetary issue"?[95] Planetary issues are, at their base, defined by four core characteristics: they are critical to multispecies flourishing; they are enmeshed in the history of life on Earth; they operate on scales of time or size that are beyond direct, individual human experience; and they exhibit some degree of human involvement.[96] Throughout the book we focus on two planetary issues—climate change and pandemic diseases—but there are many more: stratospheric ozone depletion, atmospheric aerosol loading, space junk, growing antibiotic resistance, biodiversity loss, anthropogenic genetic disruptions (whether they are due to deliberate interventions, like gene drives and gene editing, or are the unintended consequences of environmental pollutants, such as radioactive materials and ozone-thinning substances), declining soil health, upended nitrogen and phosphorus cycles, freshwater depletion, ocean acidification, and oceanic plastics—perhaps even emerging technologies that hold the potential for terraforming Earth, like artificial intelligence and bioengineering.[97]

Planetary issues, first, are objects, processes, or conditions that are vital for enabling the flourishing of life. This interest in the whole biosphere, however, is not out of sentimental commitments to nature. It is because humans can flourish only as part of a broader multispecies flourishing. Human beings are entangled in webs of dependence and interdependence with other species, from the bacteria in the ocean that help oxygenate the atmosphere, to the corn, rice, wheat, pigs, chicken, and cows humans cultivate and eat, to the fungi that decompose our bodies back into the soil. And so human flourishing must occur—as a factual matter, to say nothing of ethical duty—in the context of multispecies flourishing.

But there are limits to our commitments to all living beings. The goal of planetary governance is not to improve the lot of *E. coli*, *M. tuberculosis*, or ebolaviruses. (The eradication of smallpox, caused by *Variola* virus, was in our view an unconditional blessing.) Humans should not feed ourselves or our children to hungry animals. While one may rightly deplore reigning industrial agricultural practices, there is no denying the metabolic need for humans to consume other living matter. Multispecies flourishing must be prioritized and promoted, but in the end, in terms of governance arrangements, it is a means to achieve human flourishing.[98] At the same time, we must keep in mind that humans are best served by respecting the biospheric whole. This is the reframing in planetary terms of what nineteenth-century French political thinker Alexis de Tocqueville called "self-interest rightly understood."

This first criterion also specifies that the planetary phenomena of concern are those that affect life. Ones that don't, such as the chemical composition of Earth's inner core, fall beyond our interest in this book. This is also why, for the moment, we are uninterested in climate change on Mars or the geochemistry of Venus: these planets are neither inhabited nor habitable for human beings or, as far as we know, for any other living matter. When other planets are pummeled by comets or asteroids, we do not shed a tear. When, for example, Jupiter was struck by the Shoemaker-Levy 9 comet in July 1994, the human response—natural and correct, in our view—was not angst for Jupiter's poor gases but concern about the risk of something similar happening to our planet.[99] We are interested in Earthly planetary processes because of their effects on the ability of life, human and nonhuman, to thrive. We need Earth to remain habitable.

Our concern with the Planetary, then, is with the planet as a vessel of life—human life, yes, but also the entire biosphere on which humans depend and of which they are a part. We need the planet because it sustains life; the planet does not need us and will not miss us when we're gone. As Margulis, coauthor of the Gaia hypothesis, put it: "We delude ourselves if we believe that as 3 million year old punks we can threaten the 3,500 million year old planetary patina in which we are embedded." However, she warns, "That we can foul our nest, convert the garden of Babylon to the sands of the Sahara . . .—in short that we can make our habitat hideous for our children—is certain."[100] This latter fate is what we wish to avoid: this planet is our habitat, our home, so let's not make it hideous.

Planetary issues, second, are entangled in the long history of life on Earth. The example of the relationship between oxygen (O_2) and living matter is instructive. Oxygen, which is nonliving, is essential for life: as waste product of photosynthesis by plants and cyanobacteria, and as an input for all other multicellular organisms, which need it to produce energy. Thus complex living matter and this elemental molecule are tightly and inseparably coupled. Without its constant production by photosynthesis, O_2 would be only a rare trace gas in Earth's atmosphere, not the over one-fifth of the atmosphere that it is.[101] And without such a highly oxygenated atmosphere, complex life could not exist. In fact, it took billions of years of photosynthesis by simple organisms to get atmospheric O_2 to levels high enough for more complex multicellular plants to evolve.[102] The oxygen-rich atmosphere that we breathing organisms rely on demonstrates our entanglement with inorganic matter and the deep past of life on Earth. More generally, it demonstrates that human beings and all other life forms are inextricably embedded in the biogeochemistry of the Earth system.

Our interest here in the long history of life on Earth links us to a term Margulis used above: habitat, or rather, habitability.[103] Earth today is habitable for complex life forms because of the billions of years of life that came before: oxygenating the atmosphere, cycling carbon,

helping to maintain liquid water, and much more. From a human perspective, the deep history of life has enabled us to enhance the planet's
habitability: our use of fossil fuels, which store the energy produced by
photosynthesis over the course of hundreds of millions of years, means
humans can live comfortably in regions that would otherwise be too
hot, too cold, too dry, too wet, or too urban.[104] The problem is that in
doing so, human action has reduced Earth's habitability for many other
life forms that humans live with and rely upon—in part through the destruction of their habitats. Humans today rely on the biosphere past and
present; our descendants will too. The planetary issues that concern us
in this book are those that underscore humans' interdependence with
other living beings and the interdependence of all living beings with
nonliving matter.

Planetary issues, third, are spatially and temporally outside the
bounds of individual humans' lived experience. They entail, in Chakrabarty's phrase, "vast processes of unhuman dimensions."[105] Spatially,
planetary issues can span or travel the face of the Earth. In this geographic dimension, the Planetary shares a sense of enormity with the
global—though the realm of the Planetary extends below and above the
surface to encompass the lithosphere through the atmospheric layer
where geosynchronous satellites float ("high earth orbit").[106] But it is
the temporal dimension that really marks the Planetary as distinct from
the global. Planetary issues are linked to time scales of biological evolution and geology, scales far beyond human lived experience. Essential
processes of planetary issues can play out over thousands, millions, or
billions of years. Decisions and actions taken today could have consequences for Earth's habitability for hundreds, if not thousands of years
to come.[107]

Comprehending this vastness is a primary cognitive challenge of the
planetary age. The embodied experience of space and time (past, present, and future) is ontologically limited: individual physical bodies inhabit only a single, relatively small place at a time and for only a single,
relatively brief period. Paleontologist Stephen Jay Gould argued that
"geological time" is in fact comprehensible only through metaphors or

analogies that point beyond the tangible, the material, and the experiential.[108] As anthropologist Lisa Messeri rightly observes, "One reason 'the planetary' causes us to stumble is because it requires that we grapple with intangible modes of being."[109] This intangibility is inherently difficult for unavoidably tangible humans—and yet it must be apprehended. Or as Chakrabarty puts it, "Our embodied selves and our institutions did not evolve to deal with problems that could span geological scales of time" or planet-sized geographies.[110]

Planetary issues, finally, entail some anthropogenic causation.[111] To be sure, there exist planetary processes for which human agency has no role. Plate tectonics and volcanic eruptions, for example, are clearly Earthly phenomena that can affect human and other types of flourishing, but human beings have no bearing on their operation. As a result, they fall outside the scope of interest of this book. That said, our knowledge of these processes as well as the degree of human impact on them could change—and so our scope of interest could expand. We must remain open to this possibility. Until the middle of the twentieth century, the idea that humans could affect something as large as Earth's climate was considered outlandish. Perhaps new theories and evidence will one day bring additional planetary processes into our understanding of the anthropogenic fold. Likewise, it is possible that future humans, because of their numbers or technological inventions, will have an impact on certain processes that we currently do not. We already know that industrial activities such as fracking and mining can cause earthquakes, an Earth phenomenon previously thought to be beyond human interference.[112]

Planetary issues, in sum, are defined by four basic qualities: they are necessary for a flourishing biosphere; are inseparable from the long history of life; occur over immense timescales and geographies; and are affected by some human intervention. But they share at least two additional characteristics. First, they are properly described, not as international or global, but as supranational, transnational, or, as we prefer, planetary. That is, planetary issues do not just flow between national states or exist in the interstitial space between them (which would classify them as international). They extinguish the distinction between foreign and domestic; they are bounded only by the Earth system. Second, planetary issues and their effects are not evenly distributed; they are patchy.[113] Sometimes the patches are determined by geography, topography, and ecology, other times by social, economic, and political factors, and typically by an intersection of the two. But the patches do not map onto national states.

———

Unlike previous terms—like *globalization*, or before that, *modernization*—the Planetary does not refer to a process, a transition from one state to another. Rather, it refers to a condition: our ineluctable embeddedness in the Earth system, a system we either steward to our benefit or not, but that in either case is indifferent to us even as we depend on it. As Messeri puts it, "Planetarity, perhaps because it appeals to a word associated with 'nature' (planet) rather than 'culture' (globe), serves to remind us that we are guests of the Earth. It is humbling and therefore, one hopes, saving."[114] What is at stake in the Planetary is not the survival of life, much less the planet itself—which will outlast the brief human appearance—but whether we can find a way to manage our place on this planet in a way that ensures our flourishing for as long a term as (humanly) possible. And that latter ambition requires, before anything else, facing our real conditions with sober senses.

What should we do in the face of our budding recognition of the condition of planetarity, and of our recognition of planetary issues? While the Planetary provides us a problem, it doesn't point to solutions. The category of the Planetary helps us recognize multispecies agency as well as human embeddedness in the kaleidoscopically interwoven ecosystems that make up the biosphere, but by themselves these realizations do not help us to prioritize which planetary issues to address and how. This task requires other tools: tools we pick up from the study of governance.

The question of prioritization is central to governance: the reality of limited resources, both material and intellectual, means that addressing some problems must take precedence over addressing others. This is also the necessary and inescapable work of politics. We cannot keep tinkering with political ideas founded on a conception of the world in which humanity and nature were falsely considered and treated as separate, and unequal, spheres. Such ideas (and the institutions built on them) rest on a crumbling foundation—and, contra Friedman's counsel, we should not "bow down" to them. What we need today are new political concepts and institutions that are founded instead on the real human condition, that understand us as fragile nodes in a mind-bogglingly complex network, inextricably embedded and enmeshed in planet Earth. What the rest of this book does is invite a conversation for thinking about exactly this: how we can design political institutions that are capable of adjudicating what matters in light of the Planetary and then operationalizing those decisions.

Four

Planetary Subsidiarity

While world war raged for the second time in his life, David Mitrany spent his days planning for the peace. In 1943, the Bucharest-born, London-trained political scientist—the inaugural professor in the School of Economics and Politics at the Institute for Advanced Studies, in Princeton, New Jersey—published *A Working Peace System*, his vision for a new postwar international order. The influential pamphlet addressed what Mitrany identified as "the problem of our generation": "how to weld together the common interests of all without interfering unduly in the particular ways of each."[1] What governance systems can meet the worldwide need "to regulate the politics of its common life" while simultaneously not disturbing "the parochial politics of its members"?[2] How, in other words, to govern the whole of humanity without sacrificing any of the parts?

Picking up Mitrany's problematique today, we must consider yet another factor. We still face shared challenges in need of collective solutions, and humans are still wildly diverse, but in the eight decades since he wrote, we have also become fully aware of our planetary condition. The problem of our generation is "how to weld together the common interests of all without interfering unduly in the particular ways of each" on one systemically interdependent planet. There are eight billion of us—a riot of hopes, fears, and unique ways of life—living amid countless other species in varied ecosystems throughout the Earth system: the interconnected, planetary complex that permits the flourishing of life. We can't wish away, ignore, or run roughshod over this reality. Instead, we must confront an intractable question: How can we foster diverse dreams, in diverse communities, while simultaneously building large-scale institutions for the management of planetary risks?

The status quo system fails to achieve either goal well. The existing governance architecture concentrates authority at one point in the macro-institutional system, the sovereign national state. National states can and do delegate tasks and powers to international bodies and subnational institutions, leading to the emergence of what chapter 2 described as *ad hoc multilevel governance*. But this system, by privileging state sovereignty, neither recognizes the self-determination of diverse local communities nor provides for the adequate management of planetary problems.

Envisioning a system of common governance that can deal with the twin constraints of global human pluralism and planetary limits is the challenge that this chapter takes up. Our goal is to describe a system that allows us to think big and small in the same register—that enables us to manage planetary challenges while promoting local self-government. Accomplishing this requires a transition from the current system of ad hoc multilevel governance where authority is allocated on the basis of the principle of state sovereignty to a *deliberate multiscalar governance* system where authority is allocated on the basis of the principle of subsidiarity in a planetary key.

This chapter provides a rough diagram of *planetary subsidiarity* rather than a detailed blueprint or instructions for how to get there. The latter is perhaps the more arduous task, but before we can debate the political path forward, we must first hold a clear picture of the future we want. This, then, is an exercise in imagining the desired state of affairs as well as describing the gap between it and present-day circumstances. At the same time, this takes a necessary step toward anticipating how to overcome the objections of those who prefer to hold on to some version of the unsustainable status quo. Whereas previous chapters made empirical claims about the nature of the national state system and the condition of planetarity, here we begin to present a normative vision for transforming the former in light of the latter.

Multilevel versus Multiscalar Institutions

Multilevel governance isn't new; in fact, it's the global norm.[3] For the past half century, as chapter 2 demonstrated, multilevel structures have been increasingly common forms for the organization of governance within national states. Likewise, the current global governance system that coordinates among national states is itself a multilevel system. For nearly every important policy area today, decisions are made and policies are implemented at multiple levels of government institutions and nonstate actors, with varying degrees of authority. Think of the dizzying array of institutions at all sorts of levels involved in shaping COVID-19 responses: mayors, city councils, and local public health authorities; state, provincial, and regional leaders; national presidents and prime ministers; the UN secretary-general and the WHO director-general; international networks of doctors, scientists, and pharmaceutical companies involved in vaccine invention, trials, production, and distribution; government and nongovernmental social service providers, from neighborhood mutual aid organizations that were formed as the pandemic began to aid organizations with long-standing, global reach; philanthropists and foundations, funding efforts across all levels; and more. All of these actors, through their collaborations and their conflicts, collectively generated the overall response to the pandemic. They constitute the actually existing ad hoc multilevel governance system for global health emergencies.

The world's response to COVID-19 might not seem like the best advertisement for multilevel governance, but it in fact demonstrates some of the benefits of such a system. For instance, it allows for different responses in different jurisdictions to accommodate diverse preferences and norms. This enabled East Asian countries to pursue policies that differed from most of the rest of the world (more severe quarantines, etc.), reflecting divergent preferences and experiences of the populations (such as recent experiences with other pandemic diseases). Operating at multiple levels also meant that various levels could have different responses. In the best of circumstances, that meant they could each work at their comparative advantages, with larger jurisdictions, like the US federal government and the European Union, doing things that required substantial resources—like supporting vaccine development—while smaller jurisdictions made decisions that required locally specific information—like when to enter or exit specific phases of lockdown and reopening. In less ideal circumstances, the differently scaled institutions could serve as fail-safes to each other, with municipalities, provinces, and nonstate actors taking action in the face of poor performance by national governments and international organizations.

Alas, the current, status quo system lacks capacity at several levels. As a result, the existing global governance architecture is multilevel, but some of the functionally necessary institutions are missing, while others aren't sufficiently robust and authoritative. Today, in particular, we lack planetary governance institutions—that is, institutions tasked with and capable of managing planetary challenges. In addition, most subnational governance institutions—regional, provincial, municipal, neighborhood, and village governments—lack the authority and resources to resolve local challenges in a way that is satisfactory and responsive to their constituents. There do exist multilateral, global governance institutions and local governments, but both sorts remain firmly subordinated to sovereign national states, the basic units of today's ad hoc multilevel governance system. International and subnational institutions govern the issues that national states are unable to govern or are uninterested in governing—as long as this doesn't interfere with state sovereignty. This latter impediment means that the local scale often isn't governed effectively and the planetary scale rarely is.

In contrast to the current ad hoc multilevel governance system, we propose a *deliberate multiscalar governance* system that enables effective governance at all necessary scales. It would fill in the missing scales so that the entire governance map would be more robust: subnational institutions should be strengthened, supported, and reimagined, and planetary institutions should be created. By labeling the current system "ad hoc," we call attention to the fact that in most cases today's governance institutions emerged organically from older institutional arrangements, based on past political compromises and expediencies to work around the strictures of sovereignty. What we have ended up with is like a palimpsest that has accrued its layered features over time, the result being characterized by improvisation more than intentional design. By contrast, what we call "deliberate" multiscalar governance architecture should be based on explicit and consistent functional criteria for determining where authorities for various decisions should be allocated within the system. The idea is to develop the parts in light of the goals of the whole.

This new vision is not only about shifting from an ad hoc system to a deliberate one; we also propose shifting the emphasis from levels to scales. Levels, in our usage, imply hierarchy: cities are a lower level than, and must obey, national states. Scales, by contrast, suggest less hierarchy and more equivalence. In a multiscalar system, cities are a smaller or narrower (not lower) scale, while national states are a larger or wider (not higher) scale. This difference in scale doesn't necessitate a difference in authority or importance: each institution is fit for a specific spatial or temporal scale, and isn't automatically subordinate to larger ones.[4] In our proposed governance architecture, we focus on public authorities rather than private ones. That is, we focus on governments at varying scales. Nonstate actors can play a role in governing, such as supporting or supplementing the various scales, but the emphasis of the design we present here is layers of public institutions.

Deliberate Multiscalar Governance

For simplicity's sake, we conceptualize three primary scales of governance: local, national, and planetary. Here we introduce the general systemic architecture. The basic idea is a system of robust, well-resourced, high-capacity institutions at all scales, from the planetary to the local, that can manage governance challenges at all scales, from the planetary to the local.

At the widest scale, *planetary institutions* are the minimum viable organization for the direct management of planetary challenges. These are institutions with specifically delimited authority at the planetary scale over specific and specifically planetary phenomena. In other words, planetary institutions are not world government. A world state would be a general-purpose jurisdiction with planet-wide authority; planetary institutions, by contrast, are functionally specific institutions with limited scope of authority. At the same time, planetary institutions as we are conceiving them also differ in crucial ways from how most "global governance" operates today: whereas global governance institutions are generally multilateral associations of sovereign national states, representing the interests of those states, planetary institutions of the sorts we will propose in chapter 6 will directly address planetary challenges, answering to planetary stakeholders as a whole, rather than representing the sectional interests of national states and national elites.[5]

At the meso-scale, *national institutions* would have the authority to manage issues that fit their scale. Of course, calling national states "meso-scale" obscures the vast diversity of national states in terms of their own size and complexity. What is entailed in the national governance of China and India, each with 1.4 billion people, is vastly different from what is required of the national government of Tuvalu, which has 12,000 people. Larger countries will inevitably develop tiered systems of internal governance. The United States, for example, in addition to the federal government based in Washington, D.C., has fifty states, each of which has on average more than sixty counties, each of which in turn includes on average ten municipal governments. Likewise, in China, there are five levels of ever-smaller units of government; provinces, prefectures, counties, townships, all the way down to villages, of which there are more than one million. Placing national states within a broader multiscalar framework allows them to take on just the functions that are appropriate for their specific situation, rather than assuming that mega- and micro-states have the same scale advantages. But essentially, the national state would focus primarily on what it was formulated to do in the mid-twentieth century: national economic investment, development, and redistribution.

The appearance of the national state in our systems architecture may come as a surprise, given the objections we raise to it as a political form throughout the book. Yet the primary problem with the national state is its claim to absolute sovereignty, not its size or scale. There are, in fact, distinct advantages to meso-scale institutions—institutions fit to mediate between the abstract vastness of the planetary and the situated intimacy of the local. In particular, national states are the only political institution that have historically succeeded in redistributing the gains and losses of economic growth in any meaningful and sustained way. Without doubt, states have not often done a fair, equal, or even competent job in this regard. But redistribution schemes outside national units have almost always failed (which was a major reason why the proposed and attempted multinational federations discussed in chapter 1 all disintegrated into separate national states).[6] As a result, economic governance, particularly over questions of distribution and redistribution, is especially well suited for national-scale institutions to manage. For our proposals in this chapter, and later in the book, the starting point of our analysis is the world as it is. We aim to remain within the realm of what we think might work in reality, and, as a result, national states still serve an indispensable function in multiscalar governance system based on planetary subsidiarity.

At the narrowest scale, *local institutions* should be empowered so that local governments, which focus on local problems and local demands, have the authority and resources to develop locally appropriate responses and to adapt nimbly as local circumstances change. This isn't to suggest that we dump problems into the laps of ill-equipped local leaders so that other authorities can wash their hands of them. It is about building capable local governments that can tackle their residents' shared problems. One method for strengthening local capacity (that we will discuss at length in chapter 5) is to increase the horizontal linkages between subnational governments by creating or enhancing peer networks of local governance institutions to exchange and coordinate ideas, expertise, and resources.

Deliberate multiscalar governance represents a vision for a single worldwide governance architecture, but one that doesn't form a unitary or federal world state dominated by a single center of power. It is, rather, a framework for the dispersion of power based on the need to govern specific functional issues. The takeaway from our understanding of humankind's planetary condition isn't just that we need to create new governance institutions at the planetary scale but that we need to reconstruct the whole architecture of how governance decision rights are allocated worldwide. Tackling the challenges of the future doesn't merely require a new scale for planetary action, it requires action at appropriate scales across the entire system.[7] We do not propose a one-size-fits-all institutional solution, but rather a flexible architecture of multiple institutions, operating at multiple scales, tailoring effective governance for diverse populations living in varied circumstances on a single planet.[8]

Designing such a structure means inverting our usual thinking about governance: we must learn to prioritize governance functions over governance units. Rather than trying to match functions to units, which is how most governance allocation decisions work today, we should do the opposite. In the current system, one type of unit—the sovereign national state—is the default governor: it is given the right to decide whether or how to manage any issue that emerges, including the metadecision of whether to delegate decision rights to others. National states get first and exclusive rights to decision-making, not because they are best suited for it, but because the international system, by recent tradition and international law, favors national sovereignty.

Our argument, by contrast, is to begin with the issue or problem in need of governance and then consider all governance units that might have a role in the matter. The result of this fundamental rethink is that *national states should give up many of their governance functions, tasks, and decision rights:* planetary functions should move to planetary institutions, while many other functions should move to local institutions. The allocation of authority isn't a one-time event, however; the system must be dynamic. Putting function first means recognizing that the appropriate unit or scale can change over time. A robust multiscalar system has the capacity to morph to resolve new problems as they emerge or existing problems as they change over time, moving functions between units as warranted.

This approach—subsuming form to function—extends the one that Mitrany devised to answer the question with which we began this chapter, a tradition of international relations theory called functionalism. Functionalism, which Mitrany and others developed in the interwar period—as well as its intellectual descendent, neofunctionalism—advocates for the international integration of national states for the management of specific, concrete tasks, or functions. The basis for international cooperation, Mitrany argued, must be "along the lines of specific ends and needs, and according to the conditions of their time and place," rather than on the traditional "basis of a set constitutional division of jurisdiction of rights and powers."[9] Like functionalists, we eschew designs for world government and focus instead on context-specific, task-oriented institutions. The scope and authority of planetary institutions, in particular, follow from this tradition's position that "the jurisdiction of the various agencies [should be] no wider than the most effective working limits of the function."[10]

Yet we do not subscribe to functionalism wholesale. We reject functionalism's teleological theory and political strategy: what Ernst B. Haas, the father of neofunctionalism, described as an "integrative impulse" that drives integration in one functional area to "spill over" into others.[11] Mitrany, for instance, held the view that functional integration was only the first step toward "the ultimate goal" of world "federation."[12] Enfolding functionalism within subsidiarity, however, tempers functionalism's tendency to assume, if not outright desire, ever-increasing centralization. Where functionalism sees integration within a center as the desired state of affairs, subsidiarity seeks to balance the need for central solutions with the virtues of local autonomy.

Deliberate multiscalar governance also builds on the reality that non-national institutions already handle many governance functions. Governance includes many more actors than just national institutions. Once we recognize that governance and the national state aren't synonymous and needn't be congruent, it becomes easier to think about moving governance authorities out of national states and to other institutions. The idea is to match units to governance functions deliberately, unconstrained by the restrictive elements of sovereignty and an overly nationalist politics. This, to us, isn't a radical proposition; it's a recognition and acceleration of decades-old trends. We propose to place national states within a broader architecture that includes more empowered supranational and subnational institutions than at present exist. We want to push ourselves, and others, to think of politics, government, and governance beyond national capitals.[13]

The Principle of Subsidiarity

In any multiscalar governance system, two questions of foremost importance are which powers are allocated to which institutions and how the allocations are decided. Several principles could guide allocations of authority. The largest scale could hold all authority, including to assign and reassign powers at its discretion. Smaller scales could hold all authority except for those they consent to transfer. A written constitution could enumerate specific powers to specific points in the system. Authority could be distributed by a utilitarian logic, to maximize the welfare of the most. Authority could be assigned by democratic rule, following the majority's will. One could adopt a wait-and-see approach and let the scales duke it out among themselves. The status quo principle, state sovereignty, allocates rights and responsibilities to national states, which can then decide whether and where to delegate them. But, as we argue, this method doesn't work for planetary issues that transcend individual states. We need a new principle.

To guide allocations of authority in a multiscalar system of planetary governance, we are inspired by the *principle of subsidiarity*. The principle of subsidiarity is the idea that larger-scale governing institutions should not intervene unless and until a smaller scale is unable to carry out a particular task. It is a method for adjudicating between the advantages and disadvantages offered by all the scales at which an issue could be governed.

Policy challenges come at a range of scales, from the hyperlocal to the planetary. Each should be addressed at an appropriate institutional scale. The principle of subsidiarity is a tool to assess what the appropriate scale is: a method to determine the proper match between governance institutions, governance functions, and issues in need of governance. To return briefly to the current status quo, the question of issue-to-function-to-institution alignment gets short shrift: every issue and function goes to the national state by default. There is an unconditional presumption in favor of the national state that is undone only at a national state's discretion. It doesn't matter that national states aren't well matched for many vital issues; the ball is in their court. By contrast, the principle of subsidiarity deprivileges the national state and opens the door to allocating much greater governance responsibilities to local and planetary institutions.

We offer a new interpretation of subsidiarity, but one rooted in the history of the principle. As we will now show, the concept is plastic: many people have wielded it creatively for varied causes over four centuries. Our version draws on this history of ideational change to recast it yet again. Like many before us, we take what remains useful of the core of subsidiarity and fashion it for contemporary challenges. Through this long evolution, however, subsidiarity's central concern has remained consistent: a diverse world requires diverse solutions—there is no single answer.

A Brief History of Subsidiarity

In the late sixteenth century, the German city of Emden, a strategic port on the North Sea, found itself in a political jam. The city was a leading center of Calvinism—in 1542, it had been among the first German cities to adopt the new faith—but its provincial lord, the Count of East Frisia, was staunchly Lutheran and, up the hierarchy, in Prague, the Holy Roman Emperor was Roman Catholic. With these larger, more powerful political units increasingly trying to impose their will on the city, Emden's leaders were looking for a strategy to defend their rights and privileges of self-government. In 1604, the city council found what they were looking for in the Calvinist jurist Johannes Althusius, whom they hired to serve as a city official until his death thirty-four years later.[14]

Althusius's appeal for the city fathers was in his original theory of rightful political authority, published in 1603 as *Politics Methodically Set Forth* (*Politica Methodice Digesta* in the original Latin). In it, Althusius argued that sovereignty belonged not to central states but to cities and other small political associations. "I recognize the prince as the administrator, overseer, and governor of these rights of sovereignty," he argued. "But the owner and usufructuary of sovereignty is none other than the total people associated with one symbiotic body from many small associations."[15] In other words, the sovereignty of smaller governing units wasn't granted to them by larger units; it was theirs by natural right. As a result, smaller units were the primary body politic, and larger units existed only to serve them, especially by establishing the basis for cooperation and unity among the federated subnational units. In practice, this meant that every city was "able to establish statutes concerning those things which pertain to the administration of its own matters," whereas the monarch was "not permitted for his own pleasure to alienate or diminish the provinces, cities, or towns of his realm."[16] The leader of a larger unit of government was entitled only to "as much authority as has been explicitly conceded to him by the associated members or bodies of the realm. And what hasn't been given to him must be considered to have been left under the control of the people or universal association. Such is the nature of the contractual mandate."[17]

Though it wasn't yet called this, what the Calvinists of Emden deployed against their non-Calvinist superiors in defense of their autonomy was the principle of subsidiarity.

Widely known in his time, Althusius's *Politics* was largely forgotten over the following generations. His arguments for the autonomy of local communities and against centralized authority were out of step with the ascendent political currents in Europe, which ran toward centralizing states and empires. Beliefs like "The king represents the people not the people the king" and the king "can even be deposed" had no place in the courts of the seventeenth- and eighteenth-century absolute monarchs and their ballooning bureaucracies.[18]

Althusius's thought began to reemerge only in the mid-1800s, in the context of the rise of modern statehood. Amid the debates on liberalism and on autonomy for minority nationalities thrust to the fore by the revolutions of 1848, German Catholics seized on subsidiarity to address their concerns with maintaining regional and confessional autonomy in the centralizing, secular German state being consolidated under a Protestant Prussian monarchy. The leading thinker was Wilhelm von Ketteler, the Catholic bishop of Mainz from 1850 to 1877. Trained as a lawyer before he entered the priesthood, Ketteler studied under Protestant legal thinkers who introduced him to Althusius and the tradition of local primacy. In subsidiarity, Ketteler found an intellectual foundation for asserting the autonomy of local government and religious institutions against a Protestant state growing in power. The state, as he saw it, was "merely an institution, and its existence is dependent upon the community," which was organic and natural. It was in local communities that people, guided by local churches, could flourish. As a result, the state's purview should be limited: "The state fulfills its role and purpose when it protects the rights of its people within the communities that foster full human living."[19] Local law and custom must triumph; imposition "from above" can only cause harm to human flourishing and disrupt the delicate social balance.

In a forceful letter about schools to the revolutionary Frankfurt Parliament of 1848, for instance, Ketteler argued that "divine and natural law" gives parents "the holy and inviolable right to decide how [their] children are to be educated." Ketteler couldn't endure handing over "the bodies of our children" to "the state as the guide for [their] soul." Granting control over education to the central state rather than local communities stripped parents of their "holy right and . . . holy duty" and turned a project aimed at children's "soul's growth" into "merely a service in the interest of the state."[20]

Three decades later, Althusius was rediscovered again, this time by the German legal historian Otto von Gierke. Gierke transposed the Calvinist scholar's ideas about religious autonomy into debates about the design principles for a secular state. Like Ketteler, Gierke pulled Althusius's theory from what he called "undeserved oblivion" in order to fight contemporary political battles against the centralizing impulses of the Prussian state.[21] In particular, Gierke emphasized the "striking . . . spirit of federalism which pervades" Althusius's thought. He saw in Althusius's theory of society as a "corporatively articulated whole . . . [constructed] from the bottom upward" as well as in his formulation of popular sovereignty a "great lever of all centralizing efforts."[22] Althusius's "sense of right, and . . . his zeal for liberty" provided Gierke with the "foundation for the constructive theory of the Constitutional State" that he believed Germany should build.[23]

Around the same time, Catholic theologians were grappling with the place of the church in secularizing European states and societies overcome by a "spirit of revolutionary change" that they could no longer ignore.[24] Pope Leo XIII sought to address these social, economic, and political transformations in his papal encyclical of 1891, *Rerum novarum*. His goal was twofold: to address the conditions of the European working class and to protect the church from socialism. More broadly, however, Leo XIII sought to set the terms for the Catholic Church's compromise with modernity. Abandoning the church's outright opposition to state authority, *Rerum novarum* accepted modern national states and aimed instead to check their power. *Rerum novarum* was thus a defense of the church's autonomy against assertive secular European states and socialist parties.

In formulating his argument, Leo XIII was heavily influenced by Ketteler, calling him "my great predecessor" in Catholic social thought.[25] Like Ketteler, Leo XIII was concerned with interventions by higher forms of social organizations into what they saw as more basic and natural ones, particularly families. Smaller, local units (families, communities, churches), he argued, were distinct and independent social spheres with their own rights and privileges that couldn't be usurped by larger units. Government intrusion into family life, for instance, was "a great and pernicious error." Socialists' ambitions for "setting aside the parent and setting up a State supervision" represented an "act against natural justice and destroy[ed] the structure of the home."[26] Welfare assistance for the poor, likewise, was properly provided by individuals, associations, or the church, not "a system of relief organized by the State."[27] In holding that corporate bodies—families, local associations, the church—had a natural and moral precedence over states, *Rerum novarum* placed the idea of subsidiarity (though not yet named as such) at the heart of Catholic doctrine.

To mark the fortieth anniversary of *Rerum novarum* in 1931, Pope Pius XI decided to revisit many of Leo XIII's themes in his own papal encyclical, *Quadragesimo anno*. In a world mired in economic depression and totalitarian political ideologies—the Vatican was encircled by Mussolini's fascist state, though the specter of Stalin's Soviet Union also loomed large—Pius XI took the opportunity to articulate a far-reaching Catholic vision for the "reconstruction of the social order." To protect the position of the church and its favored forms of social organization (families and associations) from encroachment by states, *Quadragesimo anno* developed "the principle of 'subsidiary function,'" better known as the "principle of subsidiarity."[28] "Just as it is gravely wrong to take from individuals what they can accomplish by their own initiative and industry and give it to the community," the pope argued, "so also it is an injustice and at the same time a grave evil and disturbance of right order to assign to a greater and higher association what lesser and subordinate organizations can do."[29]

Limiting the governance responsibilities of the national state wasn't just about weakening it, but also about focusing it. Pius XI argued that placing limits would in fact restore the authority of modern states that are "overwhelmed and crushed by almost infinite tasks and duties."[30] Implementing subsidiarity meant that "the State will more freely, powerfully, and effectively do all those things that belong to it alone because it alone can do them."[31] In *Quadragesimo anno*, Pius IX defined a positive role for the state as the institution responsible for creating the conditions in which primary communities could seek their own flourishing. Enhancing the common good required achieving a just balance between state restraint and state assistance. Subsidiarity, now a core tenet of Catholic social doctrine, provided the church's principle for finding the balance.[32]

By the late twentieth century, this now thoroughly Catholic idea was again stripped of faith, as Gierke had done, and transplanted into secular debates about the institutional design for European integration.[33] The principle first appeared in a 1971 article by the Anglo-German sociologist Ralf Dahrendorf, who was serving at the time on the European Commission (EC). Warning about the EC's "dogma of harmonization," which threatened to impose homogeneous administrative rules on a politically and culturally heterogeneous continent, Dahrendorf proposed moving "towards the principle of subsidiarity" as an antidote to the increasingly interventionist and bureaucratized nature of the EC.[34] The idea was pressed further into European officialdom in the 1970s and 1980s by Altiero Spinelli, an Italian member of the EC and European Parliament and a leading advocate for internationalism and European federation since he penned a famous manifesto "for a free and united Europe" while Mussolini's political prisoner during World War II.[35]

If Dahrendorf and Spinelli theorized the secular application of subsidiarity to the European project, Jacques Delors, EC president from 1985 to 1995, would be the key figure in driving the EU's adoption of the principle.[36] Amid debates in the late 1980s about the next step forward in European integration, Delors latched on to subsidiarity as a way to blunt opposition to his vision for further European centralization from German Länder and British conservatives. In a 1989 speech, Delors offered the principle of subsidiarity as a solution for these concerns. "I see it [the principle of subsidiarity] as a way of reconciling . . . the need for a European power capable of tackling the problems of our age and the absolute necessity to preserve our roots in the shape of our nations and regions." This, Delors observed, was "precisely what subsidiarity is about."[37]

This, then, was the context in which subsidiarity entered the negotiations over the Treaty on European Union (the Maastricht Treaty), the institution's 1992 founding document. After numerous debates and proposals over the principle, the final treaty included several mentions of subsidiarity. The principle is first mentioned explicitly in the preamble; then, more consequentially, it appears in the substantive body of the text, where it was given strict criteria demanded by the German government. First, the treaty obliged the EU to "act within the limits of the powers conferred upon it by this Treaty and of the objectives assigned to it therein." Second, it restricted the EU's ability to act outside its areas of exclusive authority, permitting EU action "only if and in so far as the objectives of the proposed action cannot be sufficiently achieved by the Member states and can therefore, by reason of the scale or effects of the proposed action, be better achieved" at the supranational scale. Pushing this restrictive attitude further, the clause concludes, "Any action by the Community shall not go beyond what is necessary to achieve the objectives of this Treaty."[38]

The Maastricht Treaty's ambiguous usage of *subsidiarity* reflects the circumstance of the principle's inclusion: its main support came from two groups with very different interpretations and interests. One consisted of parties influenced by Catholic social doctrine, particularly Germany's ruling Christian Democrats, who supported federal institutions for Europe. The other consisted of parties opposed to strong, supranational European institutions, chiefly British and Danish conservatives. The UK's Tory prime minister, John Major, hailed subsidiarity's inclusion in Maastricht as central to "the Conservative vision of Europe": "For the first time, we have begun to reverse that centralizing trend. We have moved decision-taking back towards the Member States in areas where Community law need not and should not apply."[39] During early post-Maastricht debates, Major's government even proposed interpreting subsidiarity as a veto that any member state could use, but the other eleven members rejected the notion.[40] In trying to satisfy actors holding these divergent interpretations of the principle, the treaty neglected an actual definition of subsidiarity—the meaning has to be read from the context.[41] A British former president of the European Court of Justice dismissed Maastricht's discussion of the principle as "a disgraceful piece of sloppy draftsmanship."[42]

In the 1997 Treaty of Amsterdam and the 2007 Treaty of Lisbon, both of which are significant amendments to Maastricht, European negotiators expanded on the meaning of subsidiarity in the EU. At Amsterdam, the negotiators agreed that for EU action to be justified, first, "the objectives of the proposed action cannot be sufficiently achieved by Member States' action" and, second, the objectives "can therefore be better achieved by action on the part of the Community." These conditions are met when, for example, "the issue under consideration has transnational aspects which cannot be satisfactorily regulated by action by Member States," the EU's failure to act "would conflict with the requirements of the Treaty," or EU action "would produce clear benefits by reason of its scale or effects."[43] Despite these narrow guidelines for permissible policymaking at the European level, the protocol expressly affirmed that subsidiarity wasn't an absolute check on EU authority: "Subsidiarity . . . allows Community action within the limits of its powers to be expanded where circumstances so require, and conversely, to be restricted or discontinued where it is no longer justified."[44]

Then, at Lisbon, the EU again revisited the principle of subsidiarity. The 2007 Treaty explicitly included subnational governments in the application of the principle, permitting EU measures only if "the objectives of the proposed action cannot be sufficiently achieved by the Member States, either at central level *or at regional and local level.*"[45]

What's more, the treaty introduced a legislative "Early Warning Mechanism," which gives national parliaments the formal opportunity to object to proposed EU legislation for not complying with the principle of subsidiarity.[46]

In sum, though not known by the term *subsidiarity* until *Quadragesimo anno* in 1931, the core principle has been debated in Europe for the past four hundred years. In that time, subsidiarity has been repeatedly adopted and tweaked to suit the needs of people and institutions resisting the centralization of power by others. Indeed, a consistent theme in the history of the concept of subsidiarity, from 1603 to the present, is its regular reformulation and reinterpretation. Under Althusius, it served as a Calvinist and regionalist Germanic principle for securing autonomy from an overweening Lutheran provincial lord and a Catholic Holy Roman Emperor; under Ketteler, its religious valence was inverted to support demand for Catholic autonomy from a Protestant centralizing bureaucracy; under Gierke, the concept was secularized as a principle for functionalist administrative practices; under Leo XIII and Pius XI, it was used to resist the secularist principles of modern states and political ideologies; and finally in the Maastricht Treaty it was resecularized to provide the normative basis for multilevel governance under an "ever closer" European Union. The salient point is that the principle of subsidiarity is a concept capable of ample reinterpretation.

Despite subsidiarity's many reformulations, however, one tenet remains unchanged: subsidiarity eschews the ambition for total political victory. At its core, the concept is a pragmatic way to manage pluralism via local empowerment. This antiuniversalist, antitotalizing vision is an important check on any political project. For us, the principle of subsidiarity provides a safeguard against the impulse toward political centralization and homogenization that the expansive, holistic concept of the Planetary might otherwise seem to justify.

The EU's Misconceived Subsidiarity: Multilevel, Not Multiscalar

While the EU is the best-known and largest-scale attempt to govern using subsidiarity, it is also a cautionary tale. Our interpretation of the principle of subsidiarity emerges from an appreciation of the limits of the European project, which is often criticized for being out of touch with and unresponsive to the needs and desires of its citizens.[47] Making matters worse, the EU's legitimacy problems result at least in part from its application of subsidiarity. Why, then, would we seek to implement a principle whose foremost implementation has failed?

The basic problem is that despite the EU's stated commitment to take decisions "as closely as possible to the citizen," policymaking within the union is perceived as moving away from the citizens, as Brussels has steadily centralized more and more authority.[48] Rather than moving decisions to the "lowest" level possible, the EU has more often moved them to "higher" levels—and often to the European-level institutions with the least democratic accountability, such as the European Central Bank. In order for our governance architecture not to repeat this mistake, this section assesses how subsidiarity in the EU came to produce outcomes at odds with what we take to be the core meaning of the principle.[49]

The EU's subsidiarity problem is rooted in the intertwined history, structure, and goals of the institution. Historically, EU leadership in the early 1990s turned to the concept of subsidiarity out of political desperation, rather than principled belief. After Denmark rejected the Maastricht Treaty in a 1992 popular referendum, what had been a largely ignored clause about subsidiarity in the Treaty became a central justification. Further negotiations resulted in an emphasis on subsidiarity as a way to ameliorate the fear that national interests would be ignored by the supranational union.[50]

Structurally, the way subsidiarity operates in the EU is that the European institutions set goals and only then ask which level, European or national, will be most efficient at implementing those goals.[51] EU officials have thus treated subsidiarity not as a mechanism for balancing European and national objectives, but rather as a tool for achieving European objectives efficiently. This design presumed that there would be no conflicts between the levels, that everyone supported the objectives of the center.[52] In this regard, EU subsidiarity was a product of its time: the "end of history" moment of the early post–Cold War years, when many assumed that the great ideological battles of the past were permanently put to bed. In a political zeitgeist with general agreement that liberal democratic technocracy was the one best system for governance, EU leaders assumed that technical adjustments to reach shared goals were all that mattered.

Furthermore, the EU's goals themselves proved resistant to the centrifugal force of subsidiarity. From its inception, European integration has focused on economic integration, and the EU has been especially single-minded in pursuit of its overriding objective: the creation of a single European market for the frictionless movement of goods, capital, services, and people. Two features of economic integration counteract a presumption toward local control. First, the Treaty on European Union's criterion for permissible centralization centers on efficiency: the EU is to act if and only if an objective can "be better achieved" at the EU level, rather than a lower one.[53] But economies are typically more efficient at greater scale, and so economic objectives will typically "be better achieved" by centralized, EU action.[54] Second, the goal of economic integration encourages mission creep, as more and more policy areas can come to be defined as necessary for the goal's completion—an explicit feature of the functionalist approach to integration in the eyes of its proponents. And once a new activity is seen as part of the goal, it can easily be sucked into the EU's efficiency/centralization vortex.[55]

For the purposes of planetary governance, we draw four lessons from the EU's experience with subsidiarity. First, subsidiarity must be applied seriously and intentionally: the presumption for smaller-scale decision-making must be real. This means that the bias toward smaller-scale governance must trump some sound reasons for moving authority to larger ones.[56] If we truly value self-government, we must tolerate some inefficiencies. As a result, institutions throughout a multiscalar system must be wired for subsidiarity's presumption in favor of allocat-

ing decision rights to smaller scales. This does not mean that authority can never move to larger or wider institutional scales; it can, and it
sometimes must. Rather, there must be a good reason for moving decision rights to a larger scale that outweighs the commitment to the self-
governance of smaller scales. For a counterexample of what we mean
here, look to the European Court of Justice, the European institution
tasked with adjudicating disputes over subsidiarity between the levels.
In deciding whether decision-making authority over an issue should
rest with the EU or the member states, the ECJ has the legal authority
to consider only the EU Treaty, not national laws or constitutions. The
dispute-resolution body is thus structurally biased toward the higher
level—it is wired *against* subsidiarity.[57]

Second, we cannot elide politics; rather, politics must be front and
center. The EU's approach to subsidiarity made two political elisions.
To begin with, as noted above, it assumed away politics. It operated
from an assumption of consensus among the levels that did not in fact
exist.[58] Moreover, the EU used the principle of subsidiarity to avoid politics, moving the authority to assign authority outside the realm of politics. In particular, it relied on the logic of economic efficiency to make
political decisions about who had the authority to make decisions. This
form of meta-authority—the authority over authority, which we discuss
later—became linked to the economic concept of "comparative efficiency," which was to be assessed on the basis of economic expertise. In
other words, decisions were to be made on a technocratic basis, rather
than via citizen deliberation. The lesson here is to acknowledge that
there will always be political disputes and that an effective institutional
design must include a mechanism for adjudicating them on a political
basis.

Confronting the necessity, to say nothing of the inevitability, of
politics also addresses a shortcoming of functionalist theory. The attraction of functionalism is its claim to be able to separate "the political
from the functional approach."[59] In other words, the theory rests on the
belief that technical, functionally specific actions can somehow be isolated from politics. But history does not bear out the assumption that

the technical functions of governance can be kept at arm's length from power and politics. Indeed, the EU's much-lambasted technocratic antipolitics is a product not just of subsidiarity but of its economistic and apolitical interpretation of the functionalist tradition, which has guided the actions of many proponents of European integration.

In addition, the objectives of the centralizing institution matter. The EU's focus has been doubly perverse: it has tended toward centralization despite economic development being principally a national project. Economics is properly national because it is ineluctably distributional in character and what is considered an "appropriate" distributional outcome isn't a technical but a political question. Reaching an answer, therefore, must be managed through an explicitly political process. Even if economic efficiencies can be achieved with the greater scale of larger institutions, economic policy was always more properly the domain of national institutions. The Catholic version of subsidiarity is useful here, suggesting that allocations of authority can sometimes follow a logic of appropriateness, rather than a dogged commitment to decentralization.[60] The process of matching issues to institutions must take account of both the characteristics of the issue (its scale, spillovers, etc.) and the characteristics of the institution (its scope, abilities, strengths, and weaknesses).

Last, the nature of the condition that permits the assignment of authority to larger scales matters. The EU conditions centralization on efficiency, specifically economic efficiency. But efficiency is an empty concept with a gloss of neutrality that allows for all sorts of outcomes.[61] It assumes, moreover, that everyone shares the same goals and that politics consists only in debating the best way to implement them. However, given value pluralism among humans, there can be no consensus on fundamental values, much less on goals or priorities.[62] Economic efficiency, then, can't be the primary basis of allocating authority in a system of planetary subsidiarity. Instead, authority should be allocated on the basis of *effectiveness*. For most economic issues, efficiency and effectiveness are synonymous. But for planetary issues, efficiency and effectiveness aren't the same thing at all. And to manage planetary issues, we must strive for effectiveness, first and foremost. As a result, the criteria for overriding the presumption toward local decision-making shouldn't be that it would be more efficient to govern an issue at a larger scale, but that it would be more effective to do so. Planetary issues, in particular, must be governed at the planetary scale not because governance is more efficient that way but because the planetary is the *only* scale at which they can be governed effectively.

Our overall conclusion is that the European Union as it has historically operated has been a hierarchical multilevel structure, not a functionally multiscalar one. As a result, ultimate authority flows from the highest level down, rather than, as we recommend, a system of pluralized authority, where respect for functionally derived authority flows from multiple directions.

Planetary Subsidiarity

Planetary subsidiarity is the principle that we propose for allocating authority over an issue to the smallest-scale unit that can govern the issue effectively to achieve habitability and multispecies flourishing, goals we laid out in chapter 3. This new interpretation of the centuries-old principle of subsidiarity incorporates our understanding of the material reality of the planetary condition and of the successes and failures of subsidiarity as a principle of governance. Overall, planetary subsidiarity provides a method of threading the needle between the twin challenges with which we opened this chapter: effectively addressing pressing planetary issues, like climate change and pandemic diseases, while simultaneously maximizing local empowerment. Several features of planetary subsidiarity are worth addressing.

First, planetary subsidiarity is functional. That is, the allocation of authority over specific governance functions must be specific to each function.[63] Some issues can be governed with sufficient effectiveness at local scales, some better at national scales, others only at the planetary scale. In some cases the same function is best governed at different scales depending on context. Our architecture needn't make the mistaken assumption that there is one best or correct scale that applies to the whole system and every institution in it.[64] The point is that we first examine the issue and the necessary functional competencies needed to manage it and then assess the appropriate jurisdiction. We shouldn't first take the jurisdictions for granted and then try to squeeze the issue into its form. As we argued earlier, we must prioritize governance functions over governance units.

However, we also want to minimize the number of decision rights allocated to planetary institutions—they should remain narrowly focused, assuming only the minimal authority for the viable governance of a planetary issue. To help this goal, we can introduce an important distinction: as a general rule, governance issues and functions are either directly related to planetary challenges or not. For these two types of issues, we should apply different versions of subsidiarity. The allocation of authorities for planetary issues should be decided by *weak subsidiarity*, and the allocation of authorities for nonplanetary issues should be decided by *strong subsidiarity*. *Strong* and *weak* in this context refer to the threshold for permissible centralization of powers at a larger scale.[65] So for planetary issues, we should apply subsidiarity with a weak, or low, bar for delegating authority to a larger scale of governance. But for nonplanetary issues, we should use a strong, or high, bar for moving authority to larger scales. In other words, we want stricter criteria for centralization when the issue in question doesn't weigh on habitability or multispecies flourishing as compared to the criteria when planetary concerns are directly in question. In both cases, we want to ensure that the movement of authority is well justified, but we recognize that what counts as a good reason for centralization depends on the issue at hand.

Second, planetary subsidiarity is designed to allocate authority in a multiscalar governance architecture that includes—indeed, requires—the creation of new institutions at larger and smaller scales than existing national states. Subsidiarity's preference for smaller-scale control makes the move to local institutions (even if newly created) obvious. But subsidiarity's concern with effective outcomes also justifies the invention of institutions tailor-made for planetary governance. Both the secular and religious traditions of subsidiarity support the creation of new, larger scales of authority that are needed to solve particular problems adequately. The EU was itself a higher level founded to address Europe-wide concerns. In Catholic thinking, especially as articulated by Christian Democratic parties and thinkers, the movement of authority above national states to international organizations has always been at the heart of subsidiarity. Indeed, the logic of subsidiarity led a number of important Catholic thinkers to endorse the establishment of a world government as a necessary supplement for territorially bounded national states. "Today the universal common good presents us with problems which are world-wide in their dimensions," concluded Pope John XXIII in his 1963 encyclical *Pacem in Terris*. These problems "cannot be solved except by a public authority with power, organization and means co-extensive with these problems, and with a world-wide sphere of activity."[66] He and other Christian Democrats envisioned a fairly light-touch global authority that could step in when smaller-scale authorities were found wanting—in many ways similar to our proposal.[67]

At the other end of the spectrum, the presumption for smaller-scale governance, our third feature, isn't simply a call for decentralization. For one thing, the important insight from subsidiarity is that issues must be governed at the smallest scale *that can provide an effective solution*, not the smallest scale above all else—and in a planetary era, the smallest scale for some issues is the planet itself. In other words, decentralization at all costs isn't planetary subsidiarity. The focus should be on getting the scale right, not favoring any particular scale.

The planetary, national, and local scales are all necessary for achieving planetary governance, with each handling different, if entwined, aspects. Planetary phenomena tend to have specific impacts at all scales, so each scale of governance must be empowered to address the impacts specific to it. Climate change, for instance, is simultaneously planetary and intimate: it operates on a planetary scale but manifests in particular ways for each country, each community, even each household. As a result, the planetary phenomenon of a changing climate is experienced differently in different places and by different people—mediated not just by geography but by social, political, and economic factors as well. Addressing the situated experiences of planetary challenges is as important as addressing their large-scale drivers. The goal from an institutional design perspective is to ensure that each element is governed at the appropriate scale.

Planetary subsidiarity also isn't about pushing problems onto people and institutions who are disempowered to deal with them. The principle entails the duty for larger-scale units to provide support to smaller-scale units that need it, but without absorbing them or taking away their autonomies. Bigger scales must assist smaller scales to achieve their goals, and smaller scales must assist bigger ones in achieving theirs. Duties and responsibilities move in all directions. The principle of planetary subsidiarity thus represents *a worldwide architecture of assistance* built from the recognition of our interconnected planetary condition.

As a general rule, we envision governance units sized to fit the problems at hand. That means creating new governance units at the planetary scale as well as empowering existing and new units at the subnational scale. For example, some issues will be most effectively managed at the scale of the watershed or ecosystem or urban agglomeration.[68] In some cases, the subnational unit will be contained within existing state boundaries. In others, the new units may need to cross existing national borders: for example, the Amazon rainforest, a region critical to the planetary imperatives of habitability and multispecies flourishing, should be governed as one unit, not divided up by Brazil, Peru, Ecuador, Colombia, and several other South American countries. These sovereign national states formed a multilateral institution, the Amazon Cooperation Treaty Organization, in 1998, but its efforts at protecting the region's ecology have rarely succeeded for the same reasons that multilateral institutions rarely succeed: national resistance to delegating authority and resources, and claims to absolute sovereignty preventing integrated governance.[69] Governing the Amazon holistically thus requires a new authority that covers the Amazon.[70]

Our fourth feature: planetary subsidiarity's prioritization of (but not blind commitment to) local control is intended specifically as a check on the power of planetary institutions. The principle of subsidiarity is a way to maintain the narrow remits of planetary institutions, preventing them from expanding beyond their tailored designs. It is, to be clear, a tool for thwarting world government. Planetary institutions are necessary for the effective management of planetary problems, but many people will fear their power. Subsidiarity, then, is part of the political bargain: applying constraints on the new institutions.[71] Ultimately, the purpose of planetary governance is to maintain the planet's habitability to allow for the flourishing of plural forms of life. Thus the Earth-scale work of planetary management is in service of the intimate scales where everyday living occurs.

For humans, who live in an endlessly diverse array of communities, creating these conditions requires giving local institutions the authority to pursue their community's vision of thriving. Planetary institutions can't determine what that is. As the Catholic jurist Paolo G. Carozza argues, subsidiarity isn't merely concerned with localism but is a "principle of justice that requires larger communities to protect the legitimate autonomy of smaller communities, to provide them with assistance (*subsidium*) needed to fulfill their ends, and to coordinate and regulate their activities within the common good of the larger community, of which they are a part and which is also necessary to the flourishing of their individual members."[72] While Carozza's claim is premised on theological foundations we can't endorse, there is a strong argument to be made that the provision of planetary habitability by planetary institutions is a matter of justice that allows all smaller communities to pursue their own idea of the good life.

Fifth, the allocation of authority is a dynamic process that will unfold over time. No institution's or scale's hold on a particular governance function is set in stone. As governance challenges, our understanding of those challenges, and our capacity to manage them change over time, the loci of authority to govern should change as well. There must be room to adapt as institutions learn through practice. The ability to shift authority also reflects the fact that jurisdictions will contest the allocation of decision rights. In some cases, there will be legitimate disagreements about which unit is better placed to govern effectively. In other cases, jurisdictions will grouse about their loss of authority. In still others, conflicts will arise between functional areas: disputes between housing policy and transportation policy or land use regulation and water use allocation, for example. This is all to be expected. It is why planetary subsidiarity must put politics front and center. The overall architecture, therefore, must include arenas for peaceful, democratic political contestation.

The primary body that we envision for settling disputes about the allocation of decision rights is what might be called a *subsidiarity assembly*.[73] The subsidiarity assembly is an institution that sits outside the general multiscalar governance architecture and makes decisions about the design of the multiscalar governance architecture itself. It is the system's holder of meta-authority—the authority to resolve collisions between other sources of authority. The subsidiarity assembly, in other words, decides which units should have which decision rights in a domain. In the existing political order, sovereign national states are the sole holders of meta-authority: each sovereign state is the meta-authority within its borders and only within its borders. (More precisely, the head of government, highest court, or some other institution holds the meta-authority in and for each national state.) But this sovereigntist system is at odds with a subsidiarity-based system.

The subsidiarity assembly would be the site for democratic mediation and negotiation between units at different scales of the governance structure, with decisions guided by the principle of planetary subsidiarity. It is a mechanism for resolving conflicts over the structure of the system, not over the issues themselves. So it would decide, not which policy to pursue, but which *unit* has the authority to decide which policy to pursue or where the boundaries of the units in question should be.

Holding this meta-authority would make the subsidiarity assembly a powerful institution—on paper at least, the most powerful in the systems architecture. Yet empowering one body to make decisions on behalf of the whole system is vital for the system's success.[74] The problems in need of governing do not come neatly packaged or fit squarely into just one unit or scale. The nature of the challenges leads inevitably to contestation between and among scales.[75] Reflecting the dynamics of the phenomenon, the necessary scales for action on climate change, for example, are local, national, and planetary, and other scales to boot. What's more, the nature of problems and the tools we have to respond to them change over time as well. Sometimes the changes are linear, but other times they aren't: cyclical changes or random changes, over many different time scales, can have profound impacts for where and how an issue should be governed. Nevertheless, collisions between units and scales over who has authority to act when and where need resolution. Democratically resolving these disputes and managing the division of labor between scales and units is the necessary role taken on by the subsidiarity assembly.

The subsidiarity assembly opens the possibility for the system as a whole to be nimble and to learn from experience. At the same time, the system cannot be in constant flux. The normal functioning of governance requires some degree of continuity—institutions can't engage in long-term planning, for instance, if they don't know with reasonable certainty what authorities they will have in the future. So the system must be *flexible but stable*. The subsidiarity assembly, as a result, should be biased toward maintaining the status quo, while still making space for the political (and technical) contestation of authority assignments— and the honest potential for change.

To provide for both flexibility and stability, allocations of decision rights should be subject to only periodic reassessment, and reassignment, if found necessary. Thus the subsidiarity assembly would not need to sit on a continual basis, perhaps only every ten years. Creating a permanent secretariat for the assembly would create a mechanism for units (including collectives unrecognized as formal units by the current architecture) to submit formal petitions for the assembly to adjudicate during its next sitting. A standing staff, moreover, allows the assembly to respond to the possibility of the emergency need for the reallocation of authority.

The structural location and composition of the subsidiarity assembly are important design decisions. The assembly can't "belong" to any of the scales of the system, since that might bias it toward that scale (like the European Court of Justice, discussed previously). As a result, it must sit apart from the overall multiscalar architecture. This also means that representatives to the assembly can't come from just one scale but must come from all interested actors. The subsidiarity assembly is not, to be clear, a backhanded way for the planetary scale to dictate decisions for every other scale. In practice, the assembly should include representatives from local, national, and planetary institutions, as well as subject matter experts. The inclusion of experts on the issue at hand ensures that the assembly's decision will reflect not just subsidiarity but *planetary* subsidiarity, meaning that the allocation of decision rights should serve habitability and multispecies flourishing. How representatives are selected by each unit and how the assembly deliberates and makes decisions are not issues we take up here, other than to say that this could be an interesting place to include participatory and deliberative political practices. These could enhance the legitimacy of the meta-authority and perhaps lead to better decisions too.[76]

Thinking Through Specifics

Planetary subsidiarity isn't a perfect design. The social, economic, political, and biogeochemical realities of our planet are too varied and complex for any system to address perfectly. But while perfect institutions may be ultimately unattainable, we can still make comparative judgments.[77] And compared to the status quo world of sovereign states, planetary subsidiarity is preferable. This principle, with some tweaking, provides a suitable method for allocating authority under planetary conditions. In sum, it offers a pathway to a reconstructed governance architecture fit for a planetary future.

What might planetary subsidiarity look like for, say, the governance of climate change? Climate change is of course a complex geophysical phenomenon with consequences for the entire planet and its biosphere, but here we briefly think through two of its chief policy problems: the reduction of greenhouse gas emissions and the adaptation of human communities to the impacts of climate change.

Under planetary subsidiarity, decision rights for the minimum amount and pace of emissions reductions lie with a planetary institution. Carbon emitted anywhere has consequences everywhere: it is a problem of and for the entire Earth system. The smallest-scale unit that can effectively provide for planetary habitability and multispecies flourishing must be able to govern the whole planet. But a planetary institution for climate governance would only give broad directives and would leave the details of implementation to others—larger-scale institutions, according to the principle of subsidiary, are not to subsume smaller-scale institutions or restrict their autonomy beyond what is necessary. For example, it could decide that global emissions must be reduced by 75 percent over ten years or some other top-line directive. At that point, national states would develop their national plan for achieving the requisite reductions, which would invariably include distributional decisions affecting different sectors and regions.

Then there are decisions about climate mitigation policy that because of their place-based nature or their connection to a population's preferences are properly made at subnational scales like provinces/states or municipalities. There are likely a number of different pathways to reach the emissions reductions mandated by the planetary institution, and smaller-scale governance institutions should get to decide what works best for the local physical and social geographies, economics, preferences, and other factors. The framework set by planetary subsidiarity, however, embeds the smaller-scale governors and their locally optimized decisions within a broader, reciprocal structure. That means that they must follow the rules set by larger-scale institutions, but simultaneously the larger-scale institutions must be willing to assist the smaller-scale ones in their pursuits. Moreover, the larger-scale institutions' rules themselves should be developed, assessed, and updated in consultation with the smaller-scale, frontline implementation institutions.[78] Each institution in the architecture has obligations to all the others.

Adapting to climate change, by contrast, has a principally bottom-up dynamic. The impacts of climate change matter because of how they are felt in specific places. When climate scientists state that global average temperature has already risen by 1.1°C, they are describing a "useful fiction" that is not experienced in any particular location.[79] What matters for human beings (and all other living matter) is how that overall warming manifests in the places they dwell, which is the result of those places' specificity—the climate, natural and human geographies, topography, ecology, socioeconomic conditions, and more. The institutions best placed to decide how to adapt to changes are local. Again, these small-scale governors are part of a wider multiscalar architecture on which they can rely on for assistance. National governments will have a role in deciding the distributional elements of adaptation (which, admittedly, are substantial). Planetary institutions, which should be expert in gathering and analyzing climate data and forecasts, will provide the analytic tools that local authorities need to make well-informed decisions. Together, the various scales of governance provide communities of people facing the consequences of climate change, whether sea level rise, drought, extreme heat, or more, adapt their built environmental and social systems in a way that is appropriate to the local natural and human circumstances.

How on Earth Would We Get There?

Beyond any objections to the substance of our argument, there are plain questions about its feasibility. Two, in particular, stand out: Why would national leaders give up power? And won't nationalism get in the way? Both are important questions that we want to address head on, but readers looking for a detailed political strategy won't find one. This book presents a sketch, a vision of our desired result: a radically different architecture of governance. As previously stated, we don't provide a guide for how we get from here to there. Our modest aim in this section is merely to banish the thought that erecting planetary subsidiarity is inherently impossible.

It is at least plausible to think that national leaders could give up some of their powers to planetary and local institutions because they have done so many times before. As we showed in chapter 2, since about 1970 many governance functions have moved away from national authorities. National governments across the globe have given real decision-making powers and resources to institutions above and below themselves. A key reason they have done so is that national leaders understood something about power that many analysts miss. A state's power isn't just its control over people and territory. State power is also the ability to achieve desired outcomes. In modern governance, the two forms of power don't always go hand in hand. In fact, achieving policy goals can require relinquishing the narrow view of power as control.[80]

In addition to wanting to achieve specific objectives, national leaders might want to move authority elsewhere to avoid two forms of accountability. First, national leaders don't want to be held accountable for difficult decisions, and delegating authority, particularly to larger scales, allows them not to have to take responsibility. This is the logic that explains why political elites made central banks independent, removing themselves from the day-to-day business of monetary policy. Politicians know that from time to time politically unpopular monetary policies must be implemented, but they'd rather not be the ones giving the orders. Second, leaders don't want to be held accountable for things they do not and cannot control. Planetary challenges are outside the realm of things that national states can manage, so national elites, eventually, may want to shift responsibility onto others. Rather than take the blame again and again for planetary problems—rising sea levels, novel zoonotic diseases, climate-induced mass migration, crop failures, and more—they will want their publics to understand that these issues are delegated to someone else, someone capable of effectively addressing them.[81] It is revealing in this regard that many delegations of authority occur in the wake of crises. The League of Nations arose from the First World War, and the UN from the Second. European integration was likewise spurred by the Continent's turbulent and violent preceding decades. And central banks were often granted independence after an economic shock: the US Federal Reserve System was established in 1913 in response to the Panic of 1907, and the Bank of Italy's "divorce" from the Treasury Ministry was a consequence of soaring inflation in 1981.[82]

A different, equally understandable concern is that we live in a time of resurgent nationalism, in which "globalists" are despised and so-called populists excoriate the transfer of power away from the national state. Our argument and analysis thus far has treated governance institutions as means to an end: they serve the function of providing desired collective outcomes. But governance institutions have a second face, where they are understood as ends in themselves: they serve as expressions of human communities. This is the realm of nationalism. When people's policy preferences clash with their polity preferences, the latter often win out.[83] Brexit, with its slogan "Take back control," looms large here.

Without a doubt, many nationalists will vehemently oppose the delegation of power to planetary institutions. Some might also object to the delegation of power to subnational units, though this is a less unambiguously despised notion. Whether they win the day is, of course, a political question whose answer is unknowable. Our principle of subsidiarity, though, does offer an explicit compromise to nationalists and other partisans of subplanetary jurisdictions who are hostile to planetary governance: its whole premise is to limit the authority of planetary institutions and move decision rights to as small a scale as possible.

The idea of "the nation" and its attendant ideology, nationalism, emerged in the eighteenth and nineteenth centuries in response to particular social, economic, cultural, political, and technological conditions. The ideology was convenient and effective for state builders seeking mass mobilization of their populations, which were typically culturally diverse. But, as we saw in chapter 1, nationalists were not always interested in forming their own national state. Political allegiance to a cultural community has led to support for various institutional forms. Looking to the future, there is no guarantee that nationalism will continue to be a compelling political ideology or that it will demand a national state that possesses absolute sovereignty. As social, economic, cultural, political, and technological conditions change, it is possible that the loci of political loyalties will change as well—in fact, over the very long term, it is guaranteed.[84]

Subsidiarity itself might well nurture changing political identities. We all have many identities (national, local, ethnic, religious, gender, sexual, family, professional, partisan, ideological, and more) that we can draw on or activate depending on the context and on whom we are interacting with. That's to say, identities are situated and relational.[85] Contextual factors open and close possibilities for constellations of identity formation and expression. We expect that subsidiarity, especially under conditions of growing planetary sapience, will be an important such contextual factor shaping identities.

Most relevant to our discussion is that institutional settings are influential determinants of the politicization of identity. Institutions play a decisive role in determining which of our many concurrent identities become *political* identities.[86] The boundaries of political institutions have a strong impact on the boundaries of belonging, the affective sense of political affiliation. Nationalism emerged from a historical context dominated by the national state: political loyalties were directed at the political bodies with concentrated power and authority to shape the contours of daily life. Under subsidiarity, however, power and authority would be more distributed across institutions and scales, and political identities may likewise diffuse. Institutionalized subsidiarity could thus draw on and encourage the variegated identities we all possess. Rather than hyperfocusing all attention toward one political center (the national state), planetary subsidiarity could foster identities, and the emotional complexes that accompany them, at multiple scales, contributing to the richness of the human experience.

———

Opponents and skeptics of both the centralization and the decentralization of power share a common fear: tyranny. The concern about centralizing authority is that it can become unbound. The concern about decentralizing authority is that "local tyrants" can wield undue power in their own little fiefdoms. These twinned fears of tyranny—a system that is at once "too weak to secure us equality and too strong to allow us liberty," as Mitrany worried—can easily become a justification for maintaining the status quo forever.[87] But the reigning governance regime—ad hoc multilevel governance organized around state sovereignty—creates its own tyrannies. At the scale of national states, fewer than half of governments in the world today could be conceivably called democratic. Sovereignty means that national states get to decide their own form of rule, and many have opted for autocracy.[88]

But there is another form of tyranny, less discussed but just as pressing. Fears of overbearing authorities are well justified, and we hold them as well. But they must be balanced against fears of being ungoverned. This is the tyranny of life *outside* authority, which Hobbes famously described as "solitary, poor, nasty, brutish, and short." This, too, is oppressive. Yet at the planetary scale, this form of tyranny is what we are living with today. Concerns with despotism and misrule at the planetary and the local scales are legitimate—and we must design institutions to minimize their likelihood—but they cannot be judged in a vacuum; they must be judged in comparison with the alternatives. Deliberate multiscalar governance organized by planetary subsidiarity is not risk-free, but compared to the escalating polycrisis of the status quo and the multiple crises we are experiencing, it opens the possibility—the hope—for the effective governance of planetary problem at all scales.

Five

Local Institutions for Local Issues

In February 2007, Jakarta experienced a Noachian flood. Intense rains inundated the Indonesian capital, a coastal megalopolis built partly on reclaimed swamps, overwhelming its infrastructure: two-thirds of the total urban area was under as much as four meters of water. A global hub of more than ten million residents (totaling thirty-four million in the wider urban region), Jakarta has since experienced further catastrophic flooding in 2013, 2014, 2015, and 2020 as a result of storms that climate researchers believe have been exacerbated by planetary climate change.[1] At the time of the first of these floods, Jakarta's municipality and population were basically left on their own to deal with the deluge. Indonesia's national government, despite being located in Jakarta, was barely able to help. In 2019, in fact, the Indonesian president—a former chief executive of Jakarta—announced his intention to relocate the national capital to a new planned city in eastern Borneo, to be called Nusantara, abandoning Jakarta to sink into the sea.[2]

Facing an unprecedented challenge, the Jakarta city government (technically, the Special Capital Region of Jakarta) instead turned to international partners—including, most interestingly, the city of Rotterdam, located halfway around the world in the Netherlands. In 2013, the

mayors of the two cities, Joko Widodo of Jakarta and Ahmed Aboutaleb
of Rotterdam, signed a Memorandum of Agreement to promote interurban cooperation around climate change adaptation.[3] This agreement
extended their ongoing collaboration that began within the Connecting
Delta Cities Network, a transnational community for sharing climate
adaptation and flood risk management expertise that also includes Co-
penhagen, Ho Chi Minh City, Hong Kong, London, Melbourne, New
Orleans, and New York.[4]

Seen in national or global terms—the canonical lenses for observing and interpreting modernity—the bilateral collaboration between
Indonesia and the Netherlands might seem unlikely, especially given
the fraught history and legacy of the latter's colonial occupation of the
former.[5] On the surface, the two countries might seem to have little
in common: Indonesia is huge, the Netherlands is small; Indonesia is
lower middle income, the Netherlands is one of the wealthiest countries in the world; Indonesia is located on a series of islands strung out
along the equator, the Netherlands is a continental country in northern
Europe. The two national governments have scant practical counsel to
contribute to the governance of the other.

Seen in planetary terms, on the other hand, the cities of Rotterdam and Jakarta face common *functional* challenges: both are low-lying
seaside cities, sitting on land that is sinking because of groundwater
extraction, making them two of the most flood-prone cities on the
planet.[6] "Jakarta and Rotterdam actually have identical problems," as
Aboutaleb explained in 2017. These shared concerns over the functions
of local governance make it entirely sensible for the two cities to work
together, promoting, in Aboutaleb's words, the "exchange [of] experiences and knowledge."[7]

While mixed motives were undoubtedly involved—including trying
to rescue the value of real estate holdings of Jakarta developers—the
Jakarta-Rotterdam partnership demonstrates an emerging phenomenon in planetary governance: the advent of *translocal* networks, working
separately from the traditional state-to-state diplomacy or multilateral
member state institutions, to address shared challenges, including plan-

etary ones such as climate change and pandemics.⁸ While Jakarta and Rotterdam have operated this flood management program bilaterally, both cities also belong to the C40 Cities Climate Leadership Group, a translocal network of more than one hundred global cities whose mayors collaborate—usually apart from the foreign ministries of their home countries—to develop and deliver solutions to address the local sources and impacts of planetary climate change. "Cities all around the world are dealing with the causes and effects of climate change," Aboutaleb stated in 2020. "The ongoing exchange of knowledge and lessons learned is of unprecedented value. Being a part of international networks like C40 helps us achieve our goals together."⁹

Thus this seemingly local story of flood management in Jakarta quickly spirals out to include bilateral cooperation with Rotterdam and broader membership in a global network of mayors seeking climate action—putting it at odds with typical, national state–centered accounts of modern politics and governance. In the usual story, disasters like the ones that befell Jakarta would be dealt with by the sovereign national government, perhaps with assistance from multilateral institutions, bilateral aid from other national states, and NGOs. Instead, the Indonesian government left local authorities to manage the problem on their own, which they did with the help of transnational, interurban networks promoting city-to-city cooperation and collaboration. That these events don't fit with common notions of how governance happens is not a chance result. Rather, it is symptomatic of the hegemonic place of the sovereign national state in conventional thinking about how legitimate governance is delivered. The contemporary system of governance, as we demonstrated in chapter 1, was founded on the idea of the nation and the quest for national economic development. Leaders made national policies, crafted national development plans, and cultivated national identities and pride, transforming the national state into the center of politics, policy, and governing.

It is our contention in this chapter, however, that many policy problems currently assigned to national governments would be better addressed at local scales of administration. Local governing authorities, we argue, should have many more responsibilities and much more authority than they typically do today. This is not an argument for localism, a mindless prioritization of smaller jurisdictions, but rather a conclusion of our argument for multiscalar *planetary subsidiarity*. In other words, we do not favor the local simply because "small is beautiful" or because of some fetish for the quirky distinctiveness of subnational communities.[10] We do not believe, like many on both the political right and left, that local, face-to-face communities are inherently good or natural. Rather, we believe that administrative authority should be assigned to the governing institutions with the best functional effectiveness, such that the span of political responsibility matches the span of administrative control. In practice, this means that national states should delegate some decision rights to planetary institutions—especially over decisions where effective decision-making must take into account the planet as a whole (see the next chapter)—but many if not most others to subnational institutions that are better able (that is, are more functionally able) to take into account local conditions and preferences. In allocating decision rights according to this formula, the goal is to improve the performance of governance by allocating decision authority to the smallest-scale institution that is capable of addressing the relevant issue, which in turn should improve the legitimacy of these institutions. In sum, what we propose is a *contextual localism*, derived from the principle of planetary subsidiarity.

We detail what these local institutions might look like and also explain how the process of delegation doesn't mean abandoning locals to their own devices. Rather, it is about empowering local authorities, including by fostering laterally networked connections between different subnational and local jurisdictions that share similar challenges. The idea is to elevate not just the local but the *translocal* as a principal site of governance for dealing with the effects of planetary processes. By deconnecting localities currently tied together by the physical continuity of national boundaries and reconnecting them globally on the basis of *functional* concerns—like Jakarta's and Rotterdam's shared concern with flooding—we call for the empowerment of local institutions in a

manner that will make them more effective at serving the diverse interests and preferences of their residents in the face of the local impacts of
planetary problems.

What Is "Local"?

What are we talking about when we talk about local governance? Even
if we all agree that a particular functional authority should be handled
locally, it's still not clear where, exactly, that is. Is a province "local"? A
city? A neighborhood? A homeowners' association? This is not a mere
semantic debate. The placement of jurisdictional and functional governance boundaries is enormously consequential for processes and outcomes. Should a vote to tax the rich be taken in a wealthy community
or in a larger jurisdiction that also includes many more poor people?
Should the placement of a toxic dump be decided by the town council
where it could be located or by the council of the entire province that
produces the toxic waste? Change the jurisdiction, change the results.
Consequently, assigning authority over a specific function is an ines-
capably political act. There is no neutral way to decide who should have
authority over what.

But acknowledging that the determination of a jurisdictional
boundary is unavoidably political is not to say that there aren't ways to
do it that are more sensible or fairer than others. What we propose here
is that the principle for determining where governing authority should
be allocated should be *functionality*, derived from the principle of planetary subsidiarity discussed in the previous chapter. In the architecture
of planetary governance, jurisdictions should be drawn around specific
policy problems and should not necessarily follow existing borders.[11]

We think about appropriate local government units in terms of social
agglomerations of people who see themselves as geographically sharing
the same functional fate, primarily cities and ecologically integrated
zones.[12] While rural communities can also benefit from empowering
local governance, this chapter focuses on urban areas or cities (terms
we use interchangeably), which is where the human future largely re-

sides. According to UN estimates, just over half the world's population now lives in cities, and by 2050, cities will gain an additional 2.5 billion people, meaning that two-thirds of the world's human population will be urban.[13] Using a different definition of urbanization, the European Commission estimates that over three-quarters of the world population already lives in cities.[14] Cities are also a critical point of intersection between humans and the planet: they are where much of the impact of planetary problems will be felt because of the concentration of humanity, and they are the primary sites of greenhouse gas emissions and pandemic transmission.[15]

Of course, what counts as a "city" itself varies enormously. Consider the difference between Wellington, the capital of New Zealand, with a population of 215,000, and Beijing, the capital of China, with a population of 21 million. Beyond the two-orders-of-magnitude difference in human scale, these two cities have little in common with one another in terms of their geographies, climates, ecologies, and connections to both their immediate hinterlands and the rest of the world. What they share, however, is the fact that their residents are all beholden to the biophysical specifics of their location and the need for managing functional services, ranging from inputs such as water, fuel, and food to outputs such as sewage and air pollution.

In addition to cities as a particular locus of governance, we are interested in the meaning of local governance for ecologically integrated zones, such as watersheds or contiguous ecosystems. Like cities, these are "local planetary units" in functional terms: sites that need to be managed as a coherent, holistic unit in order to be effectively governed. The Amazon rainforest, as mentioned in the previous chapter, is one such unit.

Consider two different kinds of policy problems cities face: where and how to build housing, and how to manage access to clean running water. Following our functionalist principle of authority allocation, housing policy decisions should be allocated to the greater urban area, not individual municipalities that make up the area (since housing availability affects everyone in the region), though should smaller-scale units prove incapability of managing housing, as has happened in California, for instance, the logic of subsidiarity suggests that it is right for larger-scale units to assume this authority. Decisions about water management, by contrast, should take place at the level of the watershed, which is generally a much bigger geographic unit than an urban area. Both examples are instantiations of the principle of subsidiarity's preference for empowering the smallest governing unit capable of managing the issue. The smallest scales for good management of housing and water are different.[16]

The allocation of decision rights in our home, Los Angeles County—the largest in the United States, with ten million residents—is instructive. The county's population and territory are currently divided up among eighty-eight distinct metropolitan jurisdictions, the City of Los Angeles being just one of them, though by far the biggest and most populous. Yet for two crucial ecological and planetary issues, water usage and electricity production, the City of Los Angeles's Department of Water and Power, a municipal utility that serves four million people in the City of Los Angeles and several other jurisdictions, and the Metropolitan Water District of Southern California, a public water wholesaler that serves nineteen million residents in six counties in the region, make the key decisions. For air quality, another important ecological and planetary issue, the key decisions sit with the South Coast Air Quality Management District. This task-specific, intersecting, flexible jurisdiction, which is overseen by the California Air Resources Board and the US Environmental Protection Agency, governs air pollution control for the urban portions of Los Angeles County and all of Orange County, to the south.[17] Its borders, notably, are drawn to fit an ecological feature, a contiguous air zone, as it concerns human needs. Finally, public health—including most pandemic-related policies—is the domain of the county's Department of Public Health, which answers to the county's Board of Supervisors, not any of the many mayors and city councils in the county. As a result, the City of Los Angeles's mayor (the county's most visible elected official) was often blamed by the media and the public for COVID-related decisions he had little or no control over—his span of control did not match his span of responsibility (a political dilemma we'll return to later in this chapter).

Importantly, both urban and ecological areas change over time: physically they may grow or shrink, or research may reveal new or changing characteristics. It follows that jurisdictional boundaries for local governance should, likewise, be changeable. Rescaling local institutions to better fit the issues in need of management is preferable to conserving existing boundaries for the sake of nonfunctional criteria, like tradition. Flexibility is a corollary of functionalism, so the scope and size of local institutions must be open to periodic reassessment and reassignment.[18] Approaching jurisdictional boundaries with fresh eyes is especially urgent with our new understanding of the planetary condition.

The example of water management is again helpful. Water flows over and under the surface of the planet and through the atmosphere, without concern for human boundaries. And life, including human life, in any particular place depends on water's presence in that place. The importance of water is so great, argues political philosopher Paulina Ochoa Espejo, that the merit of a political unit's boundaries should be evaluated by their capacity to conserve water.[19] The ideal jurisdiction for this, she argues, is the watershed. Watersheds emerge from the connections between Earth and life, giving rise to certain political rights and obligations that emerge simply from dwelling in a place (rather than from holding membership in an identity group, like national citizenship, which is typically seen as the bestower of political rights and obligations). A water governance unit, then, belongs to those who, just by dwelling there, share place-specific rights and duties. In a planetary model of territorial jurisdictions, following Paulina Ochoa Espejo, "Presence and participation in systems involving geology and biota determine the relevant political bonds."[20]

The How and Why of Local Governance

Proponents of small-scale governance have made their case with all sorts of arguments, many of which date back to some of the earliest recorded musings about politics. Today, the idea of local self-governance appeals to people with wide-ranging backgrounds and ideologies, from the antistate right to the localist left to autonomist indigenous movements. Our interest in local governance, however, stems not from the special character of local communities but rather from the functional features of small-scale institutions: their potential for responsiveness to local concerns and conditions, and their potential for producing diverse and innovative forms of policies and governance arrangements.

Human beings live in innumerable different ways and conditions. We hold different values and come with different capabilities. Local governing institutions can be more sensitive to the local configurations of lifeways and conditions, values and capabilities, than larger-scale institutions. Empowering local authorities, in this sense, is an institutional embodiment of pluralism. But it's not enough for institutions to hear their constituents' voices; they must also be able to act on what they hear. That is, a local institution must have a span of operational control that aligns with its span of political responsibility.

Aligning institutions' spans of control and responsibility makes achieving functional effectiveness more likely. However, there cannot be one-size-fits-all solutions for local challenges. Solutions must be tailored to the circumstances particular to a time and place. The physical geography, ecological conditions, and social circumstances of a community affect the challenges that it faces. Governance structures must be able to accommodate these diverse conditions. The material and geographical bases of human settlement mean that there is a specificity inherent in governance.

Determining which policy problems local institutions should address requires applying the principle of planetary subsidiarity, which allocates authority over an issue to the smallest-scale unit that can govern the issue effectively to achieve habitability and multispecies flourishing. Two general rules follow from our interpretation of subsidiarity, presented in chapter 4. Rule 1: the allocation of decision rights should be decided on a functional basis. This means that rather than treating governance institutions as static and giving them authority over policy problems as they arise, we should start with the functional requirements associated with addressing the policy challenge and then empower the appropriately capable institution (possibly a new one) to govern it. The goal is to match institutions to needed governance functions, not to valorize localism or decentralization. Rule 2: authority allocations are not permanent but can and must change in response to changing functional circumstances and technological possibilities. This rule is really a corollary of functionalism—if the allocation of decision rights is based on policy problems and institutional functions, these allocations should be able to change when either the challenge or the institution changes—but it is worth stating explicitly, since foregrounding institutional dynamism affects how institutions are structured. Technological possibilities here include the technologies of governance—institutional arrangements, administrative practices, bureaucratic management, and so on—which affect how a problem can or should be governed as much as scientific developments.

The "functional test" is the primary mechanism for determining where best to vest policy authority consistent with the principle of planetary subsidiarity. For each policy problem, we must ask: What is the smallest-scale unit that can effectively govern this to achieve habitability and multispecies flourishing? And while the bias should be toward delegating decision rights to smaller-scale institutions, we shouldn't hesitate (as we will discuss at length in the next chapter) to delegate upward decisions on issues that weigh heavily on habitability and multispecies flourishing—in other words, planetary issues—to larger-scale institutions. The operational upshot of applying the functional test to the allocation of governance authority is that *causal* issues at the heart of planetary-scale phenomena are not going to be governed at the local scale, yet many of their *consequences* (which will manifest in locally particular ways) will be.

Subsidiarity, by pushing as much decision-making as possible to as small a scale as makes functional sense, empowers government actors who are close to their constituents and thus have direct line of sight and often a direct line of dialogue with the people who will be most affected by their decisions. This proximity in itself will incline public servants to try to produce results rather than to engage in ideological grandstanding. Local officials, who are held responsible for immediate, quotidian things like the quality of infrastructure, schools, public health management, and so on, have to deliver the goods that their residents demand, or risk being shown the door.[21]

A large number of empowered smaller-scale authorities permits not only diverse policies but also diverse models of governance and modes of policymaking. The current system of sovereign national states already supports many governance models, but the diversity is even starker at the local level. Likewise, national states could adopt emerging methods of deliberative and participatory democracy—and, in circumscribed circumstances, several have—but the most exciting and enthusiastic adoptions of innovative experiments in collective decision-making and rule have taken place in subnational authorities. Local institutions, where collective action and coordination challenges are smaller and fewer people have to be brought along, tend to be somewhat easier to innovate in. Encouraging lots of local-level experiments in policy and institutional architecture will produce a range of results, the most successful of which can be shared and copied.[22]

Our interpretation of the principle of subsidiarity is agnostic as to what localized forms of governance should look like. There is no reason to believe that devolving authority automatically makes governance more democratic, and clearly in some cases it will not be. But enhancing the discretion of local authorities opens the possibility for experimenting with diverse models of governance and modes of policymaking. Empowering a variety of local institutional arrangement also enhances the "antifragility" of the entire system: the different models of local governance will respond to common shocks in their own ways, creating many ongoing policy experiments that others can learn from. The diversity in the system creates incentives for self-improvement based on lessons learned by others, especially when there are institutionalized channels for exchange of ideas, expertise, and experience.[23]

Let us return to the example of climate governance that we discussed in chapter 4. Climate change poses two broad categories of policy challenges: on the one hand, mitigation—that is, reducing net greenhouse gas emissions; on the other hand, adaptation—that is, preparing to deal with the consequences of the already baked-in warming. Climate change mitigation is a quintessentially planetary problem—it doesn't matter where greenhouse gases are emitted, so the smallest scale for effective governance is the planet. Local authorities, as a result, will not determine the *what* or *how much* of climate change mitigation, but they may determine the *how*. Even with a planetary mandate to reduce emissions, there are numerous ways that a local authority could achieve it: from building cutting-edge clean energy infrastructures to deciding to live preindustrial lifestyles. The pathway to reducing emissions that makes the most sense will depend on many factors, such as current energy usage, geographic features, and economic, political, and cultural capacities. These factors are spatially specific, and the appropriate policy has to emerge from and respond to the particular time and place.[24] What works for Paris, France, will not necessarily work for Paris, Texas. As a result, each Paris should have the authority to decide how to reduce the emissions produced in their jurisdiction.

The picturesque university town of Heidelberg, Germany, for instance, made plans to all but eliminate private motor vehicles as part of its transition to net-zero emissions.[25] We happen to like this idea for this context, but we also understand it is not suitable for many other localities. Compact Heidelberg, with its medieval urban core, can abolish cars without upending daily life in a way that many other places—like our sprawling home, Los Angeles—at present cannot. It is a decision that belongs at the local scale. Just as it wouldn't make sense for the larger-scale jurisdiction of Germany to abolish private cars, it likewise would not be right for Germany to strip the city of Heidelberg of the authority to make that decision for its residents. Subsidiarity suggests that many of the mechanisms that drive the energy transition—the how, not the how much—should be tailored by local institutions responsive to local ecological and infrastructural specifics, as well as the preferences of local citizens.

The consequences of climate change are likewise locally specific: in some places, floods; in others, heat waves or fires; in others, softening permafrost; in still others, decreasing fresh water supplies. Adapting to these changes is therefore a local policy problem. The smallest-scale unit that can best manage climate adaptation is a local institution (where, as we've argued, the definition of local can vary from issue to issue). It can account for how the changing climate interacts with relevant natural topography and the built environment, patterns of population settlement and economic production, and the preferences of residents. Attentive to local histories and communal differences, local governance institutions are best placed to empower populations to seek their vision of flourishing in a changing climate. There are a wide range of possibilities, from adopting new urban plans and new agricultural crops to constructing seawalls or planning the relocation of an entire community, and the people affected should get to decide.

Under planetary multiscalar governance, local governments are not left to fend for themselves. They are embedded in a broad architecture with other institutions with different scales, scopes, and specialties. A key premise of subsidiarity is that larger-scale institutions owe assistance to smaller-scale institutions to help them pursue their self-defined goals. Robust adaptation decisions require, for instance, technical expertise and fine-grained data that local institutions often don't possess. So larger-scale institutions are responsible for the collection, processing, and analysis of necessary data (a specialty of planetary institutions), technical assistance, and other resources that local institutions might need.

National institutions will remain important for this reason. A core continued function of national governments should be the channeling of resources on an egalitarian basis across a national state—the project that helped establish the national state's hegemony in the decades after

World War II. Whether for climate adaptation or other policy areas, the national government must provide local authorities with what they need to seek flourishing community life. If some localities wish then to use those resources to invest in better public transit, while others wish to invest more in, say, a seawall, that really should be a decision made locally, by the people directly affected, since preferences and needs are unevenly distributed across a state's territory. Subsidiarity isn't going to eliminate political horse trading between and among scales of authority: local institutions are sometimes going to want to undertake ambitious climate adaptation projects that they cannot fund on their own. Cities may not be able to pay for seawalls out of their own pocket (or lines of credit). Making these decisions will require politics—another reason planetary subsidiarity cannot pretend to be a form of apolitical, technocratic governance. Subsidiarity also isn't going to make the hardest decisions in climate adaptation any easier. Reallocating authority will not ease the pain when a community should no longer receive resources to continue to adapt to climate change and must instead embark on "managed retreat."[26]

No allocation of authority is set in stone, however. Remaining attuned to the functional needs of a given policy problem and the capacity of the institutions that could manage it requires the flexibility to reallocate authority if needed. Faced with a new or changing problem, a new understanding of a problem, or changing capabilities to manage a problem, institutions must be willing and able to reassess the position of relevant decision rights (guided, perhaps, by the subsidiarity assembly sketched in chapter 4). Stubbornly fitting governance functions to the status quo governance units makes less sense than shifting a function to a more effective institution. For instance, when, early on in the COVID pandemic, US states began competing against each other to purchase ventilators, it became clear that states were not the right scale at which to manage the distribution of vital medical equipment during an emergency. A larger-scale unit, perhaps the United States, perhaps a North American institution, perhaps a planetary institution, should have taken over the coordination of the supply of ventilators and other similar items.

Translocal Networks

Local institutions have one more tool at their disposal to help them govern effectively: each other. Localities may face specific natural and social circumstances, as we've emphasized in this chapter, but these circumstances often rhyme with those of other places. Poor megacities share many of the same challenges with each other, as do cities built on low-lying coasts (like Jakarta and Rotterdam), cities that edge up to landscapes prone to wildfires, port cities, and so on. The details may differ, but many themes carry over between cities.

Cities that share challenges, however, do not necessarily share a national government—which has typically been the primary instrument for connecting and coordinating cities—and vice versa. Los Angeles, Miami, and Minneapolis are all affected by climate change, but in completely different ways that require completely different adaptation policies. These American cities' climate impacts in fact have more in common with cities in other national states (say, Cape Town, Dhaka, and Moscow, respectively) than they do with each other. Yet national states are wired to promote coordination and collaboration among the subnational entities contained within them, not across them. What is needed are networks of cities to promote lateral exchanges of information and expertise and cooperative actions among local institutions with common functional concerns.

Unlike some of the other recommendations we make in this book, translocal networks already exist. In fact, many of these networks have operated for decades, and the phenomenon is rapidly growing in number, membership, and sophistication. One 2021 study estimated there are over one hundred city networks with transnational memberships, which jointly have 10,500 member cities. In other words, networking is not just for elite "global cities," like Tokyo or São Paulo, but draws in midsized and small cities from around the world. The most common issue of focus for translocal networks is governance, followed by the environment, inequality, culture, peace building, and gender, though the majority have an interest in multiple policy areas.[27] Some are loose and informal, others are strongly institutionalized, with significant budgets and a professional secretariat. Yet all stem from a frustration among municipal officials that national states and the multilateral system are failing to make progress on shared problems. Compounding this frustration is a feeling among city leaders that they have the populations and the economic heft but that national governments don't share their priorities. Many mayors likely agree with New York's former mayor Michael R. Bloomberg, who, while in office, liked to say, "I don't listen to Washington much."[28] All of these translocal initiatives compose an "intercity order already in the making," in the words of the phenomenon's leading chronicler and advocate, political theorist Benjamin Barber.[29] Translocalism is an important trend in contemporary governance; our goal is to build on the existing momentum and boost it further.

Climate change, unsurprisingly, is one of the main policy problems that cities have come together to work on. At least nine intercity networks focused on the climate have been founded in the twenty-first century.[30] Among them, the aforementioned C40 Cities Climate Leadership Group has attracted most attention. Founded in 2005 as a network of eighteen megacities interested in climate action, the network now has ninety-seven member cities, which are home to more than eight hundred million people and are the source of over one-quarter of global GDP.[31] The network's central mission is to cut member cities' carbon emissions in half by 2030. It works toward this goal by providing a platform for horizontal exchanges and policy coordination among members. Cities in the network have taken over fourteen thousand "climate actions," and two-thirds of the actions taken in 2015, for example, were in collaboration with other C40 members.[32] What's more, policies trialed in one city often scale out to others in the network.[33]

In addition to facilitating the sharing of lessons and encouragement among peers, the C40 network provides members with technical assistance and access to financing for climate projects. C40's ability to offer technical and financial support also demonstrates its collaborative relationships with the private sector. For instance, the network's GHG Measurement and Planning Initiative, which helped cities measure and reduce their greenhouse gas emissions, was executed in partnership with the German conglomerate Siemens.[34] And the C40 Cities Finance Facility assists members in gaining access to international capital markets for infrastructure projects for climate mitigation and adaptation.[35] Some critics find fault in the network's cozy relationship to multinational corporations (and the philanthropic foundations they birth), arguing that it is merely greenwashed neoliberalism. Relatedly, others point out that the network has not resolved fundamental tensions between member cities, which lie in both the Global North and South, about how to share the cost burden of climate mitigation.[36] These critiques notwithstanding, the C40 network has produced significant results. When, for example, President Trump announced he was withdrawing the US from the Paris Agreement, C40's US members led an effort to get 407 American mayors to pledge to "adopt, honor, and uphold" the Paris goals.[37]

In contrast to the C40's technocratic and market-oriented approach, the Fearless Cities movement offers a more participatory as well as anticapitalist model of translocal networking. First convened in 2017, the Fearless Cities network "is an informal global movement of activists, organizations, councilors and mayors that are working to radicalize democracy, feminize politics and drive the transition to an economy that cares for people and our environment."[38] A number of initiatives with similar political commitments were already working on transforming their own cities, but the network, led by the leftist "municipal platform" Barcelona en Comú, sought to bring them into conversation with each other in order to share, collaborate, and amplify their power. Membership in Fearless Cities is not limited to governments: in fact,

most member organizations are not municipalities but political parties
and social movements working for change inside and outside local government.[39] The network's focus, then, tends toward solidarity building
via informal exchanges, rather than the circulation of technical best
practices and policies via formal bureaucratic channels.[40] Yet Fearless Cities is still self-consciously dedicated to tackling what they call
"global challenges." Though the members "prioritize local organizing,
action and solutions, this should by no means be interpreted as a retreat
into selfishness or parochialism," writes the International Committee
of Barcelona en Comú. "We are all too aware of the global nature of the
challenges we face in our neighborhoods, and we believe that we can
only meet them by working together."[41]

The most ambitious translocal idea to date is Barber's proposal to
create a Global Parliament of Mayors (GPM) or World Assembly of
Cities, "a formal institutional expression of the informal cooperative
networks and collaborative arrangements that for years have been
making a significant difference in addressing the challenges of an ever
more interdependent world."[42] The assembly that he envisioned would
rely on soft power and voluntary compliance, rather than hard power
and binding mandates, but has the potential for high impact nonetheless. Through consensual mechanisms like information sharing, best-
practice exchange, norm promotion, and collective purchasing power,
the GPM would increase the influence of local institutions on the global
stage and improve their capacity at home. The term *parliament* here is a
bit deceptive. Barber doesn't suggest that cities form a legislature with
jurisdiction over each other or the world; he foresees a forum that con-
venes city officials for the purposes of amplifying their collective voice
and helping each member city govern itself.

Barber's hope, which we share, is that a robust assembly of cities
"would engender optimism and rekindle democratic faith among
people who have everywhere grown cynical about government and its
capacity to deal with pressing issues."[43] With optimism and democratic
faith even more in demand today than when Barber voiced his aspirations in 2014, it is encouraging to note that interest in urban networks

has surged in the years since—including the founding, in 2016, of a Global Parliament of Mayors modeled after, though not yet fully realizing, Barber's dream.[44]

Translocal networks are an important site of ideological and institutional linkage between the local scale and the planetary. Local governments and the issues that they manage are intimately connected to the planetary scale. Small-scale actions feed into planetary processes (e.g., coal-burning power plants are located in a particular site; zoonotic crossover happens in a particular place), and small-scale communities feel their effects. We are all part of an interconnected whole, where actions anywhere can have ramifications everywhere, but local officials often have to stay focused on putting out local fires (metaphorically and literally). All politics is local, as they say. Being part of global networks of other local institutions helps keep the planetary scale front and center in the minds of municipal officials, and perhaps citizens too. Networking bridges the micro to the macro and the macro to the micro, performing interconnectedness and making the web of relations between all scales more tangible. In forging connections and underscoring interdependence, worldwide urban networks cultivate a planetary identity and a planetary politics among participants (a topic to which we will return in chapter 6).

Like all features of planetary multiscalar governance, the fundamental project of urban networks is to promote planetary habitability and multispecies flourishing. Whereas some critics suspect that mayors today join global networks to increase their city's brand and lure international business investment, planetary-centric networks must remain clear-eyed proponents of planetary goals.[45] As long as they are promoting a race to the top rather than the bottom, there's nothing wrong with encouraging competition among cities or using prestige and status to attract participation from cities. C40, for instance, gives out annual awards to recognize cities for bold and innovative climate policies, "so that other cities will be inspired and empowered to act," as the organization puts it.[46] Beyond prizes, C40 encourages the use of common standards, measures, and reporting on climate programs, enabling

each city to compare its performance to other cities in the network—
and hopefully strive for more progress.

While translocal governance networks are most developed to date
between urban areas, there's no reason why similar arrangements could
not also be forged between rural regions that share relevant common-
alities in confronting the local effects of planetary challenges. Already,
for example, there are networks of viticulturalists in California, France,
Australia, and South Africa collaborating to develop climate change
resiliency strategies for winemakers.[47] In addition to rural-to-rural
networks, there is much to be gained from networks of rural-urban
linkages, exchanging ideas on ways for cities and their rural hinterlands
to relate to each other.[48]

Problems of Local Governance

What if local majorities opt to abuse the rights of a local minority? What
if local institutions deny some or all of their constituents' basic material
needs? This, of course, is not a hypothetical. In the country we know
best, the United States, the appeal to local control or "states' rights" has
often meant granting white majorities the power to dominate African
Americans and other minorities without interference from outsiders.
This is a real problem. One response—unsatisfactory but true, nonetheless—is that abuses of power and tyranny are available at any scale.
There is nothing inherently barbaric about local institutions. National
states and transnational organizations (including both corporations
and nonprofits) can be plenty cruel.

A second response is that the multiscalar systems architecture of
planetary subsidiarity has some ability to combat this problem. Local
institutions are constructed within a broader structure of institutions
at larger scales, and if it is determined that an issue is better governed
at a larger scale, the principle of subsidiarity dictates that the authority
should move.

Planetary subsidiarity cannot and will not rid the world of local tyrannies; it's just not a promise this system can make. But neither can the

current system of sovereign national states. The whole purpose of sovereignty is to protect states' ability to do whatever they like internally. International institutions—including international law, human rights, and the Responsibility to Protect—try to circumscribe the sovereign right to oppress, but their record is mixed, to say the least.

Translocal networks, moreover, may help mitigate local parochialism and provide guardrails against abuses of power and tyranny. Focusing on the local doesn't mean having to adopt jingoism and insularity. Global networks of cities foster a sense of openness and connection to others. We can curb the chauvinist and provincialist potential of localism by promoting translocalism: delegating authority not just "down" but "out." Translocalism, in fact, is an antiparochial principle and practice. It presses against a conceited closed-mindedness that suggests, "We know it all." To the contrary, translocalism demonstrates that every community has something not just to teach but to learn. Urban networks show that one can be both rooted and cosmopolitan. Translocal connections can help to overcome the cultural insularity, social reaction, and political apathy that too often obtain in disconnected communities, especially in rural regions, and that frequently fuel demands for local control.

Solving problems of interhuman cruelty, moreover, are not the primary focus of our architecture. Our focus is the question of habitability. A bigger challenge to our proposal is what to do about local institutions that flout planetary institutions. What happens when a local self-governor decides to embark on a program of massive resistance to planetary imperatives? When it comes to local implementation of planetary-relevant policies, enforcement is certainly a central concern. While the degree and modalities of coercion are likely to be the source of serious dispute, monitoring noncompliance is becoming easier, as remote sensing technologies allow for the precise observation of things like greenhouse gas emissions and other kinds of toxins from a distance. If the first step toward enforcement is transparency, then technology can play a productive role here.

Yet there are other good reasons to be cautious of giving too much

Chapter Five

power to local institutions. Skeptics fear that local institutions lack the resources, knowledge, or staff to adequately address complex problems. Other critics argue that decentralization can give rise to overlaps, duplications, and inefficiencies. And local officials, enamored with their own autonomy, can resist cooperating with their neighbors on shared problems.[49] A body of research from around the world finds that, overall, arguments against decentralization are "partial and inclusive" and that the evidence for them is "weak and inconsistent." But it also comes to the same conclusions about arguments *for* decentralization.[50] The consequences are complex and contradictory; altogether, they are a wash. As political economist Elinor Ostrom, whose pioneering studies, starting in the 1970s, on common-pool resources helped ignite interest in decentralization, observed after years of witnessing ham-handed implementations of her insights, caution is warranted: decentralization is no panacea, she warned.[51]

"To choose to decentralize," concludes political scientist Daniel Treisman, "requires a leap of faith rather than an application of science."[52] Perhaps. But there are steps we can take to prepare for the leap. The primary one we propose in this book is that allocations of authority should follow a logic not of decentralization but of subsidiarity. Under decentralization, authority is centrifugal; it is flung to the furthest reaches of the org chart. Under subsidiarity, by contrast, authority can move in either direction, depending on the nature of the problem and available institutions. The compelling interest is to right-size rather than to localize. Local governments are just one piece of a multiscalar institutional mosaic. Institutions at the other scales of the planetary subsidiarity system will help alleviate the excesses and inadequacies of local governments, checking them when necessary and providing *subsidium* when requested.

Connecting local governments, our second proposal, also helps address some of their pitfalls mentioned above. Horizontal networks, which focus on circulating resources and expertise, can assist small-scale institutions that frequently lack adequate resources and expertise. The exchange of knowledge, ideas, and innovation, the promotion of best practices and warnings about worst practices, and facilitated collaborations mean that each locality does not have to reinvent the wheel. Sharing across the network opens each local institution up to a global repository of ideas to draw on.

———

Is all of this a recipe for chaos? Does the efflorescence of dynamic, functionally specific, potentially overlapping institutions invite confusion and competition? There certainly is a tension between flexibility and institutionalization. Having many and regularly shifting sites of authority is more complicated than having one centralized site or clearly defined hierarchical levels of authority. But governance systems should not be dismissed simply because they "look too messy and chaotic," as Ostrom argued.[53] Complex phenomena are often best managed by complex arrangements.

For an alternative approach—trying to manage complex phenomena with straightforward arrangements—we need only look to the status quo. The existing institutional structure for governing the globe's most complex problems boils down to 193 sovereign national states. It's a neat and tidy institutional architecture: mutually exclusive and collectively exhaustive divisions of the world's population and territory. But it has proved ineffective at managing the planetary challenges we face. It's no coincidence that the explosion of translocal networks is taking place while national states remain both unwilling and unable to take significant action on key problems.

Our proposal, moreover, would not create entirely independent, decentralized governance institutions, free to wreak havoc on the system as a whole. (That would be a more accurate description of the current international system.) Local governance authorities would be embedded in the larger architecture for planetary governance. Under deliberate multiscalar governance, local governors would be engaged in constant dialogue and mutual relations of assistance with larger-scale governors at the national and planetary scales, as well other local governors via horizontal networking. The flood management staffs of the

Rotterdam mayor's office and the Jakarta governor's office will be in regular contact not only with their national government but with each other as well, exchanging expertise and building translocal bonds based on shared functional interests. This arrangement protects pluralism by giving communities the maximum feasible self-governance while also providing for coordinated action on planetary concerns. The system as a whole in fact benefits from human diversity and builds off the lessons of diversity to improve overall approaches to the management of planetary problems.

Six

Planetary Institutions for Planetary Issues

The present is but a preview of what's to come: longer droughts, faster floods, angrier storms, deadlier pandemics, more broken heat records, and extinction after extinction. According to Earth system and environmental scientists, the planet has already exceeded six of nine interlinked biophysical boundaries critical for planetary stability: not just climate change, but also biodiversity, biogeochemical flows, land use change, freshwater usage, and the introduction of "novel entities."[1] A parade of international reports, scientific studies, jeremiads from moral authorities, and pleas from frontline communities, splashed across headlines daily, further reinforce that human beings—or, rather, *some* human beings—are driving the planet out of whack.

All of this is well known. And yet, little is being done about it. In large part, this is because, given the current architecture of national and international governance institutions we described in chapters 1 and 2, little can be done about it. These challenges are *planetary*, and they exceed the scope and capacity of any existing political or administrative authority, be that national or global. Without planetary institutions that meet the scale of the problems, planetary challenges will remain ungoverned. Such an unordered world is unjust and untenable.

The goal, therefore, must be to create the possibility for order in a world defined by challenges that contemporary national and international institutions are incapable of resolving.

This chapter proposes the development of *planetary institutions* capable of addressing the condition of planetarity we outlined in chapter 3. Here we sketch two potential planetary institutions: one to manage greenhouse gases in the atmosphere and another to address pandemic preparedness and management. These two are meant to be illustrative: there will need to be a whole range of planetary institutions to address other planetary challenges, ranging from space junk, to human interference in the biogeochemical cycling of nitrogen, to "planetary defense" from asteroids, to the maintenance of the planetary freshwater system.

The details of our institutional proposals matter less than the general message presented throughout the book thus far: that in the face of our awareness of the condition of planetarity, we have no choice but to reimagine the entire architecture of our governing institutions. The specific propositions that follow reflect our own opinions on how to resolve the thorny trade-offs that any new institutional order inevitably presents: between technocracy and democracy; between autonomy and authority; over the distributional consequences of planetary policies; over the proper and necessary use of force to enforce decisions; and so on. We hope our sketches here will be read not as proposals whose details are the essence of the matter but rather as provocations to spark imagination.

Two Planetary Institutions

Planetary institutions aim to provide a baseline level of stable planetary habitability. They do not guarantee universal happiness or widespread prosperity. Their goals are restrained. On the basis of what software developers call a "minimum viable product," we envision them as *minimum viable planetary governors* that enable the conditions for diverse human and nonhuman communities to live well. We seek institutions with just enough authority to govern a particular planetary problem effectively.[2] Unlike the condition of international anarchy, which defines world politics today, planetary institutions should be capable of providing an adequate solution to planetary problems. But unlike a world state, they should be minimal in the sense that they set limits, requirements, and goals for the planet as a whole but don't dictate the details of implementation.[3] In other words, planetary institutions as we propose them here will determine the compass settings of *where* to go for planetary issues, whereas subplanetary national and local institutions will have the authority to determine the detailed itineraries of *how* to get there in a way that works for their specific geographic and political circumstances. One might call this "weak" planetary governance, compared to the "strong" planetary governance of a world state. Yet it is critical to our general architectural design that each planetary institution be narrowly focused on a specific planetary issue.

A Planetary Atmospheric Steward

Anthropogenic climate change is caused by the increase of heat-trapping greenhouse gases in the Earth's atmosphere, above all carbon dioxide, but also methane, nitrous oxide, and others, primarily as a result of the burning of fossil fuels like coal, oil, and natural gas, as well as agricultural production and deforestation. From a governance perspective, the salient feature of greenhouse gases is that although they are emitted from specific, situated power plants, industrial facilities, and tailpipes, once they enter the atmosphere they become planetary— they are no longer tied to the place they were combusted but become a part of the planet's overall atmospheric chemistry. Our existing international system of climate governance, chiefly in the form of the UN Framework Convention on Climate Change (UNFCCC) and its Paris Agreement, has shown itself unable to slow, much less reverse, runaway climate change. To prevent the dangers of unchecked climate change to planetary habitability and a flourishing biosphere, we propose a governance institution with authority to manage greenhouse gases in Earth's atmosphere. A Planetary Atmospheric Steward (PAS) would marry the Intergovernmental Panel on Climate Change's (IPCC) function of increasing our knowledge of the climate with the authority to make and enforce decisions on limiting carbon emissions on the basis of what it knows.[4]

A body with authority to govern the climate at a planetary scale would need to execute several roles to operate effectively. The PAS's first role will be to *improve knowledge* of the Earth's climate and its dynamics—in other words, to enhance planetary sapience. This would include, but not be limited to, deploying more and better scientific instruments to gain historic and real-time data on temperature, atmospheric composition, and the sources of carbon emissions and carbon sinks, as well as the software and hardware necessary to process and interpret the data and to model and simulate possible climate futures. Its primary epistemic function would be to collect and analyze data about the climate as a whole, but the PAS wouldn't neglect regionally and locally specific characteristics of the changing climate.[5] Indeed, subsidiarity dictates that the PAS would have to be available to assist smaller-scale governance bodies, such as national states, regions, and municipalities, which often lack the needed information and expertise to pursue their own preferred implementation schemes within the planet-wide framework.

The IPCC already performs much of the epistemic function that we envision.[6] Where the PAS should diverge from the IPCC and the UNFCCC is in its authority to *set hard targets* for net greenhouse gas emissions—not suggestions or aspirations, but enforceable rules. The PAS's decisions on greenhouse gas emissions won't be optional: they will have to be obeyed and implemented by governance institutions at all scales. The principle of planetary subsidiarity guides the allocation of decision rights: the planetary institution sets the targets, national states decide how to handle the political-economic implications, and localities decide on the implementation details.

In our vision, the decision cascade would work like this. First, on the basis of modeling of impacts and a desire to mitigate the deleterious effects for habitability and multispecies flourishing, the PAS sets planetary greenhouse gas targets and specifies those targets down to a national level. (This will inevitably be controversial, since it speaks to major questions, such as the burden of historical versus contemporary emissions, but for now we aim to focus on organizational design.) Second, each national state takes its PAS-designated target and engages a national debate over who within the national state should bear the costs (both direct and distributional) of the transitions required to hit the target, and from there delegates the implementation to subnational levels. For example, upon receiving Brazil's targets from the PAS, Brasilia might decide that São Paulo and Rio de Janeiro—as large, rich states that have historically emitted more than their share of Brazil's carbon—should bear a greater relative burden of reduction. Then third, each state and locality decides how exactly they want to implement these mandates, hopefully in coordination and friendly competition with one another through the translocal networks outlined in chapter 5. In São Paulo this might entail more of a focus on the rapid uptake of wind and solar power generation; in Rio de Janeiro that might mean transforming the urban transportation infrastructure. Subplanetary institutions can (and should) aim to exceed the minimum baseline greenhouse gas emissions standards set by the PAS.

The PAS's twin roles are intertwined in practice. Enhancing the material infrastructure of planetary sapience—the satellites, terrestrial and oceanic sensors, computer processing power, et cetera—will enable more effective interventions at all the stages of the governing process. The systematic monitoring of Earth system processes, for example, can help with agenda setting, the first stage of the policy process, by discovering planetary problems in need of attention. At the other end of the governance process, growing planetary sapience can empower the PAS's monitoring and enforcement, even for truculent jurisdictions. Remote sensing via satellites can observe planetary harms, such as methane leaks and deforestation, that subplanetary authorities either fail to notice or ignore.[7]

Bridging the PAS's two objectives is a third role: supporting the *development, deployment, and regulation of new technologies* to help stabilize Earth's atmosphere. The PAS should promote innovation in fields such as atmospheric carbon removal, while ensuring that the technologies it sponsors will belong to the public. At the same time, its targets for decarbonization must take a holistic perspective that doesn't assume that particular technologies will pan out. The PAS could also be the forum for regulating technologies intended to directly manage the planetary climate, such as solar radiation management, also known as solar geoengineering. Regardless of whether we consider solar geoengineering to be a good or bad idea, future decisions about its use or nonuse will need to be made, and they should be made by a body with planetary authority. If one day solar geoengineering is to be developed and deployed (or it is decided to *not* use such methods), the decision should be in the hands of the PAS rather than a national state, an NGO, a philanthropist, or any other subplanetary entity. The authority to act with planetary effects should be in the hands of a planetary institution.

This brief sketch inevitably leaves many questions unanswered. How will the PAS decide its atmospheric greenhouse gas concentration goals? How should planetary habitability and economic development be balanced? How will the PAS ensure that it remains a minimal viable institution when the mandate to regulate the climate could easily expand to encompass enormous swaths of life? How will the planetary institution enforce its decisions? If net-zero emissions are achieved, will the PAS still be necessary? These and many other important debates need to be held. For now, however, we hope that this succinct outline gives a rough idea of what a governance body at the scale of the planet might look like.

A Planetary Pandemic Agency

Pandemic risk starts off small—microscopic, in fact. Infectious diseases are caused by the transmission of pathogens, bacteria, and viruses.[8] And though notable progress has been made against some diseases, like the eradication of smallpox, novel infectious diseases emerge among humans every year. Many pathogens could pose a catastrophic risk for human populations, but viruses (especially RNA viruses) are the most likely to turn into a major problem.[9] The primary pathway for new viruses and other pathogens to enter human populations, and then potentially escalate to a human pandemic, is via zoonotic spillover, that is from nonhuman animals.[10] The majority of human pathogens that currently pose the risk of a pandemic are zoonotic, in fact. Of these, most come from wildlife, though they can also infect humans via farm animals.[11] Scientists believe, for instance, that HIV-1, the retrovirus that causes AIDS, was transmitted to human beings from wild chimpanzees and that the 2009 H1N1 influenza reached humans from farmed pigs.[12] Key hotspots for zoonotic spillover, therefore, include the edges of tropical forests, where deforestation puts humans in contact with wild animals, the global wildlife trade, and livestock farms.[13]

Drug-resistant microbes represent another major risk vector for future infectious diseases. As a consequence, the highest geographic concentration of known novel diseases is not in poor, tropical regions—where zoonotic spillover from wildlife is most frequent—but in wealthy and temperate ones, including the United States, Europe, Japan, and Australia, where the evolution of antimicrobial resistance is most significant.[14] High human population density and the heavy usage of antibiotics to treat human illnesses and to keep alive livestock raised on factory farms make these regions epicenters for emerging drug-resistant pathogens. Casual and prophylactic overuse of antibiotics is raising the risk of antibacterial resistance for a variety of diseases. Although bacteria are less likely to cause a pandemic than viruses, widespread antibiotic resistance has the potential to upend modern medicine. By some estimates, antibiotic-resistant bacteria could become a leading cause of death among humans by 2050.[15]

These facts about the origins of infectious diseases likely to cause pandemics among humans suggest several critical sites for preventing their outbreak. Planet-wide monitoring and restrictions on deforestation, wildlife trade, and industrial livestock practices could reduce the number of zoonotic spillover events and lead to more rapid discovery of the pathogens that do present breakout risk. Recent studies have estimated that the cost of preventative policies such as these would be a fraction of the cost of enduring a pandemic.[16]

Despite the scientific consensus around the lifesaving (and cost-saving) potential of these measures, the current global governance framework is not conducive to their implementation. The WHO does not have the ability to override the sovereignty of national states to directly monitor disease outbreaks. What's more, its remit is too limited: measures like limiting deforestation or the trade in wildlife are often seen as too upstream of human health to enter the activities of the global public health body. Even if its mandate were extended, the WHO would continue to suffer from the same structural weaknesses as other multilateral organizations.[17]

To reduce the risk, the emergence, and the spread of pandemic diseases, we propose a Planetary Pandemic Agency (PPA). A planetary pandemic agency would need the authority to enforce these measures that the WHO can't. An effective PPA would need the capability to act against infectious diseases at the planetary scale. Across Earth, it would monitor known and emergent diseases, reduce the number of potential spillover events and outbreaks, have the authority to order quick action against possible pandemics, and produce and distribute vaccinations and therapeutics to all who might need them. As compared to the WHO, the PPA would need to change the incentives for reporting, so that countries would be motivated to identify events early (and have fewer incentives to suppress and underreport).

The PPA must be planetary in content, not just scale. It needs to adopt a holistic approach to health, embracing the interconnectedness of human health, animal health (both wildlife and livestock), and the environment, and emphasizing the life support systems of the planet as a whole, on which humans, like all creatures, rely.[18] The PPA should approach human health and well-being as "intrinsically connected" to the welfare of the various ecosystems in which humans are enmeshed, and should act on the conviction that protecting us requires protecting the planetary whole.[19] (It's important, as a result, for the PPA to collaborate with the eventual planetary institution charged with safeguarding biodiversity and limiting ecosystems disruption.) Only a planetary understanding of emergent infectious diseases—that is, an understanding that a basic cause of these emergences is the disruption of biogeochemical and ecological systems—can enable effective pandemic prevention and preparedness. As argued previously, planetary thinking helps us see ecological disruptions in holistic terms, rather than as isolated toxicities.

No matter how effective a pandemic agency could be, there will inevitably be future zoonotic and novel pathogenic outbreaks.[20] Humans and pathogens have coevolved since our species first emerged, and the Darwinian dance will never end. "Disease X," the WHO's code name for a currently unknown pathogen that could cause a future international epidemic, will forever lurk.[21] In fact, the incidence of new infectious diseases has increased over time, both because of growing antibiotic usage leading to new strains of infectious bacteria and because of intensifying interactions between humans and nonhuman animals as more forests are razed to create croplands and pastures, the trade in wild animals proliferates, and the numbers of farmed animals multiply.[22] While the actions that increase the risk that a pathogen may spill over into humans may appear to be a local matter—where to locate a new farm, which wild animals to hunt, how much antibiotics to prescribe—actions that cause the emergence of new infectious diseases can have worldwide consequences, as the history of HIV/AIDS's journey from a localized disease in central Africa to a global pandemic makes evident.[23]

The PPA's first role, then, concerns *gaining knowledge about infectious diseases and their emergence*—that is, as with the PAS, improving planetary sapience.[24] The PPA should monitor human/animal and human/wilderness interfaces everywhere, including sites of deforestation and habitat destruction, the trade in wildlife, and industrial livestock, as well as regions with heavy antibiotic usage.[25] Though conducting monitoring on a planetary scale is an immense task, existing knowledge (which will hopefully only expand) of risk factors of disease emergence will help the PPA to focus its resources. Certain species represent a much higher risk of zoonotic spillover than others, so just by monitoring nodes in trade networks for primates, pangolins, and civets, the PPA can reduce the likelihood of zoonotic disease emergence.[26] In doing so, the PPA should conduct its own public health surveillance efforts but also aggregate and analyze public health data from subplanetary institutions, though the proliferating array of distributed sensor networks, data integration platforms, and analytic tools will over time make this easier.[27] In addition to monitoring for new pathogens, the PPA must generate knowledge about existing and potential communicable diseases, supporting a library of pathogens. And when a pathogen begins to spread, the PPA can lead and coordinate efforts to understand the disease and its characteristics, such as genetic sequencing and the dynamics of transmission (roles today played by the WHO).

A second role for the PPA is to act on its knowledge by *making decisions to reduce the risks of disease emergence among humans*. The PPA must act to prevent the spillover of pathogens from animals and the evolution of new antibiotic-resistant microbes. This requires the planetary institution to adopt a holistic perspective on human health, taking action to promote the health of animals, ecosystems, and the biosphere as a whole. Only by taking action upstream of human infection can the PPA prevent epidemics from happening in the first place. To curtail the likelihood of zoonotic spillover, the PPA should promote rules to limit deforestation, hunting, and trading certain wildlife. For instance, it should regulate or even prohibit the trade in the high-risk mammals mentioned above, and unsafe industrial livestock practices (overcrowding, overmedicating, maintaining unsanitary conditions, and so on). To reduce the risk of increased antibiotic resistance, the PPA should have the authority to manage the usage of antibiotics. Planetary regulation of antibiotics could help prevent the worst-case scenarios projected from the current business as usual.

In addition, the PPA should have the authority to reduce the risk of novel disease emergence emanating from high-risk biological laboratories. The PPA must hold oversight and regulatory powers over the fifty-nine biosafety level 4, or BSL-4, labs throughout the world, in much the same way that the International Atomic Energy Agency has the authority to inspect existing nuclear facilities to ensure their peaceful use. Most of the national states that operate BSL-4 labs do not have national regulations on dual-use research (experiments whose results could be beneficial or be weaponized) or gain-of-function research (experiments designed to increase the infectiousness of a pathogen, in order to study how it might mutate to become more infectious or pathogenic). Rather, the scientists are given the leeway to regulate themselves. Even without malicious intent, the very existence of such laboratories opens the possibility for human error to release a highly infectious new disease into the population. Given this potential for worldwide spread, oversight of these laboratories and their research should belong to a planetary body.[28]

The PPA's third role concerns *centralized decision-making and coordination in the event of a pandemic or possible pandemic*. The institution's remit should include not only the ability to declare a "planetary public health emergency" (similar to the WHO's current declarations, to which it then hopes that its national members will respond appropriately) but also the authority to set standards for national and local pandemic defense plans and to mandate when subplanetary institutions should invoke these plans. What's more, during a planetary public health emergency, the PPA will promote rapid communication among subplanetary governance institutions around the world, including many nonprofit and private sector actors, who often provide health services and are more trusted than governments. Indeed, this coordinating role will perhaps be the PPA's most crucial responsibility.

A fourth role for the PPA would be to take the lead in *developing, producing, and distributing vaccines and therapeutics*. This will involve working with pharmaceutical companies or directly sponsoring research and development of vaccines for likely outbreaks before they occur and adjusting them as needed when the time comes, as well as ensuring the timely and uniform distribution of privately developed vaccines and infection-repressing therapeutics. Preventing national hoarding of medicine will be a top responsibility, and one that will distinguish the PPA from the WHO.[29]

As with the PAS for greenhouse gas management, there will be debates about the proper scope and priorities of the PPA. Should the PPA work on infectious diseases like malaria that can't spread on a planet-wide scale? The mosquitoes that transmit malaria live only in certain regions, so the disease cannot become a planet-wide pandemic—but is that reason enough to ignore a major cause of suffering and death, particular among children in Africa? Should the PPA confront animal diseases that do not directly affect humans? What about actions that adversely affect some forms of life in order to preserve others, such as the introduction of gene drives to tamp down the reproduction of disease vectors like mosquitoes? Or the introduction of a virus to kill an invasive species that is threatening biodiversity in a remote corner of the globe? What role should the PPA have in supporting functioning health care systems around the world? We propose that the PPA should operate on a planetary scale and leave the provision of basic human health care to smaller-scale institutions, but given that many populations have little access to such health care systems, emerging diseases will continue to be left untreated or unnoticed—opening the possibility for new pandemics and leading to suffering in affected populations. Is such a planetary focus without attention to on-the-ground basic health care a self-defeating initiative? These are important questions, but they are policy questions best decided by a well-functioning governance institution.

The trickier questions focus on the design and functioning of the institution itself. How should the PPA handle truculent states that refuse to share data, that slow-walk its directives, or that simply lack the capacity to do either? How should the PPA interact with legacy institutions that cover similar domains, including national public health institutions and the WHO? How will the PPA be held accountable to disadvantaged communities? These communities are often most at risk of infectious diseases yet already have little power to influence the institutions making decisions that affect their lives. These questions need to be debated and discussed. As with the PAS, our goal here is not to produce a definitive blueprint but merely to limn the approximate scope of a planetary authority for pandemic governance.

Seeing Like a Planet

A defining characteristic of planetary institutions is that their administrative ambit is worldwide: they are concerned with the planet as a whole (for a given functional domain), rather than exclusively focused on some geographic subset. Creating a governing unit that encompasses the whole Earth might seem like a mere administrative act, but the planet-wide scope of planetary institutions is what makes them unique and is the source of their effectiveness and authority.[30] The foundational work of a planetary unit is to open the possibility of imagining planetary problems as actionable, positing planetary benefits, and envisioning planetary practices. By establishing a new basic conceptual category with which we can think in terms of planetary governance, the act of creating planetary institutions is itself a valuable step, even before they do any governing.[31]

This feature also distinguishes planetary institutions from the contemporary institutions of global governance. On a surface level, the PAS and the PPA appear rather like the original visions for, respectively, the UN Environmental Programme (UNEP) and the WHO.[32] Both institutions were given broad and important mandates to enhance planetary sapience and manage international coordination and cooperation in their fields. A significant difference between what the UN system produced and what we advocate, however, is precisely the institutions' conceptual foundations. UNEP and the WHO were founded on and continue to operate with an international or global worldview. Their institutional structures, management, missions, and senses of self all stem from their fundamental commitments to internationalism and/or globalism—that is, their commitments to state sovereignty. But as we have argued, the international and the global are not the Planetary. Institutions constructed from different conceptual foundations will turn out differently. In ways that we can't yet fully foresee, planetary institutions will differ from the global governance institutions.

Effective planetary governance requires not just political authority but expert, or epistemic, authority as well. This leads to planetary institutions' first critical mission: the collection, management, and assessment of data, information, knowledge, and wisdom about the planet. Knowledge of the planet and its systems is the basis of the epistemic authority upon which the institutions' political authority rests. But even more than that, the basis for the administrative remit of planetary institutions lies precisely in our dawning recognition and understanding of the condition of planetarity. Growing planetary sapience, in other words, makes clear the imperative for planetary institutions.

Planetary sapience, as we discussed in chapter 3, is the planetary self-awareness derived from the collection and analysis of information about the planet and its many living and nonliving systems. One mandate of planetary institutions will be to advance this knowledge—the commitment to an ever-increasing understanding of Earth, its processes, and inhabitants of every species. Planetary institutions should produce, aggregate, synthesize, interpret, and share data and analysis about planetary phenomena with the public. To take our two exemplars: the PAS should pursue a comprehensive knowledge of the Earth's climate, while the PPA should pursue a comprehensive knowledge of communicable diseases and disease ecologies. Scientific understanding of our planetary conditions represents the epistemic operating system of planetary sapience.[33]

Planetary sapience is inherently valuable. We needn't believe, with Vernadsky and Teilhard, that the noösphere represents the next stage of Earth's evolution in order to know that it is a good thing to better understand our planetary home and that planetary self-awareness should be pursued for its own sake. But it is also the foundation of informed decision-making at the planetary level. Without accurate, up-to-date representations of planetary phenomena, planetary institutions would fly blind. Just as national states require national data and expend lots of resources collecting it, planetary data (and related assessments) will be a central focus of planetary institutions. If national governance institutions involve "seeing like a state," as James Scott observed, planetary sapience entails "seeing like a planet."[34]

Seeing like a planet in turn provokes the question of exactly whose eyes (and other sensory organs and devices) are activated and validated. Who are the agents of planetary sight? Who is authorized to see for the planet? Who is given warrant to speak for the planet? This mode of governance forces us to take seriously the question once raised by Dr. Seuss's 1971 children's classic *The Lorax*: Who "speaks for the trees"?[35] Here is our (undoubtedly controversial) opinion: some people know more and understand better than others about the planetary condition, and they should be empowered to speak for the planet.[36] Biologists have specialist knowledge that allows them to understand the habitus of creatures from bacteria to mycelia to cetacea better than others. Earth system and environmental scientists can measure, model, and explain the material and energy fluxes and dynamic interactions of the Earth's atmosphere, biosphere, hydrosphere, lithosphere, and so on. Astronomers, astrobiologists, and rocket scientists can account for risks ranging from asteroid strikes to space junk to interplanetary biocontamination. Virologists, microbiologists, epidemiologists, and physicians are expert in the transmission and transformation of pandemic diseases. Social scientists and humanists bring knowledge about human behavior and community dynamics. Enhancing planetary sapience means empowering the knowers of the planet to speak for planetary concerns in the arenas for planetary deliberation and decision-making created by planetary institutions.[37]

This argument does not suggest that Earth is fully knowable to science or that human beings can understand what it is like to be a bat, a tree, tundra, or an ocean.[38] But we hold that there are better and worse methods of approximating—or at least getting close to approximating— the planetary condition and the natures of Earth's many systems and living beings. Planetary sapience must include a commitment to intellectual humility, a recognition that we can't know everything. It can't replicate the hubristic belief at the heart of modernity that everything is knowable. Planetary sapience instead embraces complexity and its consequences, including the recognition that some features of complex systems are not predictable.[39] Epistemic humility, however, mustn't be allowed to produce debilitating indecision. Rather, it should inspire efforts to constantly expand and refine our ways of knowing the planet. Enhancing planetary sapience is a never-ending pursuit.

Appreciation and knowledge of the condition of planetarity are thus prerequisites for effective planetary policymaking. It is with this understanding, this sapience, that planetary institutions can take account of human and nonhuman interests, including the interests of individual species and, especially, of ecosystems and the biosphere as a whole. Doing so means not only learning more and more about nonhuman life, nonliving matter, and their interactions, but considering them in decision-making. This casts the scientific experts (and the models they build) as the representatives for the planet and its living matter. Representation, as political theorist Hanna Pitkin remarked, is "the making present in some sense of something which is nevertheless not present literally or in fact."[40] It is these experts' role and responsibility to "make present" the voice and interests of the nonhuman beings and systems. The future may bring new technologies and new ways of thinking that offer better ways for politically representing the interests and preferences of nonhumans, but for now, humans who understand the planetary condition and the technologies that they construct to do the same are the best that we have. Of course, there will need to be new modes of democratic oversight, as we discuss shortly.

The epistemic mandate of the Planetary provides the basis for the administrative mandate of planetary institutions: to govern the planet in the name of habitability and multispecies flourishing. This means that planetary institutions are to generate systems of rule that promote Earth's habitability and ensure the possibility of multispecies flourishing. This principle is the basis of planetary institutions' authority. It defines whom they govern for and in whose name they govern. Planetary institutions are stewards of the planet. This is a crucial distinction from global governance institutions, which are agents of their member states. Planetary institutions do not answer to national states, but to Earth and its biosphere. Like the planetary sovereign imagined by geographers Joel Wainwright and Geoff Mann, planetary institutions are "planetary in a dual sense: capable of acting both at the planetary scale . . . and in the name of planetary management—for the sake of life on Earth."[41]

Planetary habitability and multispecies flourishing are the twin goals of planetary governance. Every action taken by a planetary institution should promote them. There are bound to be actions that don't, but they should be taken only when there is a sound reason to do so and when the action is still within the spirit of the principle. Put another way, planetary institutions must avoid actions that deliberately harm planetary habitability and multispecies flourishing. Through the fulfillment of their dual mandate—to enhance planetary sapience and to make planetary rules—planetary institutions should wield expert authority and political authority toward effective planetary governance aimed at multispecies flourishing on a habitable Earth.

Recognizing the condition of planetarity will not always make policy choices obvious. Just as value differences drive national politics, so there will be real trade-offs to be made between different planetary objectives. Planetary institutions open the possibility for making choices on the planetary scale, but they don't hold the answers to resolve these dilemmas. For example, building massive solar arrays and other infrastructures needed for the energy transition may be at odds with protecting biodiversity in the locations where they get built: What should be prioritized? There is no objective answer for the absolute boundary of atmospheric carbon that we cannot cross: Where should it be set? These dilemmas don't come with a scientific resolution, though scientists can clarify what the planetary impacts of these different policy choices are. Deciding which policy to pursue, however, is the realm of politics.

Planetary Politics

The governance institutions we just described may appear overly technocratic. Some readers may even denounce this vision of expert-led planetary administration as "antipolitical": that is, a form of governance that intentionally removes some topics from the arena of politics and democratic debate. That is not the case. On the contrary, planetary institutions' political authority, rooted in the commitment to planetary sapience, creates the basis for a fundamentally new kind of *planetary politics.* Planetary institutions will nurture and sustain a novel form of political contestation. The development of national political and administrative institutions generally preceded national identities, consciousnesses, and politics, as we discussed in chapter 1. Likewise, we expect planetary institutions to precede planetary politics—not the other way around.[42] Just as political parties, parliamentary politics, and social movements developed in a dialectical but lagging relationship to the development of national states, a new kind of politics commensurate with planetary sapience will surely emerge with the development of planetary governing institutions.

The basic units of politics determine who belongs to a political community, as well as the basis of a community's politics—"what sorts of political actions and political problems are possible or impossible," in the words of political philosopher Zhao Tingyang.[43] Political units thus establish the limits of politics in two senses: in a jurisdictional sense, where we determine who and what is ours to rule and who and what is someone else's, and in a conceptual sense, where we decide what counts as politics. Today, the national state is the basic political unit, the one that demarcates the boundaries of political belonging and of political possibility. With planetary politics, however, neither the borders of national states nor the borders of our species mark the boundaries of political inclusion. The basic political unit is the planet. The framework for planetary politics—the who, what, where, how, and why of the political—is defined by the Earth system.

Planetary politics' contrast with national politics is clear, but its distinction from international politics is more confused because today international politics, as both concept and practice, often tries to address planetary problems like climate change and pandemics. But the international politics of planetary problems is *not* planetary politics. This is because, to again quote Zhao, international politics isn't "carried out for the sake of world interests, but only for national interests on a world scale."[44] The United Nations, to take a central site of international politics, is responsive to the interests of its member states, not to the condition of planetarity. The best that international politics can hope to achieve is voluntary multilateral cooperation, which, as we argued in chapter 2, is fine for some types of problems but unfit for planetary problems. Indeed, Lorenzo Marsili goes so far as to argue that the very structure of international politics is a significant cause of planetary problems: "It is the inter-national system itself that is accelerating the path towards disaster," he writes. "It is precisely the system of nation states that perpetuates a competitive pursuit of wealth and power that renders our societies unable to overcome their dependence on the destruction of the planet."[45]

Tellingly, there is (as of yet) no mass international politics. The UN is a forum for government-to-government interactions. States, not citizens, have a voice.[46] As a result, there is no international public and no impetus for mass mobilization in international politics. There are no significant international political parties—where would their candidates run for office? There are international social movements, but they are typically coordinated efforts to pressure national governments, the hegemonic unit of governance and thus politics.[47] Without participatory political institutions at the international level, mass international politics has not developed. With planetary institutions, by contrast, we expect a new scale of politics to emerge. Naming a new basic unit of politics—the planet—is a call to form new publics and thus a new politics. Planetary institutions will therefore be politicized in a way that contemporary multilateral institutions are not.

But it's not just that planetary politics is a postnational politics. It's also a postanthropocentric politics. By embracing the planet, rather than nations or the globe, planetary politics moves toward a *multispecies politics*. Western philosophy since at least Aristotle has considered politics the unique and exclusive domain of humans, the *zoon politikon* (political animal). But as science and philosophy have increasingly chipped away at human exceptionalism—arriving at conclusions long held by many non-Western traditions—we must face planetary politics as the politics of and for all living beings. The deep political question posed by the condition of planetarity is: How can the views and agencies of the more-than-human be included politically?

Political institutions, first, must learn to listen to creatures that Western societies have long considered voiceless. Giving voice to the voiceless isn't a fantastical idea: we do it all the time. American lawyer Christopher D. Stone, in an influential article from 1972, for instance, pointed out that "it is no answer to say that streams and forests cannot have [legal] standing because streams and forests cannot speak. Corporations cannot speak either; nor can states, estates, infants, incompetents, municipalities, or universities. Lawyers speak for them." Stone advocated giving legal rights to "forests, oceans, rivers . . . indeed, to the natural environment as a whole," making clear that these "natural objects" could be defended in courts, just like corporations, by a human guardian.[48] Likewise, French philosopher Bruno Latour, whom we encountered in chapter 3, pushed this idea from law to politics, proposing "a Parliament of Things." While "things" such as animals, plants, microbes, rivers, or the atmosphere strictly speaking cannot "speak," Latour argued, they can nonetheless be represented politically by "their representatives, scientists who speak in their name."[49] In other words, planetary politics entails empowering nonhuman others through experts or some other means of representation. It is through these representatives that we can learn to listen to and include the multispecies masses.

A rapidly growing body of scientific evidence and theory is demonstrating that the cognitive and social lives of animals are much richer and complex than was once thought.[50] Some species may even engage in politics in the sense of "social manipulation to secure and maintain influential positions," as the primatologist Frans de Waal observed among chimpanzees.[51] But as far as we know, animals cannot debate, negotiate, or make trade-offs, particularly on behalf of a collective or over the long term, all of which are hallmarks of human political activities. That said, this doesn't mean that human representatives, guardians, or spokespersons cannot engage in these political actions on their behalf. The interests of nonhumans can be made present, and they can be given weight in politics and policymaking through institutional rules and procedures. Governance institutions already have mechanisms for considering the interests of those who can't speak, as Stone pointed out five decades ago. With a range of tools, nonhuman beings and systems can be given political power and made to matter. It is question of expanding the circle of who and what we believe counts, who and what we believe should matter.[52]

The idea here is not to create political institutions among nonhumans so that, say, rabbits get to vote on whether foxes are permitted to eat them. The "natural world" already follows its own rules and doesn't need the imposition of our institutions. A multispecies planetary politics, rather, is about opening a political space in which humans are not the only voices, creating the possibility that the biosphere can represent itself. It is about expanding the sources of political power in order to restore a semblance of balance to the planet. Yet even this doesn't necessarily mean that chickens and cows, like their fellow prey the rabbits, can simply outvote humans. Our impulse isn't misanthropic, but at the same time it's clear that humans' "business as usual" relations with nonhumans can't continue. Like other concepts in this chapter, however, the contours of a postanthropocentric multispecies politics remain inchoate and aspirational.

Proposing a politics that includes nonhumans also doesn't imply a naive expectation that the interests of all will always align. There's no planetary "general will" (in Rousseau's sense): the multispecies multitude will never speak in one voice or share one desire (except, perhaps, the continuation of the lively biosphere as such). Bringing the interests of nonhuman others into politics will only make the political cacophony louder and more complex. This is always the result of greater political inclusion. And so we accept that there will be disputes—among humans, between humans and nonhumans, among nonhumans. The point of planetary institutions is to take account of all sides of a dispute, weigh the costs and benefits to all parties on a planetary basis, and come to collective decisions at the scale of the planet for issues at the scale of the planet—tasks that nationally focused political institutions are, by design, incapable of doing.

Decisions made by planetary institutions will inevitably produce winners and losers. In the end, our principal concern is human flourishing, which informs our views of how decisions should be made. But, in contrast to most contemporary policy decisions, planetary institutions must be founded on the understanding, grounded in growing planetary sapience, that human flourishing is inseparable from broader multispecies flourishing. This reorientation toward the interests of the greater biosphere doesn't disavow human interests but rather (to again quote Tocqueville) instantiates "self-interest rightly understood." What planetary politics suggests isn't a change to (human) self-interest; rather, the expanding awareness of the condition of planetarity is changing what "rightly understood" means.

This is not a naive prediction of world peace. Our claim is much more modest: that under planetary politics the terms of contestation will change. Planetary politics isn't just national politics projected on the planet. It is something new, something not yet fully imaginable.[53]

Fear of the Unknown

Planetary politics may not be completely thinkable at this point, but that doesn't stop some from preemptively fearing it. This fear—which is distinct from concerns that planetary institutions are not plausible, addressed in chapter 4—is rooted in the conviction that supranational governance institutions will inevitably (or even just possibly) become unaccountable and authoritarian. Such anxieties are understandable concerns, and smart observers of world politics who are broadly sympathetic to a cosmopolitan vision have gone out of their way to voice them.[54] Philosopher John Rawls, to take one leading example, dismissed the idea of a world state in a single sentence, arguing, following Kant's view from 1795, "that a world government . . . would either be a global despotism or else would rule over a fragile empire torn by frequent civil strife as various regions and peoples tried to gain their political freedom and autonomy."[55] Such outcomes would, without a doubt, be scary. If we believed that tyranny or war was the likely result of planetary institutions, we wouldn't advocate their creation.

It's true that we can't rule out the possibility that future planetary institutions will veer toward unchecked power, misrule, and violence. (The same lack of divination hampers planetary skeptics too, of course.) It's possible for the same reason that national states can, and frequently do, become unaccountable, undemocratic, and destructive. One shouldn't judge this dystopian future in a vacuum, however, but rather in comparison to the actually existing status quo: the modern international system of sovereign national states. Contemporary international politics *is already* unaccountable, despotic, and violent—Russia's 2022 invasion of Ukraine offers just the latest painful reminder, if one was needed.[56] And even as the status quo already represents all the things that people fear about planetary institutions, it is simultaneously unable to manage planetary problems. An uninhabitable planet is its own form of oppression and injustice. The problems of the current system, however, do not reduce the need for planetary institutions to be effective and accountable. Both attributes are necessary if these new institutions are to be legitimate.

Lost in broadsides against supranational governance is the possibility that binding ourselves in the service of planetary cooperation could represent an *expansion*, not limitation, of democratic possibilities. The thought is counterintuitive, since international organizations are often believed to undermine national democracies. Yet under some conditions international organizations have been found to strengthen domestic democracy.[57] What's more, handing over authority and responsibility for managing planetary challenges frees democratic (and, for that matter, nondemocratic) polities to contend with issues that they are practically able to address—a point originally made by Pope Pius XI in his 1931 case for subsidiarity, as we discussed in chapter 4. Rather than wasting time, resources, and democratic-participatory energy trying to solve problems with institutions that are unfit for purpose, planetary institutions supported by planetary politics will free national and subnational democratic publics and officials to focus on issues within their effective spans of control.

The status quo also provides a benchmark for judging what characteristics planetary institutions should adopt. Coming from a world centered on the sovereign national state, analysts tend to hold supranational and global governance institutions up to the ideal of the sovereign state. But that ideal, as we've demonstrated, is a myth. Rather than focus on absolute sovereignty or total control of coercion, we are better off thinking about states as they actually exist: political institutions that exercise "some degree of authoritative, binding rule making, backed up by some organized physical force."[58] This more temperate, empirically honest view of existing institutions of governance rightly suggests that there is a spectrum of compliance that we can expect from any governor, whether or not we call it a state. Governing institutions, whether states or not, need not gain complete obedience from their population. (Indeed, we don't desire states that demand and obtain complete obedience: states with no toleration for deviation are rightly condemned as totalitarian.) Rather, by setting the agenda, standards, and rules, and implementing some form of enforcement, successful governance institutions can gain (imperfect) compliance. This focus on the degree of authoritative and enforceable rule-making—rather than the black-and-white distinction between authoritative/unauthoritative and enforceable/unenforceable—points to a more productive way to think about planetary institutions.

As an interim step, we could imagine that legacy governance institutions still play a role in planetary-scale governance. For example, decisions by planetary institutions could be subject to oversight by the UN General Assembly, perhaps weighted by the size of the human population in each national state. While this would be a more national state–centric model than is ideal from a planetary perspective, it could help establish the legitimacy of the decisions made by the PAS, the PPA, and other planetary institutions. In this way, the UN General Assembly would serve a transitional function akin to the role played by the House of Lords in the United Kingdom in the twentieth century: a mechanism for acknowledging the old order, giving it the power to slow controversial decisions by the newly empowered institutions, and thus to legitimate those decisions in the eyes of those still wedded to the incumbency. As a sop to the old anthropocentric and nationalist order of things, the UN could in this guise serve then as a kind of "court of last resort" for humans opposed to the decisions of planetary institutions. Such interim mechanisms could help endow planetary institutions with legitimate political authority.

Debating Design Choices

Let's imagine that planetary institutions in the form here envisaged are eventually created. We already foresee several design challenges to planetary institutions that may emerge. Addressing these challenges and debating the questions they raise must be part of the process of getting to a planetary future. But in the course of making reforms and compromises, planetary institutions can't lose sight of their central pursuit: ensuring a habitable planet and multispecies flourishing. These goals and the institutionalized means to achieve them can never be negotiated away. Planetary institutions' core mission must always be to strive to create the conditions on Earth where other attractive pursuits are possible.

The first potential design limitation is that, in our desire to avoid the risks associated with a single, centralized world government, we have instead designed a scheme that is excessively siloed or fragmented. The idea that each planetary challenge should have its own planetary institution—the PAS for climate change, the PPA for pandemics, an institution on biodiversity, another for space junk, and so on—opens the way to coordination problems, overlapping mandates, and turf wars, challenges familiar to the operations of any multifold bureaucracy. We believe, however, that the benefits of separate governance institutions for different planetary challenges outweigh the challenges. For one, specialized institutions foreground and privilege the expertise necessary for effective planetary governance. What's more, we believe that narrowly tailored institutions that are focused on specific problems can help avoid the mission creep that is common in bureaucratic organizations, most infamously the European Union. Each institution, therefore, could carry out its epistemic and political mandates with regard to the issue under its authority. The various planetary institutions would be expected to collaborate and coordinate their work (with disputes resolved by the subsidiarity assembly, as proposed in chapter 4), but some amount of redundancy might even be preferable, given our priority is effectiveness rather than efficiency.[59] Narrow tailoring allows each planetary institution to work in a way that is appropriate to the challenge at hand. Smaller, differentiated institutions are easier to change over time in response to the changing nature of the challenge itself (and to our changing understanding of it) and in response to the work of other planetary and subplanetary institutions.

Even if our proposal isn't as cohesive or all-encompassing as the idea of a world government, we are still suggesting planet-wide authorities on specific issues. A second risk to our design, then, is that centralized authority of any kind entails centralizing opportunities for corruption and elite capture. The fossil fuel industry, for instance, will know exactly where to place pressure. The simple reply is that under the current system, the fossil fuel industry already knows exactly where to direct its influence and has done so quite effectively. Criticizing the status quo, however, doesn't supplant the need to minimize the risks of corruption and capture in planetary institutions. For this reason, it is critical that each institution establish transparent political processes for decision-making. Transparency is one way to build trust with the public and demonstrate that the institution's internal workings are for the planet's benefit. Problems posed by centralization are additionally mitigated by the application of planetary subsidiarity, which limits centralization to just the absolutely necessary decision rights. All other authority would be diffused among smaller-scale governing institutions.

A third design risk is that planetary institutions could run into problems resulting from their technocratic predilections. The urgency of planetary sapience for planetary governance means that the leadership and staff of planetary institutions must have the relevant technical expertise. This is an unapologetic call for empowering technocracy, a bad word on the left and the right. The political opposition stems, in part, from the fact that technocratic rule is too often antidemocratic and insulated from popular accountability. And there are real problems with the way that technical experts make major decisions in a manner that leaves no room for debate about their means or ends. But to our mind, it's self-evidently preferable—in terms of both functional outcome and democratic norms—to have the PAS making decisions about the optimal level of atmospheric greenhouse gases than national leaders, whether elected or installed, who actively oppose planetary habitability and multispecies flourishing. In short, it is better to give these decisions to planetary technocrats than to Donald Trump, Vladimir Putin, Jair Bolsonaro, and Mohammed bin Salman Al Saud.[60]

Nevertheless, it's important to design planetary institutions in ways that minimize the downsides of technocracy. Scientific expertise must be central to the operation of planetary institutions, but this cannot be an excuse to ignore politics. The institutions must be simultaneously technical and political.[61] Yet the marriage of technocratic competence and participatory feedback is as uneasy as it is necessary. One way planetary institutions could navigate this rocky terrain is by integrating processes that foster structured dialogues among experts and the public at all stages of the policy process. This iterative process between scientific analysis and popular engagements, often called analytic deliberation, harnesses the knowledges and values of both experts and the wider public to reach decisions that have been found to have enhanced legitimacy and quality.[62] A well-designed participatory mechanism at the planetary scale will also create space for a plurality of epistemologies, including indigenous and national traditions. The provision, explanation, and consideration of scientific information that is part of the analytic-deliberative process is part of broadening planetary sapience.

Emerging democratic methods provide another path to bridge technical expertise and popular input. In particular, citizens' assemblies, where members of the public from a wide range of backgrounds gather and deliberate on issues of concern, offer a technique for putting experts in dialogue with representatives of the public. Citizens' assemblies often receive information and arguments from expert consultations that put the selected citizens in a better position to make decisions about technical matters. While experts help frame the issues and synthesis relevant information, the "mini-public" made up of "average" (nonexpert, nonpolitician) citizens deliberates and decides on its own. A planetary citizens' assembly like this could advise, supervise, or even direct each planetary institution.[63]

"Smart democracy," a proposal by Zhao based on the thought of Jizi, a twelfth-century BCE Chinese politician, is an alternative method of accounting for both expert and public views. The idea is to make decisions with the consent of both the population and scientific experts. In a two-step process, the general public would first vote for their preferred policies from an array of options, and then two scientific committees (one of natural scientists and one of humanities scholars) would vote to accept or reject the public's result. Zhao gives the experts' views more weight than the population's, but each group plays an important political role: "The people have the independent power to decide the *desirable*, and the scientific committees have an independent power to decide the *feasible*."[64] In effect, the public moves first and the experts have veto powers. We can also envision the process reversed, so that momentum rests with the body of scientific experts and a body representing the public has consultation or veto rights.

A fourth area of design risk stems from the potential lack of attention to the question of how planetary institutions can legitimate themselves. Undoubtedly, much attention will need to be put into thinking about how to legitimate these planetary institutions, particularly insofar as their actions will often be about preventing long-term harms at the cost of liberties and enjoyments in the present—never a particularly popular mandate. Effectiveness, while necessary, is itself not sufficient to legitimate the institutions. Transparency in decision-making will also be crucial. So too will be the creation of mechanisms for appeal and redress. Those making decisions at planetary institutions, no matter how expert and honest, won't be infallible, and there will have to be ways to review and roll back unwise decisions.

A fifth critique of our institutional design might be that it puts aside or tables issues of justice or equality. While it's true that our proposal doesn't address these significant issues, neither does the existing international system. The world's existing political structures aren't equal, just, or peaceful. They're often the opposite. There's no reason to think planetary institutions will be any worse than the status quo on these questions—and arguably they might even make improvements easier to achieve. One might predict that attaining global equality, justice, or peace would be easier in the shadow of planetary institutions, with a robust planetary politics and growing planetary identities. Moreover, reordering the world's governance system provides a chance to address many of the inequalities baked into the current system. Recasting the architecture of the current system of global governance opens the possibility of building the new system on more just, equal, and democratic foundations.

Many other details will have to be worked out in the development of planetary institutions, and the outcomes will emerge from political conflict. For example, how will these institutions be funded? Who will staff these institutions? How do we ensure proper representation for different stakeholder and interest groups in staff, leadership, and decision-making processes? What languages will the institutions use? We hope that the discussions in this chapter will open intellectual and political space for asking questions like these and debating possible answers.

———

Planetary institutions are a crucial element of the overall architecture for planetary governance, but they are only one part. The roles for planetary institutions that we propose can't be understood apart from the larger architecture of planetary subsidiarity in which they are meant to be embedded. Planetary institutions both emerge from and are constrained by the principle of planetary subsidiarity, which states that authority over an issue should be allocated to the smallest-scale unit that can govern the issue effectively to achieve habitability and multispecies flourishing. The smallest scale at which planetary issues can be effectively governed is the planet itself, which justifies the creation of planetary institutions. At the same time, the principle dictates all other issues should be governed at smaller scales.

Both pieces of planetary institutions' dual mandate—to enrich planetary sapience and to manage planetary challenges—are taken up by planetary institutions only because they can't be performed effectively by smaller-scale institutions. Yet this doesn't imply that planetary institutions have no role to play at smaller scales of governance—to the contrary. The many scales of administrations must all cooperate and collaborate for the architecture as a whole to work. In particular, planetary institutions must provide assistance to the smaller-scale units that require or request it. Planetary institutions are there to help smaller-scale units achieve planetary objectives set by the planetary institutions and, importantly, to help them achieve their own preferred objectives within the planet-wide framework. For instance, smaller-scale institutions, such as municipalities, often don't have the data and expertise to pursue their goals effectively. Collecting and expertly interpreting data is, of course, one of the principal functions of planetary institutions. So planetary institutions must provide decision support to smaller-scale institutions, giving them the tools to seek locally defined flourishing.[65] Though planetary institutions operate on the vastest scale, their highest end is to provide the conditions for the situated thriving of ordinary life and ordinary lives.

Subsidiarity, however, isn't just a check on the power of larger-scale authorities, including planetary institutions. It also defines a positive role for planetary institutions as the governance authorities responsible for the habitability of Earth that enables multispecies flourishing. This central purpose of planetary institutions requires limiting the autonomy of other units. All scales are interconnected, so decisions made at the planetary scale will have ramifying effects on other levels of the architecture, including the imposition of constraints. Moreover, planetary decisions will have differential effects that will be perceived, correctly, as helping or hurting some more than others. This is where agonism is unavoidable, and a planetary politics becomes necessary.

Creating the conditions necessary for full lives with the freedom to seek diverse ends demands limits on some of those ends. This could be seen as a paradox or as a trade-off, but in fact the two points are consistent. Planetary institutions must restrict the choices of smaller-scale units so that these communities can pursue a wide range of choices. Meaningful autonomy in a planetary age requires relinquishing the barbarous relic of absolute state sovereignty. No one can flourish on an uninhabitable planet. Planetary institutions must set ground rules in order for the good life, defined in myriad diverse ways, to be within reach for any and all of Earth's living beings.

Conclusion

How Hard to Stretch Imagination

In early 1940, the English poet W. H. Auden, having emigrated to the United States a year earlier, endeavored to take stock of his new circumstances. In New York City, an ocean away from the catastrophic war heating up among the national states in what he called "torn Old Europe," Auden composed a 1,700-line "New Year Letter" in verse to his friend Elizabeth Mayer (though with the intention of making it available "to all / Who wish to read it anywhere"). "Under the familiar weight / Of winter, conscience and the State," he began, and from there, the intricate epistle takes off, running lyrically through ruminations on life, literature, ideas, and politics.[1]

Near the opening of Part II, the poet turns from conjuring a cold, dark landscape—a "barren heath / Where the rough mountain track divides / To silent valleys on all sides"—to reflect on the place of humanity in the vast, post-Einsteinian universe. He writes:

> How hard it is to set aside
> Terror, concupiscence and pride,
> Learn who and where and how we are,
> The children of a modest star,

Frail, backward, clinging to the granite
Skirts of a sensible old planet,
Our placid and suburban nurse
In SITTER's swelling universe,
How hard to stretch imagination
To live according to our station.[2]

In five staccato couplets inspired by scientific advances that were progressively dethroning humanity's central place in the universe, Auden punctures human arrogance and places our condition on Earth in proper perspective. We're nothing more than "frail, backward" creatures, "clinging" to the third planet orbiting the Sun.[3]

The last two lines are a call to action, and seeming modesty, urging us to think creatively about out how "to live according to our station." But these lines, in a different light, can be read as almost the contrary claim: not as a challenge to live small, humble lives, but to "stretch [our] imagination" to envision audacious futures. For "our station" isn't just as late-stage hominids but as a geological force. In the language we have developed in this book, learning "who and where and how we are" entails recognizing that humans are both embedded in the biogeochemistry of the Earth and a force multiplier that is changing the planet in indelible ways. Living "according to our station" means living consistently with the condition of planetarity, and that means stretching to imagine new ways of organizing life on planet Earth. The real challenge now is holding on to the modesty urged by Auden while also imagining bold new plans for planetary governance.

This book is our response to that challenge. A multiscalar governance architecture with robust institutions ranging from planet-wide to hyperlocal, we argue, provides the basis for planetary governance consistent with the condition of planetarity. Within that architecture, the principle of planetary subsidiarity guides the allocation of authority and decision rights to the most appropriate institutional scale. This dynamic model of governance is the best structure for fostering political pluralism while ensuring multispecies flourishing and the planet's habitability. We come to this conclusion on the basis of growing planetary sapience. Understanding that living matter, nonliving matter, and energy flow over and around the planet—with total disregard for humanity's beloved and bedeviling political boundaries—means that the old order of sovereign national states must be radically reconsidered.

A Statement of Principles

Behind our proposal lie five ethical and architectural principles that we believe planetary governance should work to instantiate. Some of these principles are means and others are ends. Some are seemingly utopian, others are more practical. Some have been alluded to throughout the book, while others are first articulated here. Together they form the basis for a constructive planetary governance.

Enabling Multispecies Flourishing

A thriving biosphere is the sine qua non of everything else. Anything that humans might want on and of this planet requires healthy, diverse living matter (in the sense that Vernadsky used the term: the totality of life on Earth). The commitment to multispecies flourishing must be sincere—at some level there must be an ethical obligation to our fellow living beings, from protozoa and rhizomic fungi to dolphins and chimpanzees. We should be awed by the dizzying menagerie wrought by billions of years of evolution. This planetary inheritance is precious: as best we know, it has happened only here. Disrupting ecosystems, eliminating species, and shrinking the planet's gene pool must be understood as the monstrous harms that they are. Even the Earth's climate requires less time than biodiversity to reach homeostasis after it's perturbed: "Catastrophes of the past show us that biodiversity recovers only on timescales of tens of millions of years," as geochemists Charles H. Langmuir and Wally Broecker note, "and some ancient innovations may never be recovered."[4]

A flourishing multispecies "society," moreover, is the bedrock of Earth's habitability. Maintaining a habitable planet requires stable ecosystems, which require diverse forms of life. Planetary sapience has revealed that the biosphere is an ecosystem of ecosystems, nested, interlocking, interacting communities of biotic and abiotic matter. From the planet to each individual human being, systems of living systems sustain life. The parts sustain the whole, and the whole sustains the parts. And so, a thriving biosphere is necessary for the blooming of all life, including human life.

From a human perspective, this is a rather good thing. We are part of and entirely reliant on the biosphere (the same could be said for any earthly organism). The oxygenated air we breathe and the food we eat are all products of the biosphere. But it isn't enough to care about the plants and animals we consume or find beautiful or interesting or cute. Each life form, good, bad, or ugly, is integral to the overall health of the biosphere. As the philosopher Achille Mbembe puts it, "The epoch we have entered into is one of indivisibility, of entanglement, of concatenations."[5] It's the biosphere *as a whole system* that sustains human life and enables human flourishing. Even from a selfish, human-centric point of view, multispecies flourishing is essential.

Human flourishing, however, comes in many shapes and forms. They all require a thriving biosphere, but from there they can go in all sorts of different directions. Humanity is diverse. There are many ways to live, many things to like, many desires to hold, many disgusts to avoid—in other words, many ways to flourish. There is no getting around these diversities; they are a fact of life, and a beautiful one at that. Attempts to eliminate diversities often fail or are morally indefensible (typically, the more successful they are at homogenizing a society, the less morally defensible they are). Rather, we must embrace pluralism. Tolerating difference is on its own a good goal, but it is, furthermore, the only way to manage the immense variety found among the eight billion human beings living on one interconnected planet.

Enhancing Planetary Sapience

"Humanity currently sits at a precipice," declared a 2022 article in the *International Journal of Astrobiology*: "our collective actions clearly have global consequences, but we are not yet in control of those consequences." Our ability to recognize this precipice, argue scientists Adam Frank, David Grinspoon, and Sara Walker, is the result of emerging planetary intelligence. The problem is that this emerging intelligence isn't yet actually intelligent. Earth now has what they describe as an "immature technosphere," meaning that the human population's activities (including the activities of human-made technologies) produce inadvertent planetary-scale interventions and feedbacks. What Earth needs instead is a "mature technosphere," which makes intentional planetary-scale interventions, supporting and directing beneficial feedback mechanisms.[6] This transition entails intensifying planetary sapience.

Planetary sapience is the lodestar of planetary governance. Increasing the breadth and depth of scientific knowledge about Earth provides the knowledge, understanding, even wisdom necessary for making self-aware, purposeful decisions to promote multispecies flourishing and habitability on a planet-wide scale. As such, it's an endless goal: our earthly knowledge will always be provisional, and there will always be more to learn. But the limitlessness of planetary sapience shouldn't be seen as a burden that is necessary only for the sake of competent planetary governance. Seeking planetary sapience is fundamentally good and emancipatory. There is virtue—even beauty, as Keats famously wrote—in pursuing truth.

The quest for planetary sapience may touch something deep within us, but that doesn't mean we are born equipped for it. Just as we must be taught to be good friends and good national citizens (spend time with a toddler if you think there's anything inherent about behaving well toward friends), we must be taught to become good planetary caretakers.[7] Education will thus play a crucial role in the enhancement of planetary sapience. Planetary education with both scientific and civic aspects in and of itself leads to improved planetary sapience, since wider-spread understanding of the condition of planetarity is a component of planetary sapience. Students should learn about Earth and the condition of planetarity and be instructed in planetary civics, including the ethical commitment to and empirical requirements for multispecies flourishing and habitability. Instead of focusing only on national histories, students should also study our planet's natural history, and especially be taught about the science and engineering underpinning growing planetary sapience.

Such Earth-oriented education will reflexively improve the technical apparatus of planetary sapience by training the next generations of scientific innovators and operators. An early start to planetary education (starting in primary school rather than late in high school or even university, which is when students typically encounter these ideas, if at all) will expand the base of capable technicians, engineers, and scientists—as well as informed political leaders and the members of the public. The commitment to planetary education, moreover, must be global in scope. It is unjust and self-defeating to open the door to careers in planetary governance and sapience only to people with means and access to elite schools. Producing as many planetary caretakers and governors as we need requires a broad and equitable commitment to planetary education.

As a practical step toward planetary sapience in the present, we also urge the people who already work in the field to *recognize* their work as being about enhancing planetary sapience. Everyone from Earth systems scientists to sensor technicians to primary school educators has a role. This new professional identity could provide new purpose and meaning to one's work, but it also provides a new lens with which to understand it. Adopting this perspective may open connections to other scientific fields that aren't immediately identifiable. Other holistic conceptual frameworks, such as One Health, are already working on knitting together disparate disciplines and approaches in a planetary direction, and we can only encourage more of this.[8] As part of this process, the people already doing the work of planetary sapience enhancement should form global networks with each other, exchanging ideas and information and forming political alliances for the purpose of further planetary sapience.[9]

Improving Institutional Effectiveness and Legitimacy

We believe in institutions (in case that wasn't yet clear). They are necessary for organizing large-scale, complex populations and for solving common problems. But that doesn't mean that we believe in just any institution. An institution's present-day power or longevity interests us far less than its effectiveness and legitimacy. And today, many of the powerful, legacy institutions are neither wholly effective nor adequately legitimate.

One politically prominent response to this predicament is to try to demolish the existing governance institutions and replace them with markets. Another is to enfeeble or co-opt institutions to the personal aggrandizement of already powerful and well-connected elites (a strategy that is distinct but not mutually exclusive from the first). Still another is to reject the hierarchies inherent in institutions and to prize parity over results. Perhaps the dominant response is to ignore the problem and hope that the anti–status quo insurgents go away. None of these are viable response to the challenges of a planetary age.

The institutions that govern today are breaking or already broken. That is an indictment of the current institutional system, not institutions in toto. Our existing governance institutions flail and fail because they aren't fit for purpose. They were created to address a different set of challenges than the ones we now face. These new challenges—planetary challenges—are difficult. Some are existential. Managing them will require capable institutions that govern effectively and with recognized legitimacy. There must be a commitment to effective and legitimate governance, from the planet to the hyperlocal.

Much work remains to envision, design, and build institutions of this caliber. The good news is that many of the tools already exist: lots of people think deeply and creatively about governance and governing institutions, and lots of people understand and are pushing the frontier of our understanding about the condition of planetarity. We need to unite them with a common purpose and encourage them to develop further together. This means breaking down the barriers that silo ideas and experiences about governance and the planet. We urge people who work in the field of governance—policymakers, analysts, journalists, and more—to consider the Planetary when making plans, decisions, and assessments. Yet it's important that this doesn't just become the domain of the elite. Engaged citizens, too, should start judging decisions and events with a new lens: not the national interest, but the planet's interest. Likewise, we urge people who study the condition of planetarity—scientists and philosophers, in the main—to move beyond the comfortable realm of technical papers and critique and into the messy, power-laden realm of solutions and institutions. Both governance experts and planetary experts have ideas and insights that are necessary for developing new modes of effective and legitimate governance. Drawing both areas of expertise into a common intellectual space is vital to develop the needed creative solutions.

Finally, it will also be essential to integrate the many burgeoning networks of activists and nongovernmental organizations that are working on environmental matters, not least to convince them that the condition of planetarity requires seeing the problems they work on in holistic terms. Projects like low-carbon mass transit systems cannot be blocked to protect a single snake, nor water systems to protect a single fish, nor solar farms to protect a single fox.[10] This is by no means an argument against the protection of biodiversity or a prejudgment that every green transition project is worth the costs. But taking the condition of planetarity seriously means weighing the interests of the planet as a whole, as against the interests of any particular part. Scientifically rooted planetary sapience, rather than mystical intuitions (often suspiciously aligned with NIMBY inclinations), must guide decision-making in the interest of multispecies flourishing.

Transforming the Nature of Statehood

As we outlined in chapter 1, the national state is a relatively recent political form that only since the 1960s has become globally hegemonic as *the* form for governing territory and populations. But just because the national state is of recent vintage doesn't make it easily displaceable. Institutions are sticky. Many of the problems of institutional effectiveness and political legitimacy we now face result from the fact that once institutions (especially powerful ones) are in place, they tend to be difficult to dislodge or even to meaningfully reform. The transition to planetary subsidiarity won't take place overnight. It will be a contested, political process that will unfold over time. And change is likely to come from the outside, led by people with out-of-the-box ideas.

Preemptively demolishing existing institutions would be short-sighted and dangerous. Myths and memory are powerful political forces, and contemporary political imaginations remain enthralled by the trinitarian model of governance, sovereignty, and the national state. National states have an important transitional role to play. The establishment of planetary subsidiarity doesn't mean the end of national states, but rather a dramatic if not unprecedented evolution in the nature of statehood. National states should become administrators of planetary directives. In this role, national states will play a specific function as the scale of governance tasked with making distributional decisions. In the administration of, say, planetary rules for reducing carbon emissions, national states will decide how to allocate the economic consequences of decarbonization within their jurisdiction. National states will also be charged with supporting incipient planetary institutions, subnational institutions, translocal networks, and linkages between the governance scales.

Some of this is already happening. National governments routinely support the subnational institutions within their borders, like cities and provinces or states. Some national governments already actively contribute to translocal networks. The C40 Network, for instance, counts three national governments (UK, Germany, and Denmark) among their major funders.[11] The US State Department's new Special Representative for City and State Diplomacy is actively engaged in building the capacity for more effective international partnerships among American cities and states, and in the next phases of its work should extend this capacity building to subnational actors in other parts of the world. Building this mesh of translocal institutions will help to address the challenges that low-capacity states and regions may face as they implement solutions in the service of planetary governance.

Ongoing planetary initiatives often have national governments behind them. In particular, many national states support multinational scientific programs that are central components of the existing planetary sapience infrastructure, such as NASA's planetary defense system, NOAA's Global Monitoring Laboratory, and the EU's Copernicus program of Earth-monitoring satellites. We urge national governments to expand their support for all these scientific institutions, embracing them not as rivals but as complements and fellow travelers to a better-governed world.

Rather than being the focal point of rule, national states will come to be seen as just one element in the multiscalar system. While undergoing this transition is a lot to ask of any institution, it's worth reiterating that in practice the relationship between governance and the national state is already much attenuated since its much-mythologized mid-twentieth-century apex. National states do govern (though some more than others) many domains of collective life (though some more than others), but governance is a social practice that is conceptually and practically distinct from the national state. Governance takes place without sovereign national states, and vice versa. Our proposition is to move this haphazard governance patchwork into a purposeful governance architecture: from the actually existing ad hoc multilevel governance structure that allocates authority based on the principle of national state sovereignty to a *deliberate multiscalar governance structure* that allocates authority based on the principle of *planetary subsidiarity*.

Rethinking Sovereignty, Rights, and Responsibilities

Decoupling governance and the national state shouldn't be very controversial; it's a fact of life. Decoupling sovereignty and the national state, by contrast, is widely seen as a mad proposition. But this is precisely what planetary subsidiarity entails. Subsidiarity and absolute sovereignty are rival principles.[12] They put forward incompatible visions of political organization. This, for us, is a feature, not a bug, of subsidiarity, because sovereignty needs to be fundamentally rethought in light of our emergent awareness of the condition of planetarity.

It seems impossible today to imagine that sovereignty would pass from the national state to some other entity, or that it might be radically reimagined. But sovereignty has been transformed and relocated many times throughout history. What seems natural and unalterable about today's sovereignty arrangements was, just a few hundred years ago, considered at least as utopian as what we are proposing in this book might seem to some today. To have proposed in Europe in 1715 that sovereignty be formally vested in the people rather than in the monarch would have seemed preposterous. Yet over the course of the eighteenth century, the concept of sovereignty was reconstructed in both principle and practice on those lines. By the late 1780s, revolutions in America and France put the once-outrageous theory of popular sovereignty into action: the Americans had made "We the People" the ultimate source and bearer of legitimate authority, and the French had declared, "The principle of any Sovereignty lies primarily in the Nation. No corporate body, no individual may exercise any authority that does not expressly emanate from it."[13]

The transformation of sovereignty in the early modern North Atlantic both reflected and accelerated a transfiguration in centuries-old political modalities. Under the model of monarchical sovereignty, the rule over populations and territories was conducted in ways that became inconceivable under the popular model. The Habsburg dynasty was famous for its conjugal conquests throughout Europe, which is how the head of the royal household ended up with the tedious title "Emperor of Austria; King of Hungary and Bohemia, King of Lombardy

and Venetia, of Dalmatia, Croatia, Slavonia, Galicia, Lodomeria and
Illyria; Archduke of Austria; Grand Duke of Tuscany; Duke of Lor-
raine, of Salzburg, Styria, Carinthia, Carniola..."[14] Today, by contrast,
it's impossible to imagine territory, citizenship, or governance decision
rights transferring hands via dynastic marriages. There are still monarchical regimes, particularly in the Middle East. But there are many
more royal families that sit on a throne that is constrained by constitutional government; sovereignty, in these cases, has been detached from
governance. The king of the United Kingdom, for instance, remains
the sovereign. But though he is the head of state, Charles III does not
govern. Rather, the elected British government governs in his name.

An analogous arrangement for national state sovereignty is plausible under planetary subsidiarity. Given that absolutist national state
sovereignty is as appropriate to a world defined by the condition of
planetarity as absolute monarchy was to a world defined by popular
political participation, national states can remain technically sovereign
(perhaps remaining a focal point of a population's psycho-political en-
ergies, much as the House of Windsor continues to be for many Brits),
but they won't govern many of the issues that they do now. Sovereignty
can no longer be taken to mean the absolute right to exclude external
authority from one's own territory, as conventional Westphalian definitions of sovereignty often claim. Moreover, as international relations
scholar Stephen Krasner demonstrates, this definition of sovereignty
has anyway always been at best a polite fiction, mainly honored in the
breach. Given what the condition of planetarity exposes about our in-
eradicable interdependence with nonhuman others, from microbes to
the planet itself, it's high time we dispensed with this anthropocentric
form of "organized hypocrisy."[15]

Under the conditions of intense global interconnectedness marked
by globalization, scholars of sovereignty already in the late twentieth
century observed that the classical model no longer applied. As the
international lawyers Abram Chayes and Antonia Handler Chayes
argued in 1995, the traditional understanding of sovereignty as "the
complete autonomy of the state to act as it chooses" doesn't describe

the condition of states in the complex and interdependent international system of a globalized world. In such a world, they posit, sovereignty has taken on a new meaning: it consists of "membership in reasonably good standing in the regimes that make up the substance of international life. . . . In today's setting, the only way most states can realize and express their sovereignty is through participation in the various regimes that regulate and order the international system."[16] This is correct but doesn't go far enough. Sovereignty today can't merely account for global interdependence among national states, it must account for planetary interdependence among all vital systems.

Zhao Tingyang's idea of "world sovereignty" is worth considering in this regard. "Although world sovereignty is greater than national sovereignty, it doesn't negate national sovereignty," he argues. "Rather, it serves as a sort of external limit on any national sovereignty." In his view, the two forms of sovereignty are congruent parts of "one body," in which "the internal politics of national states would still fall under the auspices of national sovereignty, but . . . political problems external to nation-states . . . and everything that concerns the collective fate of humanity would fall under the domain of world sovereignty."[17] Alternative reconstructions of the concept are found among advocates of "green sovereignty." International relations theorist Daniel Deudney, for instance, argues that the "emergent global village" requires a "terrapolitan" conception of sovereignty, meaning that "the central basis of political association . . . must be the Earth (terra) and its requirements." This form of sovereignty belongs to an "intergenerational public," and political institutions, therefore, must mediate across time, preventing "the living from altering the planet in ways that are inconsistent with the fundamental interests of the sovereign, the international public."[18] We raise both Zhao's and Deudney's redefinitions of sovereignty, not necessarily to endorse them, but to suggest emerging alternatives to the absolutist conception of Westphalian state sovereignty.

At its philosophical heart, sovereignty is about communities having the freedom to pursue their own ends. It is a form of liberty. But liberty has two faces, as the philosopher Isaiah Berlin observed in a famous lecture from 1958. There is "negative liberty," or "freedom from," and "positive liberty," or "freedom to." The former is the ability to "act unobstructed by others," while the latter is the ability to pursue self-mastery.[19] The traditional notion of sovereignty, as developed from the sixteenth century onwards, is a form of negative liberty: sovereignty as freedom from external interference. This idea arose to cope with and order a European world where the primary concern was the threat of coercion by other states. As a result, states can appeal to their sovereignty to act as they please. Following Berlin, we can call this old model *negative sovereignty.*

Negative sovereignty breaks down under the planetary conditions. Just as negative liberty is an incomplete accounting of what it means to be free, negative sovereignty doesn't make one fully sovereign. The purpose of sovereignty isn't merely to be free to pursue whatever ends one wishes. Any sovereignty worth having must enable a community to achieve its ends. And under conditions of planetary interdependence, achieving vital goals can't be achieved unilaterally. It requires cooperation; something to which negative sovereignty is often an obstacle. In other words, the management of planetary issues demands a new understanding of sovereignty, a *positive sovereignty.*

Positive sovereignty is the idea that communities should be able to seek their own diverse ends, to flourish and thrive, on a planet where many of the most important phenomena are indifferent to human concerns or boundaries. Self-mastery under such circumstances, the ability to achieve desired outcomes, necessitates the limitation of the negative sovereignty of national states. It requires diminishing the purported right of all national states to say "no," and elevating the right to force antiplanetary states to act in alignment with planetary interests. We need a new sovereignty that serves the planet and its populations, even if that means curtailing the decision-making authority of national states.

Whereas the primary concern for theorists of negative sovereignty was the threat posed by other states, the primary threat today emanates, not from states, but from planetary challenges. Negative sovereignty can provide protection against states impinging on other states' autonomy, but it doesn't provide protection against planetary challenges. Given that planetary challenges aren't self-contained within any state, the action of one state can affect all others—the atmospheric carbon and viruses travel, indifferent to border guards. Acceptance of planetary limits, which are biogeochemical in nature, springs from "incapacity," in Berlin's terms, not "coercion."[20] By contrast, having less freedom to act on planetary issues makes states freer to pursue their diverse ends. Thus limitations on negative sovereignty for planetary issues don't curtail liberty; they *enable* it.

A principal defense of the sovereign national state is the argument that individuals gain rights only when they are members of a political community and that the best and only political community for enforcing rights in the modern world is the state.[21] We agree that human beings deserve rights and political communities to enforce them. Hannah Arendt remains correct that it is a "calamity" to be deprived of "a right to have rights" via membership in a political community.[22] But this "right to belong" is not inconsistent with the need for certain limitations or required actions regarding planetary problems. A planetary institution managing greenhouse gas emissions or pandemic disease outbreaks doesn't infringe on or abrogate individuals' rights (or duties) gained via membership in a subplanetary political community. Moreover, planetary institutions would represent only a mild encroachment on the self-determination of communities, since implementation details would be largely left to smaller-scale institutions. And, it's worth underlining, individuals will also lose a right to have rights if and when the planet becomes uninhabitable.

That monarchs have remained sovereigns in so many places where they no long rule isn't accidental. The concept of sovereignty, particularly absolute sovereignty, is interlaced with monarchical attitudes. And though the idea is now embraced around the world, it's a Eurocentric holdover from the era of absolute monarchy. Instead of venerating this remnant of king-worship, we should think instead of *planetary rights and responsibilities*.

Unanswered Questions

This book is a call to action. But before a new world order can be constructed, many more details must be worked out. In particular, many questions about the practical design and operation of planetary institutions require answers. A noncomprehensive list of unresolved, pressing dilemmas includes the following.

How will planetary institutions, and the broader system of planetary subsidiarity, be funded? International efforts often collapse over the funding issues. It's all well and good for national states to agree to support, say, global climate change adaptation, but when it comes time to pay up, they balk. As a result, many international organizations are chronically underfunded and are unable to fulfill their mandate. The WHO is emblematic of this problem. Developing mechanisms for financing the governance architecture envisioned in the previous chapters is a vital, yet challenging, next step.

How will planetary institutions deal with noncompliance by smaller-scale governors? The question of enforcement is critical to any governance arrangement. How will planetary institutions get their way if other institutions are unwilling to carry out planetary imperatives? Relatedly, how will subplanetary institutions defend themselves from unjust overreach by planetary institutions? We aren't so naive as to think that severe conflicts among human beings will suddenly disappear. How will those conflicts be resolved, and how will the decisions be enforced? Put another way, what's the role of coercion in planetary subsidiarity? As one friend of ours has pressed repeatedly: Where are the guns?

How will planetary institutions deal with low-capacity governance institutions? The capacity of national and subnational institutions to perform their functions of governance varies dramatically. This fact poses a conundrum for planetary governance as we've conceived of it. On the one hand, planetary governance relies on institutions at all scales to carry out certain tasks necessary for multispecies flourishing and habitability. On the other hand, we don't expect the planetary governance architecture to engage in significant resource redistribution. Each principle seems individually necessary for plausible and effective planetary governance, but together they produce an unworkable system. How can we square this circle?

How will planetary institutions deal with capitalism? Or perhaps more pointedly, how will they resist the power of capital? Capitalism, at least in our industrial capitalist modernity, is clearly behind many planetary problems.[23] As a result, planetary institutions will have to make decisions that are at odds with the current winners of the capitalist system. But capital tends to enfeeble, co-opt, or skirt its governors, evacuating them of the power to govern. How can planetary institutions limit the power of capital to evade the rules it doesn't like?

How will planetary institutions interface with the existing international governance architecture? While planetary institutions would likely not replace the United Nations writ large (as the UN replaced the League of Nations), how do we minimize competition and maximize cooperation between the old multilateralist institutions—which are still needed to manage global issues and international relations, like war and trade—and the new planetary ones? Could relevant UN agencies be tweaked and incorporated into a new planetary governance regime, or should they be scrapped and built from scratch?

Who will staff planetary institutions? How will they be selected? How many should there be? To whom are they accountable? Personnel is policy, as the saying goes, so staffing can't be an afterthought. How can planetary institutions hire staff in ways that ensure quality and fairness, and reflect the human population of the planet—as well as represent the interests of nonhumans?

This book is a vision, not a blueprint. Thus we don't have the answers to all these questions. Instead, we aim to encourage debate and innovation to address them, in order to address the scale and scope of the challenge posed by the condition of planetarity.

Toward a Habitable Planet

It's worth considering what will happen if the seemingly unrealistic proposals for planetary institutional change of the sort we make here don't take place. There are three plausible scenarios for a future without planetary subsidiarity. (1) National states continue to hoard their sovereignty, planetary problems go unaddressed, and business as usual hums along: climate catastrophe, biodiversity collapse, recurrent pandemics with infectiousness and lethality that make us wistful for COVID-19.[24] (2) An authoritarian planetary hegemon (likely based in Beijing) emerges to bring order to the chaos.[25] (3) The status quo institutional matrix undertakes modest reforms—enhanced multilateral cooperation, for example—that prove to be sufficient. Perhaps the sustainability of national state system is given a boost by some unproven (and inevitably highly risky) technological Hail Mary paying off, making business as usual sustainable.[26] How realistic (to say nothing of democratic) is it to accept any of these alternatives?

In fact, as growing sapience of the condition of planetarity makes the scale of a planetary crisis increasingly apparent, all existing options—including most of all "do nothing"—seem patently unrealistic. This is why radically new thinking is required. Indeed, the most realistic (and ethical) thing to do today is precisely to think the unthinkable.

Even for those readers who might agree with our diagnosis and proposals, an inevitable question is: How do we get there from here? How, specifically, is it possible to overcome the pull of national interests and the jealous guardianship of the prerogatives of national sovereignty? We maintain candidly, as we have throughout, that we don't pretend to see a clear path to planetary governance today. Indeed, it may take a cataclysmic disaster to make possible the shift to planetary governance. The economist Milton Friedman was right in this regard: "Only a crisis—actual or perceived—produces real change," he wrote. "When that crisis occurs, the actions that are taken depend on the ideas that are lying around. That, I believe, is our basic function: to develop alternatives to existing policies, to keep them alive and available until the

politically impossible becomes politically inevitable."[27] The burden of
this book, then, is to argue for the kinds of institutions we should have,
so that if an opportunity arises for serious change, there will already be
a diagram of the sort of institutions and institutional architecture we
need.

That planetary governance's most likely birth is through disaster
is bleak, but of a piece with the history of major institutional reform.
Most, if not all, instances of significant changes to governance architecture, whether at the national level or the supranational, have typically
taken place only in or immediately after moments of existential crisis
or collapse of the existing institutional order. Institutions protect their
authority and power, and it's only when they're brought face to face
undeniably with their own limitations that they usually agree to cede
control. Crises in fact often midwife institutional creativity previously
thought risible. The basic idea behind the League of Nations and United
Nations, for instance, had been around for a long time (since at least
1795, when Immanuel Kant called for a "federation of nations" in his
philosophical sketch for "Perpetual Peace"), but it took the convulsions
of the two world wars for it to finally flower. Likewise, the creation of
the US Federal Reserve Bank went from a wild idea adamantly opposed
by private bankers to an institutional reality in the wake of the Panic
of 1907, which had very nearly produced a massive economic catastrophe. Similarly, it took the currency crises and stagflation of the 1970s
and 1980s to convince politicians across the Western world of the necessity of independent central banks focused on fighting inflation. We
don't wish for crises of these scales to occur, but planetary catastrophe
isn't hard to imagine. The heat wave that kills tens of millions of people
in the opening scene of Kim Stanley Robinson's 2020 cli-fi novel *The
Ministry for the Future* represents one scenario under which an effective planetary climate governance regime might emerge.[28] Should a
planetary calamity of such a scale unfold, the ideas in this book will be
available for those who seek to transform the architecture of planetary
management.

Yet even this grim account is perhaps too optimistic. Mainstream views of planetary crises, particularly climate change, present them as dystopias-to-come, in contrast to a supposedly "normal" Holocene past. For many of Earth's human inhabitants, by contrast, the present is *already* postapocalyptic. The imagined dystopian future of doom-sayers is already here. The work of indigenous thinkers, in particular, helps us situate the horrors of prospective planetary ruination as an already-experienced present—one that, alas, has prompted exactly zero national states to move in substantially new directions.[29] Indigenous epistemologies—for so long represented in many Western literatures as a relic from the past—in this sense are in fact exactly the reverse: an epistemology of the future. If the future is anything like the past, this doesn't bode well at all.

Complicating this already dire outlook, international politics is, as we write, at its darkest moment in recent memory. Great power rivalries have continuously intensified over the time that we've worked on this book. US-China relations are in a downward spiral, and Russia's war of territorial conquest in Ukraine represents a criminal and retrograde event. The consequences of renewed geopolitical tensions for the management of planetary problems can only be bad.

An era marked by a deteriorating relationship between great powers is admittedly an inopportune time to push for supranational cooperation. The US's attempt to pursue a dual-track, decoupled relationship with China—pushing for coordination on climate action and some other global public goods, while competing on trade, technology, and military might—has so far failed to bear fruit. But even if this American strategy eventually works, Beijing's view of its own future could prove debilitating for planetary cooperation. From Beijing's perspective, why would a self-perceived rising power want to sign up for planetary institutions now, when it could wait and then create such institutions on its own terms when it is in a stronger position in the future?

Take a step back, however, and these conflicts between national states tend to lose their present heat. Even the biggest, most serious questions that fuel present-day interhuman rivalries are tragicomically small when put in context of the planet, which creates the very possibility of even having them. Step back further, and human concerns begin to look even pettier. "The Earth is a very small stage in a vast cosmic arena," remarked the astronomer Carl Sagan, reflecting on the significance of a photograph of our planet taken by the *Voyager 1* spacecraft in 1990 from a distance of six billion kilometers. In that photo, which Sagan sagely commissioned, planet Earth appears in "a lonely pixel, hardly distinguishable from the many other points of light *Voyager* could see."[30]

> Think of the rivers of blood spilled by all those generals and emperors so that, in glory and triumph, they could become the momentary masters of a fraction of a dot. Think of the endless cruelties visited by the inhabitants of one corner of this pixel on the scarcely distinguishable inhabitants of some other corner, how frequent their misunderstandings, how eager they are to kill one another, how fervent their hatreds. . . . There is perhaps no better demonstration of the folly of human conceits than this distant image of our tiny world.[31]

We needn't leave Earth to gain some perspective. From the point of view of the bacteria in our microbiome, a virus seeking a new host, carbon compounds cycling through the atmosphere, water molecules churning through the oceans or falling from the clouds or sitting frozen in a glacier for millennia, our actions are meaningless. From the standpoint of mice and rats, pigeons and pangolins, deer and chimpanzees and alligators and elephants and whales, our interhuman prejudices are pointless—merely destructive. Even from the perspective of future humans, our present-day geopolitical competitions will be nothing but a historical curiosity.

Our descendants will care whether the planet we bequeath them is habitable, however. It will matter if the climate is stable, the oceans aren't clogged with plastic, habitats can support a diverse range of species, and nuclear radiation doesn't poison every living thing. In the long term, geopolitical tensions, ideological rivalries, economic growth, and everything else that occupies so much of collective thought and action will matter only to the extent that they benefit (or harm) the planet. Our politics must, in the end, promote planetary habitability.

We are not advocating the use of abstract claims about long-term planetary habitability to deprive fellow humans of what they need to thrive now.[32] This is not an argument for the Global North, which has primarily caused the present crises of habitability, to kick the ladder out from underneath the Global South, preventing billions of people from advancing their well-being or seeking justice. But it is an argument that these other imperatives must be pursued within a horizon defined by planetary habitability. We reject the claim, still made by some, that the Global South should get the right to the same destructive carbon-fueled, land-intensive, and generally exploitative growth that the North got. It may not be fair, but such a trajectory is no longer an option. The Global South deserves the fruits of growth, but they must be pursued via different energy and land use regimes—as, of course, must be the economic activities of the wealthier regions of the world. Restructuring global economic systems so that they are less rigged in favor of the winners will help foster these transitions.

"How hard it is to set aside" centuries of accumulated beliefs and desires about humanity and our place on this planet. But setting them aside is necessary if we—both "we" as humans, all humans, and "we" as living matter, the whole biosphere—are going to flourish on this "sensible old planet." The growing planetary sapience has enhanced our accounting of Earth, showing us how right Auden was. The advances in scientific understanding have an aesthetic quality in their revelation of the breathtaking complexity and interrelatedness of everything on this planet. In our day-to-day lives, we encounter only a tiny portion, and yet even this small slice consumes our waking hours. Our relentless focus on our sliver, in the grand scheme of things, obscures more than it illuminates. Observed from afar, the details fade away. Seen from space, planet Earth is an unbroken sphere—a blue and green celestial whole, orbiting a modest star.

Acknowledgments

For sharing their feedback, expertise, and wisdom; prodding us to consider new issues and take alternative perspectives; and sometimes telling us that an idea was just plain stupid (not that we always listened), we have lots of people to thank.

Our institutional home, the Berggruen Institute, played an enormous role in the life of this book. From its inception in 2010, the Institute has been dedicated to thinking about the intersection between governance and philosophy, and to cross-fertilizing these too-often segregated fields. This book is a direct reflection of those commitments. Thinking of the Planetary as not just a philosophical event but also a governance challenge began in conversations at the start of the COVID-19 pandemic with our colleagues Yakov Feygin and Tobias Rees and the Institute's leadership team. Nathan Gardels drew from his long experience in both practical politics and the journalism of ideas to keep us focused on the institutional realities of any form of planetary governance. Dawn Nakagawa's promotion of new models of political participation informed our thinking about how to integrate technocratic and democratic elements into new planetary institutions. Bing Song encouraged us to look at ideas in Eastern thought about the Planetary. Lorenzo Marsili got to many of these ideas first in his elegant little book *Planetary Politics: A Manifesto* (2021). Last but certainly not least,

Nicolas Berggruen made the book possible not only with his generosity but more importantly with his fearless dedication to supporting the exploration of new ideas, however wild.

Yakov Feygin and Claire Webb never failed to put us in our place with hard questions but were also infallibly supportive through the inevitable rigors of putting together a book. Yakov disagrees with much of our argument, which is what made him such a valuable intellectual sparring partner. Claire pushed us from the beginning to think capaciously about life on the planet and to make multispecies flourishing a core principle in the book. Benjamin Bratton contributed the key concept of planetary sapience. At *Noema* magazine, Kathleen Miles and Peter Mellgard helped sharpen our ideas when we published the first kernel of the book. In addition, a number of interviews that we conducted for *Noema* on the themes of this book proved highly generative for our thinking: thanks to Craig Calhoun, Dipesh Chakrabarty, Francis Fukuyama, Achille Mbembe, Tobias Rees, Anne-Marie Slaughter, and Roberto Mangabeira Unger for their time and ideas. Jade Clemons pressed us on some shortcomings in our argument and volunteered to help with the bibliographical apparatus. Joyce Jalleo made sure the trains ran on time.

The Institute also hosted many gatherings where the ideas in this book took shape. Particularly helpful at the outset of the project was the Planetary Governance Working Group—made up of Berggruen fellows, Los Angeles–based scholars, and friends from elsewhere who Zoomed in—who read early drafts of chapters 3 and 6, as well as the 2021 *Noema* essay where we first outlined our argument. Our thanks to both regulars and occasionals who joined us in downtown Los Angeles over the years: Aneesh Aneesh, Ziyaad Bhorat, Jenny Bourne, Dominic Boyer, Cameron Brinitzer, Inho Choi, Devika Dutt, Peter Ekman, Akhil Gupta, Jonathon Keats, Liz Koslov, Andy Lakoff, Hannah Landecker, Rob Lempert, Geoff Manaugh, Lorenzo Marsili, Ayesha Omer, Peter Redfield, Luísa Reis-Castro, Lois Rosson, Boris Shoshitaishvili, Miriam Ticktin, Claire Webb, Anna Weichselbraun, and Alden Young. Andy, Peter Ekman, and Alden were especially lavish with their ideas and reactions. A big thanks to Amelia Sargent for organizing the working group logistics and ensuring we always had something to eat. The Institute's 2021–22 Future of Democracy Working Group—Stuart Candy, Yael Eisenstat, Johanna Hoffman, Gabriel Kahan, Mike McCarthy, and Dawn Nakagawa—gave helpful feedback on chapter 5.

Many friends and colleagues beyond the Institute also gave the ideas in this book close scrutiny and helpful criticism. Bentley Allan, Bart Bonikowski, Eva-Maria Muschik, and Or Rosenboim participated in a virtual workshop where we apprehensively shared parts of the book for the first time. They gave us excellent feedback on chapters 1 and 2 and much-needed early encouragement about the overall direction of the project. The late and much missed Karen Bakker, Daniel Deudney, Daniel Immerwahr, Rob Lempert, Jessica Seddon, Jack Snyder, and Steve Weber generously read the entire manuscript and provided thoughtful criticisms and questions. It may be trite to say that it would be a better book if we had done everything they had suggested, but that doesn't make it any less true. The two anonymous reviewers for Stanford likewise provided constructive critical feedback.

At a crucial point in our writing, we had the immense pleasure and honor of spending time together at the immaculate Rockefeller Foundation Bellagio Center. Enormous thanks to Zia Khan and Sarah Geisenheimer for arranging our visit and to Pilar Palacià, Alice Luperto, and the rest of the staff for creating a small paradise for calm reflection and intellectual production. Over after-dinner drinks there, Hernan Diaz and Brando Skyhorse provided timely motivation. We received additional feedback from virtual audiences at the University of Southern California's Center for International Studies and the (alas now defunct) Strelka Institute. Others not yet mentioned who lent their ideas and critical eyes and ears include Hadas Aron (the unnamed friend referenced in the Conclusion), Erin Bromaghim, Ben Cerveny, Aaron Clark-Ginsberg, Simon Collard-Wexler, Alexis Crow, Stefanie Fishel, Bruce Jones, Trevor Latimer, Juha Leppänen, Stephen Macekura, Emile Mack, Miriam Marlier, Niccolò Milanese, Ted Nordhaus, Ben Oppenheim, Naomi Oreskes, Mark Paul, Ananya Roy, Stephanie Schwartz, Nicholas Rush Smith, and Sara Walker.

The staff of the Los Angeles Public Library shipped books across the city for our research, even while branches remained closed to the public because of the pandemic. Mereani Vakasisikakala at the United Nations' Dag Hammarskjöld Library assisted us in finding the archival documents used in the opening to chapter 1. Emily Rose Anderson was extremely helpful while Blake was a USC/Berggruen Fellow.

Ben Adams, Tim Frye, Sam Haselby, David Hollinger, and Eric Nusbaum gave us sage publishing advice. Eric Lupfer, our agent, believed in our manuscript and worked his magic to find it the right home. At Stanford University Press, the peerless Dan LoPreto has been an enthusiastic and incisive editor. His perspicacious pen made our arguments clearer, language sharper, and prose flow. Cat Pavel, our editorial assistant, was immensely helpful in the whole publishing process. Elisabeth Magnus's keen copyedits made valuable improvements to the text. Thanks also to Melissa Jauregui Chavez, Emily E. Smith, David Zielonka, and everyone else at Stanford involved in our book. Varsha Venkatasubramanian did a fantastic job with the index.

Our profound appreciation to everyone mentioned, and apologies to anyone we may have forgotten to mention.

———

Blake:

Writing this book with Nils was a treat—yet another way I've benefited from the generosity he's shown since taking me under his wing as a college senior many years ago.

The ideas in the book grew richer from many conversations with my in-laws, Ace Leveen and Arnie Eisen. My mom and dad, Judy and Mitch Blake, helped me innumerable times in innumerable ways. For their unwavering belief in me, I am beyond grateful to all my parents.

Ezra and Ari fill my life with fun and joy. Shulie, my best friend and partner in everything, provides patience, confidence, encouragement, and love. I thank and love the three of you more than I can put in words.

Notes

Preface

1. Hélène Landemore, *Open Democracy: Reinventing Popular Rule for the Twenty-First Century* (Princeton, NJ: Princeton University Press, 2020), 19.

2. A reference to Amartya Sen's criticism of "transcendental institutionalism," a form of political thought concerned more with perfection than with the real world. Amartya Sen, *The Idea of Justice* (Cambridge, MA: Harvard University Press, 2009), 5–8.

3. Landemore, *Open Democracy*, 19.

Introduction

1. Data from "Tracking," Johns Hopkins University Coronavirus Resource Center, accessed June 15, 2023, https://coronavirus.jhu.edu/data. Johns Hopkins Coronavirus Resource Center, a private initiative that provided real-time public information about the pandemic worldwide better than most governments or international organizations, stopped collecting data on COVID infections and deaths on March 10, 2023, two months before the World Health Organization declared the COVID-19 pandemic over, on May 5, 2023. On the estimated "excess deaths" from the novel coronavirus, see William Msemburi et al., "The WHO Estimates of Excess Mortality Associated with the COVID-19 Pandemic," *Nature* 613, no. 7942 (January 2023): 130–37.

2. Nathan D. Wolfe, Claire Panosian Dunavan, and Jared Diamond,

"Origins of Major Human Infectious Diseases," *Nature* 447, no. 7142 (May 2007): 279–83.

3. Fabian Z. X. Lean et al., "Differential Susceptibility of SARS-CoV-2 in Animals: Evidence of ACE2 Host Receptor Distribution in Companion Animals, Livestock and Wildlife by Immunohistochemical Characterization," *Transboundary and Emerging Diseases* 69, no. 4 (July 2022): 2275–86.

4. Eben Kirksey, "The Emergence of COVID-19: A Multispecies Story," *Anthropology Now* 12, no. 1 (2020): 11–16.

5. Aleesha Khaliq, "Wild Goats Take Over Welsh Town amid Coronavirus Lockdown," CNN, March 31, 2020, https://www.cnn.com/2020 /03/31/europe/wild-goats-wales-streets-lockdown-scli-gbr/index.html; "Chilean Capital Gets Another Visit from Cougar amid Coronavirus Lockdown," Reuters, April 2, 2020, https://www.reuters.com/article/us -health-coronavirus-chile-puma/chilean-capital-gets-another-visit-from -cougar-amid-coronavirus-lockdown-idUSKBN21K37Q.

6. Marlee A. Tucker et al., "Behavioral Responses of Terrestrial Mammals to COVID-19 Lockdowns," *Science* 380, no. 6649 (June 2023): 1059–64.

7. Kasha Patel, "Airborne Nitrogen Dioxide Plummets over China," NASA Earth Observatory, March 2, 2020, https://earthobservatory.nasa .gov/images/146362/airborne-nitrogen-dioxide-plummets-over-china.

8. Zhu Liu et al., "Near-Real-Time Monitoring of Global CO_2 Emissions Reveals the Effects of the COVID-19 Pandemic," *Nature Communications* 11 (2020): 2.

9. Benedette Cuffari, "The Size of SARS-CoV-2 and Its Implications," News Medical, last updated February 15, 2021, https://www.news-medical .net/health/The-Size-of-SARS-CoV-2-Compared-to-Other-Things .aspx. The quote is from Peter Baldwin, *Fighting the First Wave: Why the Coronavirus Was Tackled So Differently across the Globe* (New York: Cambridge University Press, 2021), 82.

10. Dipesh Chakrabarty, *The Climate of History in a Planetary Age* (Chicago: University of Chicago Press, 2021), 68.

11. Maria A. Spyrou et al., "The Source of the Black Death in Fourteenth-Century Central Eurasia," *Nature* 606, no. 7973 (June 2022): 718–24.

12. Paraphrasing Scott F. Gilbert, Jan Sapp, and Alfred I. Tauber, "A Symbiotic View of Life: We Have Never Been Individuals," *Quarterly Review of Biology* 87, no. 4 (December 2012): 327.

13. In addition to the cited sources, this section is indebted to Hannah Landecker, "Antibiotic Resistance and the Biology of History," *Body and*

Society 22, no. 4 (December 2016): 19–52; and Dipesh Chakrabarty, "An Era of Pandemics? What Is Global and What Is Planetary about COVID-19," *In the Moment* (blog), October 16, 2020, https://critinq.wordpress.com/2020 /10/16/an-era-of-pandemics-what-is-global-and-what-is-planetary-about -covid-19/.

14. There are lots of definitions of governance (likely too many) strewn about. Some that influenced our thinking include Börzel and Risse's "the various institutionalized modes of social coordination to produce and implement collectively binding rules or to provide collective goods"; Hooghe and Marks's "authoritative decision making in the public sphere"; Weiss's "the entire composite ecosystem through which a society manages its common affairs, a system that may or may not involve authoritative structures"; and Bevir's "all processes of governing, whether undertaken by a government, market, or network; whether over a family, tribe, corporation, or territory; and whether by laws, norms, power, or language. Governance is a broader term than government because it focuses not only on the state and its institutions but also on the creation of rule and order in social practices." We prefer our definition for its simplicity and plain language. Tanja A. Börzel and Thomas Risse, "Governance without a State: Can It Work?," *Regulation and Governance* 4, no. 2 (June 2010): 114; Liesbet Hooghe and Gary Marks, *Community, Scale, and Regional Governance: A Postfunctionalist Theory of Governance*, vol. 2 (New York: Oxford University Press, 2016), 5; Thomas G. Weiss, *Governing the World? Addressing "Problems without Passports"* (New York: Routledge, 2014), 9; Mark Bevir, *A Theory of Governance* (Berkeley: University of California Press, 2013), 1.

15. Karl J. Maier and Mustafa al'Absi, "Toward a Biopsychosocial Ecology of the Human Microbiome, Brain-Gut Axis, and Health," *Psychosomatic Medicine* 79, no. 8 (2017): 947–57; Federico Boem, Gabriele Ferretti, and Silvano Zipoli Caiani, "Out of Our Skull, in Our Skin: The Microbiota-Gut-Brain Axis and the Extended Cognition Thesis," *Biology and Philosophy* 36, no. 14 (March 2021): 1–32.

16. The concept of planetary sapience is drawn from Benjamin Bratton, "Planetary Sapience," *Noema* magazine, June 17, 2021, https://www.noema mag.com/planetary-sapience/.

17. Indigenous thought and scholarship have been particularly fruitful and have produced a forceful critique of the Western traditions in which our book is rooted. We do not explore this body of work in any depth in this book, but our engagement with it has been valuable. Especially important

for us are Jodi Byrd, *The Transit of Empire: Indigenous Critiques of Colonialism* (Minneapolis: University of Minnesota Press, 2011); Angayuqaq Oscar Kawagley, *A Yupiaq Worldview: A Pathway to Ecology and Spirit* (Prospect Heights, IL: Waveland Press, 1995); Robin Wall Kimmerer, *Braiding Sweetgrass: Indigenous Wisdom, Scientific Knowledge and the Teachings of Plants* (Minneapolis: Milkweed Editions, 2013); Ailton Krenak, *Ideas to Postpone the End of the World*, trans. Anthony Doyle (Toronto: House of Anansi Press, 2019); Elias Nelson, "Making Native Science: Indigenous Epistemologies and Settler Sciences in the United States Empire," PhD diss., Harvard University, 2018; Kimberly TallBear, *Native American DNA: Tribal Belonging and the False Promise of Genetic Science* (Minneapolis: University of Minnesota Press, 2013); Kyle Powys Whyte, "On the Role of Traditional Ecological Knowledge as a Collaborative Concept: A Philosophical Study," *Ecological Processes* 2 (April 2013), https://ecologicalprocesses.springeropen .com/articles/10.1186/2192-1709-2-7; and Christine J. Winter, "A Seat at the Table: Te Awa Tupua, Te Urewera, Taranaki Maunga and Political Representation," *borderlands* 20, no. 1 (January 2021): 116–39.

18. Will Steffen et al., "Planetary Boundaries: Guiding Human Development on a Changing Planet," *Science* 347, no. 6223 (February 2015): 736; Linn Persson et al., "Outside the Safe Operating Space of the Planetary Boundary for Novel Entities," *Environmental Science and Technology* 56, no. 3 (February 2022): 1510–21; Lan Wang-Erlandsson et al., "A Planetary Boundary for Green Water," *Nature Reviews Earth and Environment* 3, no. 6 (June 2022): 380–92. On the point that some humans, rather than "humanity," are to blame, see, for example, Jason Moore, ed., *Anthropocene or Capitalocene? Nature, History, and the Crisis of Capitalism* (Oakland, CA: PM Press, 2016).

19. We draw the contrast from Chakrabarty, *Climate of History*, 81–85.

20. W. H. Auden, "New Year Letter," in *Collected Poems*, ed. Edward Mendelson (New York: Vintage, 1991), 208.

Chapter 1

1. UN Secretary-General, "Report to the General Assembly of the United Nations on the Permanent Headquarters of the United Nations," A/311, July 1947, 38, https://digitallibrary.un.org/record/490632?ln=en.

2. UN Secretary-General, "Report," A/311, 19.

3. UN Security Council, Resolution 109, "On Admission of Albania,

Jordan, Ireland, Portugal, Hungary, Italy, Austria, Romania, Bulgaria, Finland, Ceylon (Sri Lanka), Nepal, Libya (Libyan Arab Jamahiriya), Cambodia, Laos (Lao People's Democratic Republic) and Spain to Membership in the United Nations," December 14, 1955, https://digitallibrary.un.org/record/112082?ln=en.

4. UN General Assembly Fifth Committee, "Major Maintenance and Capital Improvement Programme at Headquarters," A/C.5/738, 1958, annex 1, p. 6, and annex 2, p. 1. The situation was even worse—"inadequate," in the stilted language of UN budgetary documents—in the Security Council's chambers, where "it has been necessary to install temporary chairs to provide for delegates wishing to attend the deliberations of the Council. There is no provision for telecommunication facilities at these chairs, and the arrangements have given rise to many complaints." UN General Assembly Fifth Committee, "Major Maintenance," A/C.5/738, annex 1, p. 5.

5. UN, "Growth in United Nations Membership," accessed June 15, 2023, https://www.un.org/en/about-us/growth-in-un-membership. A remodel that ended in 1964 (when there were 115 members) provided space for 126 member states—a number reached in 1968. Major alterations to the General Assembly Hall were again approved in 1976 and were completed in 1980. UN Visitor Centre, "Fact Sheet: History of the United Nations Headquarters," September 2019, https://www.un.org/sites/un2.un.org/files/english_2019.pdf.

6. Andreas Wimmer and Brian Min, "From Empire to Nation-State: Explaining Wars in the Modern World, 1816–2001," *American Sociological Review* 71, no. 6 (December 2006): 870. According to the UN Special Committee on Decolonization, there remain seventeen Non-Self-Governing Territories—"territories whose people have not yet attained a full measure of self-government"—ranging from Western Sahara (pop. 582,000) to Pitcairn (pop. 43). Combined, these territories in 2023 represent a total population of 1.7 million (0.02 percent of the total global human population) and a land area of 117,000 square miles (0.2 percent of the planetary total). UN, "The United Nations and Decolonization: Non-Self-Governing Territories," accessed June 15, 2023, https://www.un.org/dppa/decolonization/en/nsgt.

7. We follow specialists in insisting that what is usually called the "nation-state" should really be called the "national state," a "relatively centralized, differentiated, and autonomous organizations successfully claiming priority in the use of force with large, contiguous, and clearly bounded

territories." Charles Tilly, *Coercion, Capital, and European States, AD 990–1992* (Oxford: Blackwell, 1992), 43. Nation-statehood in the technical sense implies that there is a culturally homogeneous people in whose name the state governs. Most states today lack this homogeneity, making them "national states" but not "nation-states."

8. Jane Burbank and Frederick Cooper, *Empires in World History: Power and the Politics of Difference* (Princeton, NJ: Princeton University Press, 2011), 288. In 1940, the total colonial population was eight hundred million. Odd Arne Westad, *The Global Cold War: Third World Interventions and the Making of Our Times* (Cambridge: Cambridge University Press, 2005), 417n1.

9. By *sovereignty*, we mean the fact of being the supreme recognized authority over a given polity or jurisdiction. The hegemony of the national state that solidified by 1965 was primarily de jure or ideological, reflecting what Jan Klabbers describes as the "epistemic priority of the state." As the next chapter will make clear, many postcolonial states were never de facto hegemonic within their borders. Another way of putting it is that what became hegemonic was the national state's "international legal sovereignty," which Stephen Krasner defines as "the mutual recognition of states." Other aspects of state sovereignty, including their ability to exercise authority in their territory, to control cross-border flows, and to exclude external actors, were not universally achieved. Jan Klabbers, "An Accidental Revolution: The ILO and the Opening Up of International Law," in *International Labour Organization and Global Social Governance,* ed. Tarja Halonen and Ulla Liukkunen (New York: Springer, 2021), 126; Stephen D. Krasner, *Sovereignty: Organized Hypocrisy* (Princeton, NJ: Princeton University Press, 1999), 9.

10. A variety of tiny de facto independent states continue to exist in the world, usually under the umbrella of protection from a powerful patron state. Places such as Abkhazia, Transdniestria, and Northern Cyprus exercise internal sovereignty over their citizens but are not recognized by most of the world as the de jure legal authority in that territory. Tellingly, however, virtually all of these states seek either to become internationally recognized independent national states or to join an existing such state. See Thomas de Waal, "Uncertain Ground: Engaging with Europe's De Facto States and Breakaway Territories," Carnegie Endowment for International Peace, December 3, 2018, https://carnegieendowment.org/files/deWaal_UncertainGround_final.pdf.

11. Philip J. Stern, *The Company-State: Corporate Sovereignty and the Early Modern Foundations of the British Empire in India* (New York: Oxford University Press, 2011).

12. Tilly, *Coercion, Capital,* 4.

13. Kent V. Flannery, "The Cultural Evolution of Civilizations," *Annual Review of Ecology and Systematics* 3 (1972): 399–426; James C. Scott, *Against the Grain: A Deep History of the Earliest States* (New Haven, CT: Yale University Press, 2017), 7.

14. Tilly, *Coercion, Capital,* 41–42.

15. Quentin Skinner, "A Genealogy of the Modern State," *Proceedings of the British Academy* 162 (2009): 325–70.

16. Mira L. Siegelberg, *Statelessness: A Modern History* (Cambridge, MA: Harvard University Press, 2020), 7.

17. Bentley B. Allan, *Scientific Cosmology and International Orders* (New York: Cambridge University Press, 2018), 2, 10.

18. Tilly, *Coercion, Capital,* 25, 103–14.

19. "Declaration of Independence: A Transcription," July 4, 1776, America's Founding Documents, US National Archives and Records Administration, https://www.archives.gov/founding-docs/declaration-transcript.

20. David Armitage, *Foundations of Modern International Thought* (New York: Cambridge University Press, 2012), 216–17.

21. Burbank and Cooper, *Empires in World History,* 247. Moreover, before South American countries assumed their present borders, most of South America was part of two large states, Gran Colombia and United Provinces of the Río de la Plata.

22. Burbank and Cooper, *Empires in World History,* 227–28.

23. Joshua Simon, "From the American System to the Anglo-Saxon Union," in *Forms of Pluralism and Democratic Constitutionalism,* ed. Andrew J. Arato, Jean L. Cohen, and Astrid von Busekist (New York: Columbia University Press, 2018), 73.

24. Armitage, *Foundations of Modern International Thought,* 225–27 (quote from p. 227).

25. Camilo Henríquez quoted in Armitage, *Foundations of Modern International Thought,* 225.

26. Charles S. Maier, *Once within Borders: Territories of Power, Wealth, and Belonging since 1500* (Cambridge, MA: Harvard University Press, 2016), 11.

27. In the premodern vision, time was cyclical rather than linear and what happened in world was the result of God or fortune. Given this un-

derstanding of the world, there was little for the state to do. Yet by the early nineteenth century, we see the emergence of new thinking about time, the human condition, and the place of God, all of which pointed to the notion that human beings did have some control in the world. This opened the possibility that the state could intervene to improve the lives of at least some people. See Allan, *Scientific Cosmology*.

28. Ben W. Ansell and Johannes Lindvall, *Inward Conquest: The Political Origins of Modern Public Services* (New York: Cambridge University Press, 2020).

29. Pieter M. Judson, *The Habsburg Empire: A New History* (Cambridge, MA: Harvard University Press, 2016), 156, who notes that the revolutionaries of 1848 "portrayed themselves as caretakers of the true Habsburg imperial ideal as it ought to be practiced." On Hungary, see Miklós Molnár, *A Concise History of Hungary* (Cambridge: Cambridge University Press, 2001), 177.

30. František Palacký quoted in Judson, *Habsburg Empire*, 156.

31. Judson, *Habsburg Empire*, 199, 213; Eric J. Hobsbawm, *The Age of Revolution: 1789–1848* (New York: Vintage, 1996), 132–48. As Hobsbawm warns, "The assumptions, hopes, needs, longings and interests of ordinary people . . . are not necessarily national and still less nationalist." E. J. Hobsbawm, *Nations and Nationalism since 1780: Programme, Myth, Reality* (Cambridge: Cambridge University Press, 1990), 10.

32. Woodrow Wilson, "Address of the President of the United States Delivered at a Joint Session of the Two Houses of Congress, February 11, 1918," in *Papers Relating to the Foreign Relations of the United States, 1918*, Supplement 1, *The World War*, vol. 1, https://history.state.gov/historical documents/frus1918Supp01v01/d59.

33. Robert Gerwarth, "1918 and the End of Europe's Land Empires," in *The Oxford Handbook of the Ends of Empire*, ed. Martin Thomas and Andrew Thompson (New York: Oxford University Press, 2019), 30.

34. Siegelberg, *Statelessness*, 53.

35. Wilson, "Address of the President."

36. Jeremy W. Crampton, "The Cartographic Calculation of Space: Race Mapping and the Balkans at the Paris Peace Conference of 1919," *Social and Cultural Geography* 7, no. 5 (2006): 731–52.

37. Gerwarth, "1918," 34.

38. Siegelberg, *Statelessness*, 59; Jan-Werner Müller, *Contesting Democracy: Political Ideas in Twentieth-Century Europe* (New Haven, CT: Yale Uni-

versity Press, 2011), 22. To protect the minority nationalities, the victorious powers imposed a series of Minority Treaties on the new states, imping-ing on their sovereignty by restricting the maltreatment of minorities—restrictions that the victors did not apply to themselves.

39. This is not to say that the transition was smooth or seamless. As the Habsburg Empire collapsed in October 1918, nationalists "groped—and often bumbled—their way toward establishing new states." Judson, *Habsburg Empire*, 431.

40. There were still trivial exceptions such as the Free City of Danzig, which was placed under the direct international control of the League of Na-tions. Siegelberg, *Statelessness*, 55–56; Maier, *Once within Borders*, 267. This moment also produced perhaps the most famous definition of the state, one given by Max Weber in a lecture that coincided with the start of the Paris Peace Conference. In "Politics as a Vocation," which the German so-ciologist delivered in Munich in January 1919, Weber provided a functional account of the state, which remains a touchstone today. Many members of his audience in the Free Students' Union had just experienced—perhaps even participated in—an uprising to declare a socialist Bavarian Republic in November 1918. Yet rather than address this "bloody carnival," Weber demurred, retreating to theory and ethics. Amid the political turmoil of military defeat and the German Empire's collapse, he described the state as an organization with the means to achieve social order: "a human commu-nity that (successfully) claims the monopoly of the legitimate use of phys-ical force within a given territory." Max Weber, "Politics as a Vocation," in *From Max Weber: Essays in Sociology*, ed. and trans. H. H. Gerth and C. Wright Mills (New York: Oxford University Press, 1946), 78. On the politi-cal context of Weber's lecture, see Müller, *Contesting Democracy*, 8–9 (with Weber's "bloody carnival" quote found on p. 8).

41. Eric Hobsbawm, *The Age of Extremes: A History of the World, 1914–1991* (New York: Vintage, 1995), 209; Odd Arne Westad, *The Cold War: A World History* (New York: Basic Books, 2017), 264; Westad, *Global Cold War*, 77–78.

42. Erez Manela, *The Wilsonian Moment: Self-Determination and the International Origins of Anticolonial Nationalism* (New York: Oxford Uni-versity Press, 2007), 67, 80. While this is generally true of establishment anticolonial activism, some early movements did take a more radical stance against empire, such as the Indian Swadeshi movement that emerged in 1905. See Manela, *Wilsonian Moment*, 80–81.

43. In a telling action two months after President Wilson announced his Fourteen Points, the United States paid the government of Denmark $25 million for formal possession of the Danish West Indies—the last time that a territory and its population were transferred between sovereign states as a pure cash transaction, without any consideration of the desire of the local peoples, who in this case were mostly of African descent. This action demonstrated the meaning and limits of the idea of self-determination. At the very moment when the United States was exalting the principle of national self-determination, it also made clear that this principle applied only to certain ("civilized") peoples, notably Europeans and their descendants. See Charles Callan Tansill, *The Purchase of the Danish West Indies* (Baltimore: Johns Hopkins University Press, 1932).

44. Gopal Krishna Gokhale quoted in Manela, *Wilsonian Moment*, 80.

45. Indian National Congress, "Declaration of Purna Swaraj," December 19, 1929, https://www.constitutionofindia.net/historical-constitution/declaration-of-purna-swaraj-indian-national-congress-1930/; Manela, *Wilsonian Moment*, 217.

46. Covenant of the League of Nations, June 28, 1919, preamble, https://avalon.law.yale.edu/20th_century/leagcov.asp.

47. Léon Bourgeois quoted in Mark Mazower, *Governing the World: The History of an Idea, 1815 to the Present* (New York: Penguin, 2013), 137.

48. See Mazower, *Governing the World*, 137; Megan Donaldson, "The League of Nations, Ethiopia, and the Making of States," *Humanity* 11, no. 1 (Spring 2020): 6–31; and Susan Pedersen, *The Guardians: The League of Nations and the Crisis of Empire* (New York: Oxford University Press, 2015), esp. 261–86.

49. Covenant of the League of Nations, art. 22, https://avalon.law.yale.edu/20th_century/leagcov.asp; Pedersen, *Guardians*.

50. Westad, *Cold War*, 265.

51. Herbert Morrison quoted in Tony Judt, *Postwar: A History of Europe since 1945* (New York: Penguin, 2006), 280.

52. Committee to Frame a World Constitution, *Preliminary Draft of a World Constitution* (Chicago: University of Chicago Press, 1948), 41.

53. Committee to Frame a World Constitution, *Preliminary Draft*, 3. For background and analysis, see Or Rosenboim, *The Emergence of Globalism: Visions of World Order in Britain and the United States, 1939–1950* (Princeton, NJ: Princeton University Press, 2017), 168–208.

54. Joseph Preston Baratta, *The Politics of World Federation: From World*

Federalism to Global Governance (Westport, CT: Praeger, 2004); Graham Nicholson, "Remedying the Retreat in the Protection of Citizens International Human Rights," *International Journal of Peace and Development Studies* 9, no. 3 (2018): 34; Samuel Zipp, *The Idealist: Wendell Willkie's Wartime Quest to Build One World* (Cambridge, MA: Belknap Press of Harvard University Press, 2020).

55. Albert Einstein, "A Reply to the Soviet Scientists," in *Out of My Later Years* (New York: Philosophical Library, 1950), 175.

56. Einstein, "The Way Out," in *Out of My Later Years*, 143.

57. Quoted in Mazower, *Governing the World*, 233–34.

58. *A Concurrent Resolution to Seek Development of the United Nations into a World Federation: Hearings on H. Con. Res. 64, before the Committee on Foreign Affairs*, 81st Cong. (October 12–13, 1949), 1.

59. Charter of the United Nations, chap. 1, art. 2, https://www.un.org/en/about-us/un-charter/full-text.

60. See Rosenboim, *Emergence of Globalism*.

61. Kwame Nkrumah quoted in Adom Getachew, *Worldmaking after Empire: The Rise and Fall of Self-Determination* (Princeton, NJ: Princeton University Press, 2019), 17.

62. Mamadou Dia quoted in Frederick Cooper, *Citizenship between Empire and Nation: Remaking France and French Africa, 1945–1960* (Princeton, NJ: Princeton University Press, 2014), 1.

63. Cooper, *Citizenship between Empire and Nation*, 11.

64. Quoted in Getachew, *Worldmaking after Empire*, 107.

65. Eric Williams quoted in Getachew, *Worldmaking after Empire*, 126.

66. Monte Palmer, "The United Arab Republic: An Assessment of Its Failure," *Middle East Journal* 20, no. 1 (Winter 1966): 50–67; John C. H. Oh, "The Federation of Malaysia: An Experiment in Nation-Building," *American Journal of Economics and Sociology* 26, no. 4 (October 1967): 425–37; Donn M. Kurtz, "Political Integration in Africa: The Mali Federation," *Journal of Modern African Studies* 8, no. 3 (October 1970): 405–24; Tai Yong Tan, *Creating "Greater Malaysia": Decolonization and the Politics of Merger* (Singapore: Institute of Southeast Asian Studies, 2008); Aremu Johnson Olaosebikan, "Kwame Nkrumah and the Proposed African Common Government," *African Journal of Political Science and International Relations* 5, no. 4 (2011): 218–28; Sunil S. Amrith, *Crossing the Bay of Bengal: The Furies of Nature and the Fortunes of Migrants* (Cambridge, MA: Harvard University Press, 2013), 243; Michael Collins, "Decolonisation and the 'Federal

Moment,'" *Diplomacy and Statecraft* 24, no. 1 (2013): 21–40; Getachew, *Worldmaking after Empire*, 107–41.

67. Even the United States, long a federal state, felt the attraction of federation anew in the late 1950s: Alaska and Hawaii were both admitted to the union in 1959, the first new states in nearly fifty years. Europeans, too, saw the appeal of a multinational political structure at this moment: in 1957, six European states signed the Treaty of Rome to form the European Economic Community.

68. David Ben-Gurion quoted in Dmitry Shumsky, *Beyond the Nation-State: The Zionist Political Imagination from Pinsker to Ben-Gurion* (New Haven, CT: Yale University Press, 2018), 218. Even until the 1940s, just a few years before Israel's independence, Ben-Gurion was not committed to the national state as the definitive form of Jewish self-determination. It was the war, specifically the Holocaust, that foreclosed all other options in his mind. His earlier openness to national autonomy within the Ottoman Empire and other federative arrangements was killed in the death camps. The transformation of Ben-Gurion's political thought is traced in Shumsky, *Beyond the Nation-State*, 172–219.

69. Aimé Césaire quoted in Westad, *Global Cold War*, 85.

70. On the thought of Césaire and Senghor, see Gary Wilder, *Freedom Time: Negritude, Decolonization, and the Future of the World* (Durham, NC: Duke University Press, 2015).

71. Benedict Anderson, *Imagined Communities: Reflections on the Origin and Spread of Nationalism*, rev. ed. (London: Verso, 1991), 53, 51–52 (italics in original).

72. Nils Gilman, *Mandarins of the Future: Modernization Theory in Cold War America* (Baltimore: Johns Hopkins University Press, 2003); Michael E. Latham, *The Right Kind of Revolution: Modernization, Development, and U.S. Foreign Policy from the Cold War to the Present* (Ithaca, NY: Cornell University Press, 2011).

73. See Allan, *Scientific Cosmology*, 165.

74. Timothy Mitchell, in a prominent argument, dates the modern understanding of the economy to the 1930s through 1950s, while Adam Tooze demonstrates that the concept was already in use, especially among German economic thinkers, by the 1880s and 1890s. Timothy Mitchell, "Fixing the Economy," *Cultural Studies* 12, no. 1 (1998): 82–10; Timothy Mitchell, *The Rule of Experts: Egypt, Techno-Politics, Modernity* (Oakland: University of

California Press, 2002); Adam Tooze, "The Crisis: The Unmaking of the Economy?," working paper, June 2016, https://adamtooze.com/wp-content/uploads/2016/03/Tooze-Unmaking-the-Economy-2016.pdf.

75. Stephen Constantine, *The Making of British Colonial Development Policy, 1914–1940* (Abingdon: Routledge, 2005).

76. Alden Young, *Transforming Sudan: Decolonization, Economic Development, and State Formation* (New York: Cambridge University Press, 2018), 36.

77. Latham, *Right Kind of Revolution*, 68.

78. Amrith, *Crossing the Bay*, 192. Coastal cities that had long been oriented outward, toward the other coastal cities that ringed the Bay, were reoriented inward, toward the land at their backs rather than the sea they faced.

79. Jawaharlal Nehru quoted in Latham, *Right Kind of Revolution*, 68.

80. Crucially, working toward economic development also satisfied the desires of both postwar superpowers. For the United States, development promised a way to manage the aspirations of anticolonial leaders, spread the gospel of American modernity, and blunt the appeal of Soviet communism. For the Soviet Union, development promised more or less the inverse. It was for this reason that the Cold War struggle for ideological dominance was mainly fought in the postcolonial world. See Westad, *Global Cold War*.

81. Nehru quoted in Westad, *Cold War*, 156–57.

82. Nkrumah quoted in Latham, *Right Kind of Revolution*, 65.

83. Nkrumah quoted in Westad, *Global Cold War*, 91.

84. Nkrumah quoted in Getachew, *Worldmaking after Empire*, 108.

85. Mazower, *Governing the World*, 293; Guy Fiti Sinclair, *To Reform the World: International Organizations and the Making of Modern States* (Oxford: Oxford University Press, 2017); Eva-Maria Muschik, *Building States: The United Nations, Development, and Decolonization, 1945–1965* (New York: Columbia University Press, 2022).

86. Quoted in Pedersen, *Guardians*, 358.

87. The nation-state's role as a symbol of sovereignty helps explain why so many "development" initiatives in postcolonial states went into the building of economically unnecessary "vanity" projects like fancy presidential palaces and football stadiums. The point was not so much to make a government that could "see like a state" (as James Scott put it) but rather to make a government that could *seem* like a state. See Steven Pierce, "Look-

ing Like a State: Colonialism and the Discourse of Corruption in Northern Nigeria," *Comparative Studies in Society and History* 48, no. 4 (October 2006): 887–914.

88. As Eslava and Pahuja explain in an excellent recent essay: "The outcome of colonial subjects' struggles against their respective metropoles was, therefore, not the right to decide for themselves the mode in which they could organize their political communities and economic relations after independence. Instead of a right to 'self-definition,' the outcome of the process of decolonization was the principle of 'self-determination,' which could be practiced only within the confines of the national state form, and often according to pre-established colonial boundaries that enclosed in single national formations highly disparate ethnic groups and incongruous geographical spaces." Luis Eslava and Sundhya Pahuja, "The State and International Law: A Reading from the Global South," *Humanity* 11, no. 1 (Spring 2020): 121.

89. Tanisha M. Fazal, *State Death: The Politics and Geography of Conquest, Occupation, and Annexation* (Princeton, NJ: Princeton University Press, 2007).

90. Maier, *Once within Borders*, 257.

91. Almost half (44 percent) of international boundaries in Africa "are straight lines that either correspond to an astrologic measurement or are parallel to some other set of lines." Jeffrey Herbst, "The Creation and Maintenance of National Boundaries in Africa," *International Organization* 43, no. 4 (Autumn 1989): 675.

92. Ron E. Hassner and Jason Wittenberg, "Barriers to Entry: Who Builds Fortified Boundaries and Why?," *International Security* 40, no. 1 (Summer 2015): 168.

93. UN General Assembly, Resolution 1514 (XV), "Declaration on the Granting of Independence to Colonial Countries and Peoples," December 14, 1960, https://documents-dds-ny.un.org/doc/RESOLUTION/GEN/NR0/152/88/PDF/NR015288.pdf?OpenElement.

94. UN General Assembly, Resolution 2064, "Question of the Cook Islands," December 16, 1965, https://digitallibrary.un.org/record/203557?ln=en; Vernon Van Dyke, "Self-Determination and Minority Rights," *International Studies Quarterly* 13, no. 3 (September 1969): 231–32; Mazower, *Governing the World*, 269.

95. Mazower, *Governing the World*, 269.

96. Stephen Kotkin, *Armageddon Averted: The Soviet Collapse, 1970–2000* (New York: Oxford University Press, 2008), 90–92.

97. Edward W. Walker, *Dissolution: Sovereignty and the Breakup of the Soviet Union* (Lanham, MD: Rowman and Littlefield, 2003), 139.

98. For a thoughtful consideration of how we might recover the "imaginary futures" that once were, see Manu Goswami, "Imaginary Futures and Colonial Internationalisms," *American Historical Review* 117, no. 5 (December 2012): 1461–85.

99. Todd Shepard, "The Birth of the Hexagon: 1962 and the Erasure of France's Supranational History," in *Vertriebene and Pieds-Noirs in Postwar Germany and France: Comparative Perspectives*, ed. Manuel Borutta and Jan C. Jansen (New York: Springer, 2016), 53–69; Frederick Cooper, *Colonialism in Question: Theory, Knowledge, History* (Oakland: University of California Press, 2005), 188.

100. For the American version of this story, see Daniel Immerwahr, *How to Hide an Empire: A Short History of the Greater United States* (New York: Random House, 2019).

101. Armitage, *Foundations of Modern International Thought*, 216–17; Andreas Wimmer and Nina Glick Schiller, "Methodological Nationalism and Beyond: Nation-State Building, Migration and the Social Sciences," *Global Networks* 2, no. 4 (October 2002): 301–34.

102. Anderson, *Imagined Communities*, 12.

Chapter 2

1. Roger Revelle and Hans E. Suess, "Carbon Dioxide Exchange between Atmosphere and Ocean and the Question of an Increase of Atmospheric CO_2 during the Past Decades," *Tellus* 9, no. 1 (1957): 18–27 (quote is from p. 24); Spencer R. Weart, "Roger Revelle's Discovery," American Institute of Physics, last modified August 2021, https://history.aip.org/climate/Revelle.htm; Spencer R. Weart, *The Discovery of Global Warming* (Cambridge, MA: Harvard University Press, 2008), 26–30. See also Roger Revelle, "How I Became an Oceanographer and Other Sea Stories," *Annual Review of Earth and Planetary Sciences* 15 (1987): 11–12; and Joshua P. Howe, *Behind the Curve: Science and the Politics of Global Warming* (Seattle: University of Washington Press, 2014), 16–20.

2. UN Framework Convention on Climate Change (UNFCCC), June 12, 1992, preamble. For how the global climate became an issue for global

governance, see Bentley Allan, "Producing the Climate: States, Scientists, and the Constitution of Global Governance Objects," *International Organization* 71, no. 1 (Winter 2017): 131–62; and Clark A. Miller, "Climate Science and the Making of a Global Political Order," in *States of Knowledge: The Co-production of Science and the Social Order*, ed. Sheila Jasanoff (London: Routledge, 2004), 46–66.

3. UNFCCC, art. 2.

4. UNFCCC, preamble.

5. UNFCCC, "Report of the Conference of the Parties on Its Twenty-First Session, Held in Paris from 30 November to 13 December 2015," FCCC/CP/2015/10/Add.1, January 29, 2016, 3.

6. A similar dynamic unfolded during the previous emergence of new national states after World War I. The collapse of the Habsburg Empire meant that flows of things like people, capital, crime, and disease, which had long been managed in the territorially expansive imperial context, were suddenly transnational phenomena. Each new national state could try to manage the problems within its borders, but that meant dealing with only a part of a problem, not the whole. Transnational governance projects, including the forerunners to Interpol and World Health Organization, emerged to deal with the causes and consequences of activities that spanned the newly sovereign jurisdictions. See Natasha Wheatley, "Central Europe as Ground Zero of the New International Order," *Slavic Review* 78, no. 4 (Winter 2019): 900–911.

7. Michael Zürn, "Global Governance as Multi-level Governance," in *Oxford Handbook of Governance*, ed. David Levi-Faur (New York: Oxford University Press, 2012), 732.

8. Mark Mazower, *Governing the World: The History of an Idea, 1815 to the Present* (New York: Penguin, 2013), 417. The growth of international nongovernmental organizations began in 1945 but accelerated dramatically starting in the 1960s. See John Boli and George M. Thomas, *Constructing World Culture: International Nongovernmental Organizations since 1875* (Stanford, CA: Stanford University Press, 1999), 22–23. Weiss, presumably using different data, finds that of the thirty-eight thousand international intergovernmental and nongovernmental organizations founded in the twentieth century, thirty-three thousand were founded after 1950, and half of the total were after 1980. Thomas G. Weiss, *Governing the World? Addressing "Problems without Passports"* (New York: Routledge, 2014), 16.

9. For the rise of this concept in the 1970s, see Daniel J. Sargent, *A Su-*

perpower Transformed: The Remaking of American Foreign Relations in the 1970s (New York: Oxford University Press, 2014), 165–97.

10. Liesbet Hooghe and Gary Marks, *Community, Scale, and Regional Governance: A Postfunctionalist Theory of Governance*, vol. 2 (New York: Oxford University Press, 2016), 44–62.

11. We draw and adapt these terms from management science, especially as presented by Francis Fukuyama, "Why There Is No Science of Public Administration," *Journal of International Affairs* 58, no. 1 (Fall 2004): 189–201.

12. Jeremy Bentham quoted in Mazower, *Governing the World*, 20 and 21; David Armitage, *Foundations of Modern International Thought* (New York: Cambridge University Press, 2012), 42.

13. Immanuel Kant, *To Perpetual Peace: A Philosophical Sketch*, trans. Ted Humphrey (Indianapolis, IN: Hackett, 2003); see Georg Cavallar, "Kant's Society of Nations: Free Federation or World Republic?" *Journal of the History of Philosophy* 32, no. 3 (July 1994): 461–82.

14. Friedrich von Gentz quoted in Mazower, *Governing the World*, 4.

15. Charles S. Maier, *Once within Borders: Territories of Power, Wealth, and Belonging since 1500* (Cambridge, MA: Harvard University Press, 2016), 273. This timing, writes historian Kiran Klaus Patel, suggests that "the emergence of modern sovereign national statehood went hand in hand with elements relativizing it." Kiran Klaus Patel, *Project Europe: A History* (New York: Cambridge University Press, 2020), 24.

16. Sunil S. Amrith, "Internationalizing Health in the Twentieth Century," in *Internationalisms: A Twentieth-Century History*, ed. Glenda Sluga and Patricia Clavin (New York: Cambridge University Press, 2017), 246–47; Mazower, *Governing the World*, 110–11. The engaging book on quarantine practices by Manaugh and Twilley discusses nineteenth-century international efforts on pp. 104–7; Geoff Manaugh and Nicola Twilley, *Until Proven Safe: The History and Future of Quarantine, from the Black Death to the Space Age* (New York: MCD Picador, 2021).

17. Two judicious assessments of the UN's successes and failures are Paul Kennedy, *The Parliament of Man: The Past, Present, and Future of the United Nations* (New York: Random House, 2006); and Stanley Meisler, *United Nations: A History*, rev. ed. (New York: Grove Press, 2011).

18. Charter of the United Nations, June 26, 1945, art. 2.1, https://www.un.org/en/about-us/un-charter/full-text.

19. Charter of the United Nations, preamble; Mark Mazower, *No En-*

chanted Palace: The End of Empire and the Ideological Origins of the United Nations (Princeton, NJ: Princeton University Press, 2009).

20. Charter of the United Nations, preamble; Stephen Wertheim, *Tomorrow, the World: The Birth of US Global Supremacy* (Cambridge, MA: Harvard University Press, 2020).

21. As Michael Barnett argues, the UN's constituency—the political community to which it is accountable—is unclear, contested, and often defined in contradictory ways. Throughout its charter and history, the UN has claimed to represent the world's individual persons, collective "peoples," and sovereign national states. These three international communities often have divergent interests, and when a tension arises the UN generally sides with states. Michael N. Barnett, "The UN Security Council, Indifference, and Genocide in Rwanda," *Cultural Anthropology* 12, no. 4 (November 1997): 565.

22. Scott Barrett, *Why Cooperate? The Incentive to Supply Global Public Goods* (New York: Oxford University Press, 2007), 19, quoted in Weiss, *Governing the World?*, 9.

23. As Thomas Schelling, in a well-known example of two people trying to find each other in New York City without communicating or prior instruction, puts it, in coordination problems "any solution is 'correct' if enough people think so." (The two people should try to meet at the information booth in Grand Central Station at noon—at least if they are New Haven–based academics in 1960.) Thomas C. Schelling, *The Strategy of Conflict* (Cambridge, MA: Harvard University Press, 1960), 55; see also Duncan Snidal, "Coordination versus Prisoners' Dilemma: Implications for International Cooperation and Regimes," *American Political Science Review* 79, no. 4 (December 1985): 923–42.

24. The ITU was originally established as the International Telegraph Union. Mazower, *Governing the World*, 102.

25. Helen Milner, "The Assumption of Anarchy in International Relations Theory: A Critique," *Review of International Studies* 17, no. 1 (January 1991): 67–85.

26. Treaty Establishing the European Economic Community (Treaty of Rome), March 25, 1957, preamble.

27. On the EU's power outside its borders, see Anu Bradford, *The Brussels Effect: How the European Union Rules the World* (New York: Oxford University Press, 2020).

28. Jacques Delors quoted in William Phelan, "What Is *Sui Generis*

about the European Union? Costly International Cooperation in a Self-Contained Regime," *International Studies Review* 14, no. 3 (September 2012): 367.

29. At the very least, we can say, with Patel, *Project Europe*, 23, that the EU "approximate[s] the ideal of supranational governance." See, for example, Wayne Sandholtz and Alec Stone Sweet, eds., *European Integration and Supranational Governance* (New York: Oxford University Press, 1998); Roger J. Goebel, "Supranational? Federal? Intergovernmental? The Governmental Structure of the European Union after the Treaty of Lisbon," *Columbia Journal of European Law* 20, no. 1 (2013): 77–142; and, for an early account, Ernst B. Haas, *The Uniting of Europe: Political, Social, and Economic Forces, 1950–1957* (Stanford, CA: Stanford University Press, 1958). For the view that the EU is not supranational, see, for example, Andrew Moravcsik, "Preferences and Power in the European Community: A Liberal Intergovernmentalist Approach," *Journal of Common Market Studies* 31, no. 4 (December 1993): 473–524; Andrew Moravcsik, *The Choice for Europe: Social Purpose and State Power from Messina to Maastricht* (Ithaca, NY: Cornell University Press, 1998); and Christopher J. Bickerton, *European Integration: From Nation-States to Member States* (New York: Oxford University Press, 2012).

30. The precise nature of the political institution that evolved out of this decades-long process of European integration is the subject of fierce (though often highly technical) debate. At issue, ultimately, is the question of who is sovereign, the EU itself or its twenty-seven member states. That is, which entity can override or ignore the decisions of the other? This is a major political and legal question, though one that we do not need to dwell on here. At momentous decision points, when a clash of sovereignty is real and unavoidable, it seems clear to us that national states get to decide: Hungary refused the EU's decisions on migration in 2015, and in 2020 the United Kingdom withdrew from the EU altogether. In neither case did the EU take up arms, and the two states were allowed to assert their sovereign prerogatives. But those cases are quite rare in the day-to-day business of governing the union. As Tanja A. Börzel, *Why Noncompliance: The Politics of Law in the European Union* (Ithaca, NY: Cornell University Press, 2021), 3, finds, the EU doesn't have a problem with noncompliance with its laws: "Almost all member states comply with almost all EU law almost all the time."

31. Patel, *Project Europe*, 26–27.

32. Robert Schuman quoted in Luuk Van Middelaar, *The Passage to Europe: How a Continent Became a Union* (New Haven, CT: Yale University Press, 2013), 16.

33. Patel, *Project Europe*, 35–36.

34. Patel, *Project Europe*, esp. 14–22 and 42; Desmond Dinan, "Understanding European Union Governance: Political Challenges of the Integration Project," in *Crisis of the European Union: Challenges, Analyses, Solutions*, ed. Andreas Grimmel (London: Routledge, 2017), 18.

35. True, EU member states retain an exit option, like national states that are party to multilateral institutions. The United Kingdom, of course, exercised that option and separated from the union in 2020. The stupidity of Brexit was that it was premised on a reassertion of sovereignty, but the only sovereignty that could be attained was a nominal one that came with little change in governance. By withdrawing, the UK merely lost its voice in a system of governance that it remains subject to. In other words, Brexit may have achieved "sovereignty," but it did not result in more national control for the UK. Perhaps there is pride associated with nominal sovereignty, but the fact is that the UK remains a rule-taker, not a rule-giver, and the country still must do what Brussels decides. As a result, Brexit, rather than demonstrating the viability of reasserting sovereign statehood for EU members, seems to have tarnished the political program, at least for the time being. Since the Brexiteers' victory in the 2016 referendum, Euroskeptic parties elsewhere in the Union have dropped their campaigns for EU withdrawal. See Nicholas Westcott, "A Peculiar Definition of Sovereignty Is the Root Cause of a Failed Brexit," *LSE Brexit Blog*, November 27, 2020, https://blogs.lse.ac.uk/brexit/2020/11/27/a-peculiar-definition-of-sovereignty-is-the-root-cause-of-a-failed-brexit/.

36. Bickerton, *European Integration*.

37. See Patel, *Project Europe*, 40; Bickerton, *European Integration*, 72; and Liesbet Hooghe and Gary Marks, *Multi-level Governance and European Integration* (Oxford: Rowman and Littlefield, 2001), 27.

38. The EU has actually pushed for the transfer of more authority from national states to regional and municipal governments, including establishing and supporting institutions that advocate for subnational bodies, such as the European Committee of the Regions and EuroCities. National governments have been the primary impediment to subnational delegation.

39. Treaty of Rome, art. 3(c).

40. Adam Tooze, *Crashed: How a Decade of Financial Crises Changed the World* (New York: Penguin, 2018).

41. Marija Bartl, "The Way We Do Europe: Subsidiarity and the *Substantive* Democratic Deficit," *European Law Journal* 21, no. 1 (January 2015): 23–43. To be fair, there has always been a parallel push within the European project resisting bureaucratization and calling for greater democratization. While the latter has usually lost, there have been advances, including increasing the powers granted to the European Parliament (the only EU institution with directly elected representatives), as well as embryonic forms of transnational participatory democracy, such as the European Citizens Initiative, introduced in 2007. Whether such initiatives will be effective in the long term in terms of either shaping policy or increasing the legitimacy of European institutions remains an open question. See Erik Longo, "The European Citizens' Initiative: Too Much Democracy for EU Polity?" *German Law Journal* 20, no. 2 (April 2019): 181–200.

42. Lorenzo Marsili, "There Is Now a Way for the UK to Rebuild Its Bridges with the EU—Labour Should Take the Lead," *The Guardian*, October 6, 2022, https://www.theguardian.com/commentisfree/2022/oct/06/uk-eu-labour-russia-europe.

43. Alison E. Post, "Cities and Politics in the Developing World," *Annual Review of Political Science* 21 (May 2018): 116.

44. Hooghe and Marks, *Community, Scale*, 44–62; Gary Marks, Liesbet Hooghe, and Arjan H. Schakel, "Patterns of Regional Authority," *Regional and Federal Studies* 18, nos. 2–3 (2008): 170–71.

45. Hooghe and Marks, *Community, Scale*, 55.

46. Marks, Hooghe, and Schakel, "Patterns of Regional Authority," 171–73.

47. Lily L. Tsai, *Accountability without Democracy: Solidary Groups and Public Goods Provision in Rural China* (New York: Cambridge University Press, 2007), 187–227.

48. Hooghe and Marks, *Community, Scale*, 51; Neil Brenner, *New State Spaces: Urban Governance and the Rescaling of Statehood* (New York: Oxford University Press, 2004).

49. Anwar Shah, "Balance, Accountability, and Responsiveness: Lessons about Decentralization," World Bank Policy Research Working Paper No. 2021 (November 1999).

50. Luis Eslava and Sundhya Pahuja, "The State and International Law:

A Reading from the Global South," *Humanity* 11, no. 1 (Spring 2020): 124–30. But international institutions didn't just use sticks, there were carrots as well: for instance, the World Bank from 1990 to 2007 allocated $7.4 billion to support decentralization in twenty countries. World Bank Independent Evaluation Group, *Decentralization in Client Countries: An Evaluation of World Bank Support, 1990–2007* (Washington, DC: World Bank, 2008), 9.

51. Patrick Le Galès, "The Rise of Local Politics: A Global Review," *Annual Review of Political Science* 24 (2021): 357.

52. Parag Khanna, "Dismantling Empires through Devolution," *The Atlantic*, September 26, 2014, https://www.theatlantic.com/international/archive/2014/09/stronger-than-democracy/380774/; Guy Grossman and Janet I. Lewis, "Administrative Unit Proliferation," *American Political Science Review* 108, no. 1 (February 2014): 196, 199; Jan H. Pierskalla, "The Proliferation of Decentralized Governing Units," in *Decentralized Governance and Accountability: Academic Research and the Future of Donor Programming*, ed. Jonathan Rodden and Erik Wibbels (New York: Cambridge University Press, 2019), 115–43.

53. Brenner, *New State Spaces.* New nodes of authority within the state have also transformed the conduct of international politics, creating new issues, sites, and channels for transnational contestation. See, for example, Henry Farrell and Abraham L. Newman, "Domestic Institutions beyond the Nation-State: Charting the New Interdependence Approach," *World Politics* 66, no. 2 (April 2014): 331–63; and Kathleen R. McNamara and Abraham L. Newman, "The Big Reveal: COVID-19 and Globalization's Great Transformations," *International Organization* 74, no. S1 (December 2020): E59–E77.

54. See, for example, R. A. W. Rhodes, "The New Governance: Governing without Government," *Political Studies* 44, no. 4 (September 1996): 652–67.

55. Alison E. Post, Vivian Bronsoler, and Lana Salman, "Hybrid Regimes for Local Public Goods Provision: A Framework for Analysis," *Perspectives on Politics* 15, no. 4 (December 2017): 952–66.

56. Melani Cammett and Lauren M. MacLean, "The Political Consequences of Non-state Social Welfare: An Analytical Framework," in *The Politics of Non-state Social Welfare*, ed. Melani Cammett and Lauren M. MacLean (Ithaca, NY: Cornell University Press, 2014), 39–42; Peggy Levitt et al., "Transnational Social Protection: Setting the Agenda," *Oxford Development Studies* 45, no. 1 (2017): 2–19.

57. Post, Bronsoler, and Salman, "Hybrid Regimes"; Cammett and MacLean, "Political Consequences"; Levitt et al., "Transnational Social Protection."

58. An important point is found in the qualifier *often*: insecurity does not automatically lead to the arrival of nonstate security providers. In some times and places no actor is able or willing to generate order, and disorder reigns. See, for example, Ana Arjona, *Rebelocracy: A Theory of Social Order in Civil War* (New York: Cambridge University Press, 2016). On states opting to withhold security to a population, see Rachel Kleinfeld and Elena Barham, "Complicit States and the Governing Strategy of Privilege Violence: When Weakness Is Not the Problem," *Annual Review of Political Science* 21 (2018): 215–38.

59. Mattathias Schwartz, "A Massacre in Jamaica," *New Yorker*, December 12, 2011, https://www.newyorker.com/magazine/2011/12/12/a-massacre-in-jamaica.

60. Stephen Rodriques, "Building Partnerships for Restoring Ecosystems in Liberia," *New Dawn*, July 5, 2021, https://thenewdawnliberia.com/building-partnerships-for-restoring-ecosystems-in-liberia/.

61. Rivke Jaffe, "The Hybrid State: Crime and Citizenship in Urban Jamaica," *American Ethnologist* 40, no. 4 (November 2013): 735.

62. Other scholars refer to the result of these trends as "polycentric governance" or "regime complexes." On the former, see Elinor Ostrom, "Polycentric Systems for Coping with Collective Action and Global Environmental Change," *Global Environmental Change* 20, no. 4 (October 2010): 550–57; on the latter, see Robert O. Keohane and David G. Victor, "The Regime Complex for Climate Change," *Perspectives on Politics* 9, no. 1 (March 2011): 7–23.

63. We draw here in particular on Daniel Bodansky, "The Legal Character of the Paris Agreement," *Review of European, Comparative and International Environmental Law* 25, no. 2 (July 2016): 142–50; Robert O. Keohane and Michael Oppenheimer, "Paris: Beyond the Climate Dead End through Pledge and Review?" *Politics and Governance* 4, no. 3 (2016): 142–51; Robert O. Keohane and David G. Victor, "Cooperation and Discord in Global Climate Policy," *Nature Climate Change* 6, no. 6 (2016): 570–75; and David Held and Charles Roger, "Three Models of Global Climate Governance: From Kyoto to Paris and Beyond," *Global Policy* 9, no. 4 (November 2018): 527–37.

64. Analysts have long held that US opposition to Kyoto was the result

of concerns among legislators that China and other countries in the Global South would free-ride on US emission reduction efforts. But recent research by Aklin and Mildenberger shows that US opposition emerged out of domestic distributive politics that had nothing to do with China's actions. Regardless, Kyoto demonstrates that the fundamental problem with multilateral institutions is that national states can opt in or out of them at will. Michaël Aklin and Matto Mildenberger, "Prisoners of the Wrong Dilemma: Why Distributive Conflict, Not Collective Action, Characterizes the Politics of Climate Change," *Global Environmental Politics* 20, no. 4 (November 2020): 17.

65. Despite putting the power to set and meet goals entirely in the hands of individual national states in order to increase buy-in, the United States still pulled out of the agreement for several months at the end of the Trump administration.

66. These limits are themselves ambiguous. The signatories to the Paris Agreement commit to keeping global temperatures from rising above 2°C above the "preindustrial" temperature, but that "preindustrial" baseline was never defined. Finnemore and Jurkovich point out that this is not a problem for the Paris Agreement because it is an "aspirational document" rather than a commitment or promise to keep temperatures below any specific level (and therefore a specific preindustrial baseline is unnecessary for judging whether specific obligations have been met). Whether or not they intend it this way, their observation is a damning critique of Paris. Martha Finnemore and Michelle Jurkovich, "The Politics of Aspiration," *International Studies Quarterly* 64, no. 4 (December 2020): 768.

67. Paris Agreement, April 22, 2016, art. 4, para. 2. Italics are ours, though drawn from Keohane and Oppenheimer, "Paris," 147.

68. Xin Lan, P. Tans, and K. W. Thoning, "Trends in Globally-Averaged CO_2 Determined from NOAA Global Monitoring Laboratory Measurements," Version 2023-05, Earth System Research Laboratories, National Oceanic and Atmospheric Administration, accessed May 10, 2023, https:// doi.org/10.15138/9N0H-ZH07. Another striking way of capturing the problem: in 1995, the year of the first UNFCCC meeting, 86 percent of global primary energy consumption came from fossil fuels. By 2019, it had fallen to only 84 percent. Helen Thompson, "The Geopolitical Fight to Come over Green Energy," *Engelsberg Ideas*, March 5, 2021, https://engelsbergideas .com/essays/the-geopolitical-fight-to-come-over-green-energy/.

69. UNFCCC, "'Climate Commitments Not On Track to Meet Paris

Agreement Goals' as NDC Synthesis Report Is Published," February 26, 2021, https://unfccc.int/news/climate-commitments-not-on-track-to -meet-paris-agreement-goals-as-ndc-synthesis-report-is-published; Fiona Harvey, "Current Emissions Pledges Will Lead to Catastrophic Climate Breakdown, Says UN," *The Guardian*, October 26, 2022, https://www.theguar dian.com/environment/2022/oct/26/current-emissions-pledges-will-lead -to-catastrophic-climate-breakdown-says-un.

70. "Climate Action Tracker," accessed July 9, 2021, https://climateac tiontracker.org/.

71. World Health Organization, "Countries," accessed June 15, 2023, https://www.who.int/countries. The WHO is built upon some of the same contradictions as the broader UN. Its constitution places the "right to health" with individuals, but the organization's governing body, the World Health Assembly, is a parliament of national states, where each delegate represents their national ministry of health. Each national state gets a vote, yet many of the governments represented are not the most import- ant health care or public health provider within their borders. Moreover, only national states get a vote; the local NGOs, international NGOs, cor- porations, and UN agencies that provide health on the ground do not. See Amrith, "Internationalizing Health," 255–56 and 262.

72. Dali L. Yang, "China's Early Warning System Didn't Work on Covid-19," *Washington Post*, February 24, 2020, https://www.washington post.com/politics/2020/02/24/chinas-early-warning-system-didnt-work -covid-19-heres-story/; Dali L. Yang, "Wuhan Officials Tried to Cover Up Covid-19—and Sent It Careening Outward," *Washington Post*, March 10, 2020, https://www.washingtonpost.com/politics/2020/03/10/wuhan-offi cials-tried-cover-up-covid-19-sent-it-careening-outward/.

73. Laurie Garrett, *The Coming Plague: Newly Emerging Diseases in a World Out of Balance* (New York: Farrar, Straus and Giroux, 1994), 42.

74. Selam Gebrekidan et al., "In Hunt for Virus Source, W.H.O. Let China Take Charge," *New York Times,* November 2, 2020, https://www.ny times.com/2020/11/02/world/who-china-coronavirus.html.

75. Gebrekidan et al., "In Hunt for Virus Source"; Nicholas Wade, "The Origin of COVID: Did People or Nature Open Pandora's Box at Wuhan?" *Bulletin of the Atomic Scientists,* May 5, 2021, https://thebulletin.org/2021 /05/the-origin-of-covid-did-people-or-nature-open-pandoras-box-at -wuhan/; Javier C. Hernández and James Gorman, "On W.H.O. Trip, China Refused to Hand Over Important Data," *New York Times*, February

12, 2021, https://www.nytimes.com/2021/02/12/world/asia/china-world
-health-organization-coronavirus.html. Upon the publication of the preliminary report by the team of international experts enlisted by the WHO,
Lawrence Gostin, a leading American public health law authority, remarked that "the lack of political cooperation from China continues to stifle
any meaningful progress" toward understanding the origins of COVID-19.
Benjamin Mueller and Carl Zimmer, "Mysteries Linger about Covid's Origins, W.H.O. Report Says," *New York Times*, June 9, 2022, https://www
.nytimes.com/2022/06/09/science/covid-origins-who-report-china.html.

76. Montreal Protocol on Substances That Deplete the Ozone Layer,
September 16, 1987, preamble, https://treaties.un.org/doc/publication/
unts/volume%201522/volume-1522-i-26369-english.pdf.

77. Kofi Annan quoted in Michael Oppenheimer et al., *Discerning Experts: The Practices of Scientific Assessment for Environmental Policy* (Chicago: University of Chicago Press, 2019), 110.

78. Charles F. Sabel and David G. Victor, *Fixing the Climate: Strategies
for an Uncertain World* (Princeton, NJ: Princeton University Press, 2022),
19.

79. World Health Organization, "Thirty-Third World Health Assembly Resolutions and Decisions Annexes," WHA33/1980/REC/1, May 5–23,
1980, 1.

80. Erez Manela, "Smallpox Eradication and the Rise of Global Governance," in *The Shock of the Global: The 1970s in Perspective*, ed. Niall Ferguson et al. (Cambridge, MA: Harvard University Press, 2010), 257–58.

81. Erez Manela, "Smallpox and the Globalization of Development," in
The Development Century: A Global History, ed. Stephen J. Macekura and
Erez Manela (New York: Cambridge University Press, 2018), 101.

82. Rachel Carson, *Silent Spring* (Boston: Houghton Mifflin, 1962), 297.

83. Manela, "Smallpox and the Globalization of Development," 95–96.

84. Randall Packard, *A History of Global Health: Interventions into the
Lives of Other Peoples* (Baltimore: Johns Hopkins University Press, 2016);
Andrew Lakoff, "Two Regimes of Global Health," *Humanity* 1, no. 1 (Fall
2010): 59–79.

85. Amitav Acharya, "After Liberal Hegemony: The Advent of a Multiplex World Order," *Ethics and International Affairs* 31, no. 3 (Fall 2017):
271–85.

86. Ann Swidler, "Global Institutional Imaginaries," in *Culture and
Order in World Politics*, ed. Andrew Phillips and Christian Reus-Smit (New

York: Cambridge University Press, 2020), esp. 188–97; Weiss, *Governing the World?*, 4–5.

87. Rosa Ehrenreich Brooks, "Failed States, or the State as Failure?" *University of Chicago Law Review* 72, no. 4 (Fall 2005): 1166–67.

88. Weiss, *Governing the World?*, 1.

Chapter 3

1. Thomas L. Friedman, *The World Is Flat: A Brief History of the Twenty-First Century*, rev. and expanded ed. (New York: Macmillan, 2006), 53, 459.

2. Friedman, *World Is Flat*, 468–70. Though brief, his discussion of the problems that could emerge from the reliance on just-in-time globalized supply chains during a pandemic was quite prescient.

3. See the discussion in Dipesh Chakrabarty, *The Climate of History in a Planetary Age* (Chicago: University of Chicago Press, 2021), esp. 71.

4. Chakrabarty, *Climate of History*, 71.

5. Vaclav Smil, *The Earth's Biosphere: Evolution, Dynamics, and Change* (Cambridge, MA: MIT Press, 2003).

6. For a definition of the Earth system, see Tim Lenton, *Earth System Science: A Very Short Introduction* (New York: Oxford University Press, 2016), 14–17.

7. Benjamin H. Bratton, *The Terraforming* (Moscow: Strelka Press, 2019); Chakrabarty, *Climate of History*.

8. Scott F. Gilbert, Jan Sapp, and Alfred I. Tauber, "A Symbiotic View of Life: We Have Never Been Individuals," *Quarterly Review of Biology* 87, no. 4 (December 2012): 326–27. See also Margaret McFall-Ngai et al., "Animals in a Bacterial World, a New Imperative for the Life Sciences," *Proceedings of the National Academy of Sciences* 110, no. 9 (February 2013): 3229–36.

9. Putting our microbiota into perspective, Quigley observes, "The number of bacteria within the gut is approximately 10 times that of all of the cells in the human body, and the collective bacterial genome is vastly greater than the human genome." See Eamonn Quigley, "Gut Bacteria in Health and Disease," *Gastroenterology and Hepatology* 9, no. 9 (September 2013): 561.

10. Anna Tsing, "Unruly Edges: Mushrooms as Companion Species," *Environmental Humanities* 1, no. 1 (May 2012): 144. Her magnificent elaboration is Anna Lowenhaupt Tsing, *The Mushroom at the End of the World: On the Possibility of Life in Capitalist Ruins* (Princeton, NJ: Princeton University Press, 2015).

11. As mentioned in the Introduction, holistic and environmentally focused intellectual and spiritual traditions exist in most if not all cultures. We have chosen in this chapter to focus specifically on the Western lineage of this tradition of thought because of the way that tradition has been in dialogue with both the precision-oriented Western sciences and the Western political traditions that underpin the predominant political and governance institutions of the present.

12. Novelist Richard Powers, on a podcast, contrasts the "humbling sciences . . . that point our attention away from ourselves and onto other living things" with "the human sciences that amplify our ability to control and master and manipulate our situation here and to understand ourselves." "Transcript: Ezra Klein Interviews Richard Powers," *New York Times*, September 28, 2021, https://www.nytimes.com/2021/09/28/podcasts/transcript-ezra-klein-interviews-richard-powers.html.

13. Charles Darwin, *The Origin of Species* (1859; repr., New York: Oxford University Press, 1996), 395.

14. Ernst Haeckel quoted in Carolyn Merchant, *The Columbia Guide to American Environmental History* (New York: Columbia University Press, 2005), 160.

15. Ernst Haeckel quoted in Robert J. Richards, *The Tragic Sense of Life: Ernst Haeckel and the Struggle over Evolutionary Thought* (Chicago: University of Chicago Press, 2019), 8n28.

16. Paul Warde, Libby Robin, and Sverker Sörlin, *The Environment: A History of the Idea* (Baltimore: Johns Hopkins University Press, 2018), 33.

17. For background on Vernadsky, see Kendall E. Bailes, *Science and Russian Culture in an Age of Revolutions: V. I. Vernadsky and His Scientific School, 1863–1945* (Bloomington: Indiana University Press, 1990); Lynn Margulis et al., "Foreword to the English-Language Edition," in Vladimir Vernadsky, *The Biosphere*, trans. David. B. Langmuir (New York: Copernicus, 1998), 14–19; and Giulia Rispoli and Jacques Grinevald, "Vladimir Vernadsky and the Co-evolution of the Biosphere, the Noösphere, and the Technosphere," *Technosphere Magazine*, June 20, 2018, 1–9.

18. W. I. Vernadsky, "The Biosphere and the Noösphere," *American Scientist* 33, no. 1 (January 1945): 4.

19. Vernadsky, "Biosphere and the Noösphere," 1.

20. Vernadsky, *Biosphere*, 39, 44, 43, and 142.

21. Vernadsky, "Biosphere and the Noösphere," 3, 8, 9 (italics in the original).

22. Philosopher and mathematician Edouard Le Roy was also involved with these intellectual exchanges and is credited with coining the term *noösphere*.

23. Pierre Teilhard de Chardin, *The Vision of the Past*, trans. J. M. Cohen (New York: Harper and Row, 1967), 181; Vernadsky, "Biosphere and the Noösphere," 8.

24. Vladimir Vernadsky, "The Transition from the Biosphere to the Noösphere," *21st Century Science and Technology*, Spring-Summer 2012, 18. This article is an excerpt from Vernadsky's *Scientific Thought as a Planetary Phenomenon* (published in 1938), trans. William Jones (Moscow: Nongovernmental Ecological V. I. Vernadsky Foundation, 1997).

25. Vernadsky, "Biosphere and the Noösphere," 8.

26. Ursula King, *Spirit of Fire: The Life and Vision of Pierre Teilhard de Chardin* (Maryknoll, NY: Orbis Books, 2015).

27. Pierre Teilhard de Chardin, *The Phenomenon of Man*, trans. Bernard Wall (New York: Harper, 1959), 183.

28. Teilhard, *Phenomenon of Man*, 183.

29. Though Tansley was the first to use the term in print, the underlying concept that living and nonliving elements of a given place constitute a single, integrated unit preceded him. Moreover, the term was coined by Tansley's junior colleague A. R. Clapham. See Kurt Jax, "Holocoen and Ecosystem: On the Origin and Historical Consequences of Two Concepts," *Journal of the History of Biology* 31, no. 1 (Spring 1998): 113–15; and Peter G. Ayres, *Shaping Ecology: The Life of Arthur Tansley* (Oxford: Wiley-Blackwell, 2012), 138.

30. See, for instance, this usage by ecologist John Phillips in 1930: "I do not restrain ecology to a study of vegetation, I mean the *full* ecology . . . that of man, other animals and vegetation." Quoted in Peder Anker, *Imperial Ecology: Environmental Order in the British Empire, 1895–1945* (Cambridge, MA: Harvard University Press, 2001), 130 (italics in original).

31. All quotes are from A. G. Tansley, "The Use and Abuse of Vegetational Concepts and Terms," *Ecology* 16, no. 3 (July 1935): 299 (italics in original).

32. Tansley, "Use and Abuse," 299. See Warde, Robin, and Sörlin, *Environment*, 82–85.

33. Tansley, "Use and Abuse," 304.

34. Quoted in Warde, Robin, and Sörlin, *Environment*, 38.

35. Quoted in Warde, Robin, and Sörlin, *Environment*, 10.

36. Fairfield Osborn, *Our Plundered Planet* (Boston: Little, Brown, 1948), vi. See Warde, Robin, and Sörlin, *Environment*, 13.

37. Jerry Brown and Stewart Brand, "The Origins of 'Planetary Realism' and 'Whole Earth' Thinking," *Noema* magazine, February 9, 2021, https://www.noemamag.com/the-origins-of-planetary-realism-and-whole-earth-thinking/; Fred Turner, *From Counterculture to Cyberculture: Stewart Brand, the Whole Earth Network, and the Rise of Digital Utopianism* (Chicago: University of Chicago Press, 2010), 69.

38. "Purpose," *Whole Earth Catalog*, Fall 1968, 2.

39. J. E. Lovelock, "Gaia as Seen through the Atmosphere," *Atmospheric Environment* 6, no. 8 (August 1972): 579.

40. James Lovelock, *Gaia: A New Look at Life on Earth*, rev. ed. (New York: Oxford University Press, 1987), 6. Leah Aronowsky uncovers the troubling impact of Lovelock's professional relationship with the fossil fuel industry, who had and still have a direct interest in the idea that Earth can self-regulate, on the development of the Gaia hypothesis. Leah Aronowsky, "Gas Guzzling Gaia, or: A Prehistory of Climate Change Denialism," *Critical Inquiry* 47, no. 2 (Winter 2021): 306–27.

41. Lovelock, *Gaia*, 9.

42. Lovelock, *Gaia*, viii.

43. Disputation over the scientific status of the Gaia hypothesis continues. A prominent early critic was W. Ford Doolittle, "Is Nature Really Motherly?," *CoEvolution Quarterly* 29 (January 1981): 58–63. (*The CoEvolution Quarterly* was Stewart Brand's follow-up magazine to the *Whole Earth Catalog*.) More recently, Earth system scientist Toby Tyrrell judged that only one of Lovelock's three primary assertions was supported in his review of the most up-to-date evidence: Toby Tyrrell, *On Gaia: A Critical Investigation of the Relationship between Life and Earth* (Princeton, NJ: Princeton University Press, 2013). Interestingly, Doolittle himself eventually reversed his earlier skepticism, concluding that the Gaia "hypothesis does make sense if one treats the clade that comprises the biological component of Gaia as an individual and allows differential persistence"; W. Ford Doolittle, "Making Evolutionary Sense of Gaia," *Trends in Ecology and Evolution* 34, no. 10 (May 2019): 889. Doolittle explained why he had changed his mind in W. Ford Doolittle, "Is the Earth an Organism?," *Aeon* magazine, December 3, 2020, https://aeon.co/essays/the-gaia-hypothesis-reimagined-by-one-of-its-key-sceptics.

44. James E. Lovelock and Lynn Margulis, "Atmospheric Homeostasis

by and for the Biosphere: The Gaia Hypothesis," *Tellus* 26, nos. 1–2 (February 1974): 3.

45. Lovelock, *Gaia*, 126.

46. Lovelock, *Gaia*, 8, 64–65.

47. See Stephen Macekura, *Of Limits and Growth: The Rise of Global Sustainable Development in the Twentieth Century* (New York: Cambridge University Press, 2015). In 1971, for instance, international relations scholars Harold and Margaret Sprout observed that "there is evidence of spreading awareness . . . that progressive destruction of the ecology of the biosphere poses a comparably lethal threat to human well-being, and possibly to future human tenure upon the earth," as "nuclear catastrophe." That same year, international law scholar Richard Falk warned of "the endangered-planet crisis" caused, in part, by "prevailing presuppositions that the earth has an infinite capacity to satisfy the ever-increasing human wants of a growing population." Harold Sprout and Margaret Sprout, *Toward a Politics of the Planet Earth* (New York: Van Nostrand Reinhold, 1971), 484–85, 484; Richard A. Falk, *This Endangered Planet: Prospects and Proposals for Human Survival* (New York: Random House, 1971), 22. The titles of both books are clear reflections of the era's planetary zeitgeist.

48. U Thant quoted in Glenda Sluga, "The Transformation of International Institutions: Global Shock as Cultural Shock," in *The Shock of the Global: The 1970s in Perspective*, ed. Niall Ferguson et al. (Cambridge, MA: Belknap Press of Harvard University Press, 2010), 233.

49. Barbara Ward and René Dubos, *Only One Earth: The Care and Maintenance of a Small Planet* (New York: W. W. Norton, 1972), 11. Barbara Ward, *Spaceship Earth* (New York: Columbia University Press, 1966), was another inspiration for Brand to start *Whole Earth Catalog*. See Steven Kotler, "The Whole Earth Catalog Effect," *Plenty Magazine*, November 2008. The phrase was further popularized in an influential essay by economist Kenneth E. Boulding, "The Economics of the Coming Spaceship Earth," in *Environmental Quality in a Growing Economy*, ed. Henry Jarrett (Baltimore: Johns Hopkins University Press, 1966), 3–14; and especially by R. Buckminster Fuller, *Operating Manual for Spaceship Earth* (New York: Simon and Schuster, 1969).

50. Barbara Ward, "Only One Earth, Stockholm 1972," in *Evidence for Hope: The Search for Sustainable Development*, ed. Nigel Cross (London: Earthscan, 2003), 4, 7.

51. Aurelio Peccei quoted in Glenda Sluga, "'Sleepwalking' from Plan-

etary Thinking to the End of the International Order," HEC Working Paper, European University Institute, February 2021, 5.

52. Donella Meadows et al., *The Limits to Growth: A Report for the Club of Rome's Project on the Predicament of Mankind* (New York: Universe Books, 1972), 21–22.

53. Club of Rome Executive Committee, "Commentary," in Meadows et al., *Limits to Growth*, 185.

54. Meadows et al., *Limits to Growth*, 23.

55. Meadows et al., *Limits to Growth*, 23.

56. Club of Rome Executive Committee, "Commentary," 190.

57. Club of Rome Executive Committee, "Commentary," 188.

58. The back cover quote is from journalist and world peace advocate Norman Cousins.

59. Arne Naess, "The Shallow and the Deep, Long-Range Ecology Movement: A Summary," *Inquiry* 16 (1973): 95. The term *ecology*, despite its earlier history, was only just entering public consciousness. In late 1969, the *Los Angeles Times* observed, "The newest word among social activists is *ecology*—a word most people hadn't heard of a year ago." Rasa Gustaisis quoted in Benjamin Lazier, "Earthrise; or, The Globalization of the World Picture," *American Historical Review* 116, no. 3 (June 2011): 617n41.

60. Naess, "Shallow and the Deep," 96. In an influential 1975 book, philosopher Peter Singer, *Animal Liberation: A New Ethics for Our Treatment of Animals* (New York: HarperCollins, 1975), 6, condemned such anthropocentrism as "speciesism," which he defined as "a prejudice or attitude of bias in favor of the interests of members of one's own species and against those of members of other species."

61. Naess, "Shallow and the Deep," 95.

62. Naess, "Shallow and the Deep," 96.

63. Wallace S. Broecker, "Climatic Change: Are We on the Brink of a Pronounced Global Warming?," *Science* 189, no. 4201 (August 1975): 460–63.

64. On ecofeminism, see, for example, Susan Griffin, *Woman and Nature: The Roaring inside Her* (New York: Harper and Row, 1978); and Val Plumwood, *Feminism and the Mastery of Nature* (London: Routledge, 1993).

65. On the founding of the UN Environmental Program, see Maria Ivanova, *The Untold Story of the World's Leading Environmental Institution: UNEP at Fifty* (Cambridge, MA: MIT Press, 2021), 25–54.

66. Max R. Langham and W. W. McPherson, "Energy Analysis," *Science* 192, no. 4234 (April 1976): 8–11.

67. Paul J. Crutzen and Eugene F. Stoermer, "The 'Anthropocene,'" *Global Change Newsletter* 41 (May 2000): 17.

68. Paul J. Crutzen, "Geology of Mankind," *Nature* 415, no. 6867 (January 2002): 23.

69. Quoted in Gregg Mitman, "Hubris or Humility? Genealogies of the Anthropocene," in *Future Remains: A Cabinet of Curiosities for the Anthropocene*, ed. Gregg Mitman, Marko Armiero, and Robert S. Emmett (Chicago: University of Chicago Press, 2018), 63.

70. Clive Hamilton and Jacques Grinevald, "Was the Anthropocene Anticipated?" *Anthropocene Review* 2, no. 1 (January 2015): 59–72.

71. Working Group on the "Anthropocene," "Results of Binding Vote by AWG, Released 21st May 2019," http://quaternary.stratigraphy.org/working-groups/anthropocene/. See Meera Subramanian, "Anthropocene Now: Influential Panel Votes to Recognize Earth's New Epoch," *Nature*, May 21, 2019. For a criticism of how the AWG has gone about their work, as well as their placement of the golden spike, see Simon L. Lewis and Mark A. Maslin, *The Human Planet: How We Created the Anthropocene* (New Haven, CT: Yale University Press, 2018), 290–93.

72. The Anthropocene is one of those rare academic concepts, like existentialism and postmodernism, that breaks out of the ivory tower to become a popular term. There are numerous novels dealing with the Anthropocene, a musical (*Anthropocene, The Musical*, a "dystopic eco-tainment about how man is destroying Earth"; https://clubgewalt.nl/en/project/anthropocene-the-musical/), even an Anthropocene fashion label (https://anthropocene.fr/). See Adam Trexler, *Anthropocene Fictions: The Novel in a Time of Climate Change* (Charlottesville: University of Virginia Press, 2015); and Alexandra Nikoleris, Johannes Stripple, and Paul Tenngart, "The 'Anthropocene' in Popular Culture: Narrating Human Agency, Force, and Our Place on Earth," in *Anthropocene Encounters: New Directions in Green Political Thinking*, ed. Frank Biermann and Eva Lövbrand (New York: Cambridge University Press, 2019), 67–84.

73. See Jason Moore, ed., *Anthropocene or Capitalocene? Nature, History, and the Crisis of Capitalism* (Oakland, CA: PM Press, 2016); and Donna Haraway and Anna Tsing, "Reflections on the Plantationocene: A Conversation with Donna Haraway and Anna Tsing, Moderated by Gregg Mittman," *Edge Effects*, June 18, 2019, https://edgeeffects.net/wp-content/uploads/2019/06/PlantationoceneReflections_Haraway_Tsing.pdf. One recent study counts at least eighty alternative terms that have been sug-

gested. Franciszek Chwałczyk, "Around the Anthropocene in Eighty Names—Considering the Urbanocene Proposition," *Sustainability* 12, no. 11 (April 2020): 4458.

74. She continued: "Some people, some companies, some decision-makers in particular, have known exactly what priceless values they have been sacrificing to continue making unimaginable amounts of money. And I think many of you here today belong to that group of people." The crowd of stunned plutocrats sat for a moment in silence until U2 frontman Bono started clapping. Ivana Kottasova and Eliza Mackintosh, "Teen Activist Tells Davos Elite They're to Blame for Climate Crisis," CNN, January 25, 2019, https://www.cnn.com/2019/01/25/europe/greta-thunberg-davos-world -economic-forum-intl/index.html.

75. J. R. McNeill and Peter Engelke, *The Great Acceleration: An Environmental History of the Anthropocene since 1945* (Cambridge, MA: Belknap Press of Harvard University Press, 2014); Will Steffen et al., "The Trajectory of the Anthropocene: The Great Acceleration," *Anthropocene Review* 2, no. 1 (April 2015): 81–98.

76. Kathleen D. Morrison, "Provincializing the Anthropocene: Eurocentrism in the Earth System," in *At Nature's Edge: The Global Present and Long-Term History*, ed. Gunnel Cederlöf and Mahesh Rangarajan (New York: Oxford University Press, 2015), 1–18.

77. Scott A. Elias, "Basis for Establishment of Geologic Eras, Periods, and Epochs," in *Encyclopedia of the Anthropocene*, vol. 1, *Geologic History and Energy*, ed. Scott Elias (Oxford: Elsevier Science, 2017), 9–17.

78. Jan Bogaert, Isabelle Vranken, and Marie André, "Anthropogenic Effects in Landscapes: Historical Context and Spatial Pattern," in *Biocultural Landscapes: Diversity, Functions and Values*, ed. Sun-Kee Hong, Jan Bogaert, and Qingwen Min (New York: Springer, 2014), 89–112.

79. For example, Erle Ellis et al., "People Have Shaped Most of Terrestrial Nature for at Least 12,000 Years," *Proceedings of the National Academy of Sciences* 118, no. 17 (April 2021): e2023483118.

80. Donna Haraway, *Staying with the Trouble: Making Kin in the Chthulucene* (Durham, NC: Duke University Press, 2016), 100.

81. Indeed, the effort by the geologists to fix the date of the advent of this supposed new era as late as possible can be seen as a tacit effort to hold open the notion of modern humanity's exceptional agency, even as it condemns the way in which that agency has so far been exercised. See Simon L. Lewis and Mark A. Maslin, "Defining the Anthropocene," *Nature* 519,

no. 7542 (March 2015): esp. 177–78. Chakrabarty, *Climate of History*, 155–81, questions the strictly geological approach to dating the Anthropocene, proposing that historians should be involved in deciding where to place the golden spike.

82. Donna Haraway, "A Manifesto for Cyborgs: Science, Technology, and Socialist Feminism in the 1980s," *Socialist Review*, no. 80 (1985): 69, 72.

83. Gayatri Chakravorty Spivak, "'Planetarity' (Box 4, WELT)," *Paragraph* 38, no. 2 (July 2015): 290–92 (all quotes from p. 291); Gayatri Chakravorty Spivak, *Death of a Discipline* (New York: Columbia University Press, 2003).

84. Bruno Latour and Dipesh Chakrabarty, "Conflicts of Planetary Proportions–A Conversation," *Journal of the Philosophy of History* 14, no. 3 (November 2020): 419–54. On high modernism, see James C. Scott, *Seeing Like a State: How Certain Schemes to Improve the Human Condition Have Failed* (New Haven, CT: Yale University Press, 1998).

85. Examples from the social sciences and humanities include Joseph Masco, "Bad Weather: On Planetary Crisis," *Social Studies of Science* 40, no. 1 (February 2010): 7–40; Elizabeth DeLoughrey, "Satellite Planetarity and the Ends of the Earth," *Public Culture* 26, no. 2 (Spring 2014): 257–80; Anthony Burke et al., "Planet Politics: A Manifesto from the End of IR," *Millennium* 44, no. 3 (June 2016): 499–523; William E. Connolly, *Facing the Planetary: Entangled Humanism and the Politics of Swarming* (Durham, NC: Duke University Press, 2017); Bratton, *Terraforming*; Daniel Deudney, *Dark Skies: Space Expansionism, Planetary Geopolitics and the Ends of Humanity* (New York: Oxford University Press, 2020); Milja Kurki, *International Relations in a Relational Universe* (New York: Oxford University Press, 2020); Chakrabarty, *Climate of History*; Lorenzo Marsili, *Planetary Politics: A Manifesto* (Cambridge: Polity Press, 2021); Oran R. Young, *Grand Challenges of Planetary Governance: Global Order in Turbulent Times* (Cheltenham, UK: Edward Elgar, 2021); Mary Kaldor and Sabine Selchow, "Planetary Politics: Reviving the Spirit of the Concept of 'Global Civil Society,'" in *Civil Society: Concepts, Challenges, Contexts*, ed. Michael Hoelscher et al. (Cham, Switzerland: Springer, 2022), 189–204; and Stewart Patrick, *To Prevent the Collapse of Biodiversity, the World Needs a New Planetary Politics* (Washington, DC: Carnegie Endowment for International Peace, 2022).

86. Benjamin H. Bratton, *The Stack: On Software and Sovereignty* (Cambridge, MA: MIT Press, 2016); see also Karen Bakker, *Gaia's Web: How Digital Environmentalism Can Combat Climate Change, Restore Biodiversity,*

Cultivate Empathy, and Regenerate the Earth (Cambridge, MA: MIT Press, 2024).

87. Gloria Hicks, "Getting at Groundwater with Gravity," *Sensing Our Planet*, February 13, 2007, https://earthdata.nasa.gov/learn/sensing-our -planet/getting-at-groundwater-with-gravity. (*Sensing Our Planet* was a NASA publication for the general public from 1994 to 2018, when it was discontinued by the Trump administration, which was actively hostile to the enhancement of planetary sapience.)

88. Celso H. L. Silva Junior et al., "Persistent Collapse of Biomass in Amazonian Forest Edges Following Deforestation Leads to Unaccounted Carbon Losses," *Science Advances* 6, no. 40 (October 2020): eaaz8360.

89. The quote is from Benjamin Bratton, "Planetary Sapience," *Noema* magazine, June 17, 2021, https://www.noemamag.com/planetary-sapience /. See Spencer R. Weart, *The Discovery of Global Warming* (Cambridge, MA: Harvard University Press, 2008); Sarah Dry, *Waters of the World: The Story of the Scientists Who Unraveled the Mysteries of Our Oceans, Atmosphere, and Ice Sheets and Made the Planet Whole* (Chicago: University of Chicago Press, 2019); and Paul Edwards, *A Vast Machine: Computer Models, Climate Data, and the Politics of Global Warming* (Cambridge, MA: MIT Press, 2013). Some scholars refer to the sum total of all these technologies of perception as the "technosphere." See, especially, Adam Frank, David Grinspoon, and Sara Walker, "Intelligence as a Planetary Scale Process," *International Journal of Astrobiology*, 21, no. 2 (April 2022): 47–61, who argue that Earth currently possesses only an "immature" technosphere, that is, one capable of *sensing* the condition of planetarity; a "mature" technosphere, by contrast, would enable not just sensing but *control* over planetary phenomena. See also P. K. Haff, "Technology as a Geological Phenomenon: Implications for Human Well-Being," *Geological Society, London, Special Publications* 395, no. 1 (May 2014): 301–9.

90. Baptiste Monsaingeon, "Oceans of Plastic: Hetergeneous Narrations of an Ongoing Disaster," *Limn* 3 (June 2013), https://limn.it/articles/ oceans-of-plastic-heterogeneous-narrations-of-an-ongoing-disaster/.

91. Bratton, "Planetary Sapience."

92. Lynn Margulis places planetary sapience in Earth-historical context, describing the long-standing existence of a planetary "proprioceptor capability": "Proprioceptors work as sensory systems not for outside information about others or the environment but inside the body. . . . The Earth has enjoyed a proprioceptor system for millennia, since long before

humans evolved. The air circulated gas emissions and soluble chemicals from tropical trees, mating-ready insects, and life-threatened bacteria. Love compounds have wafted in Spring breezes since the Archean age. But the speed of proprioception has increased with the electronic age." Lynn Margulis, *Symbiotic Planet: A New View of Evolution* (New York: Basic Books, 2002), 113–14.

93. As Langmuir and Broecker observe, "Biodiversity is perhaps our most precious planetary resource, for which the timescale of replenishment, known from past mass extinctions, is tens of millions of years." Charles H. Langmuir and Wally Broecker, *How to Build a Habitable Planet: The Story of Earth from the Big Bang to Humankind,* 2nd ed. (Princeton, NJ: Princeton University Press, 2012), 580.

94. See Scott, *Seeing Like a State*; John McPhee, *The Control of Nature* (New York: Farrar, Straus, and Giroux, 1989).

95. Throughout the book, we use the terms *planetary issues*, *planetary challenges*, and *planetary problems* interchangeably.

96. We draw here on Chakrabarty, *Climate of History*, 85.

97. Part of our list comes from the nine processes identified by the Stockholm Resilience Centre's planetary boundaries framework. See Johan Rockström et al., "Planetary Boundaries: Exploring the Safe Operating Space for Humanity," *Ecology and Society* 14, no. 2 (December 2009), http://www.ecologyandsociety.org/vol14/iss2/art32/; Johan Rockström et al., "A Safe Operating Space for Humanity," *Nature* 461, no. 7263 (September 2009), 472–75; Will Steffen et al., "Planetary Boundaries: Guiding Human Development on a Changing Planet," *Science* 347, no. 6223 (February 2015): 736; and Johan Rockström and Mattias Klum, *Big World, Small Planet: Abundance within Planetary Boundaries* (New Haven, CT: Yale University Press, 2015), 59–79. Although many of the issues listed commonly appear on lists of global environmental problems, the inclusion of issues like space junk and anthropogenic genetic disruption differentiates the planetary perspective from the environmental one.

98. Environmentalist schemes that prioritize other species above humans beings are all too easily used to justify oppression of some humans by others. See, for example, Ramachandra Guha, "The Authoritarian Biologist and the Arrogance of Anti-humanism: Wildlife Conservation in the Third World," *The Ecologist* 27, no. 1 (January/February 1997): 14–20.

99. The crash galvanized scientists and governments to monitor asteroids that could come near Earth in the name of "planetary defense."

"How Historic Jupiter Comet Impact Led to Planetary Defense," NASA, June, 30, 2019, https://www.nasa.gov/feature/goddard/2019/how-historic -jupiter-comet-impact-led-to-planetary-defense.

100. Lynn Margulis quoted in Raymond F. Dasmann, "Toward a Biosphere Consciousness," in *The Ends of the Earth: Perspectives on Modern Environmental History*, ed. Donald Worster and Alfred W. Crosby (Cambridge: Cambridge University Press, 1988), 280.

101. Lenton, *Earth System Science*, 2.

102. Langmuir and Broecker, *How to Build*, 578.

103. Chakrabarty suggests that "habitability," which is centrally concerned with what makes "life—complex, multicellular life, in general— . . . not humans alone, sustainable," provides an important contrast to the idea of "sustainability." Habitability is a planetary concept, whereas sustainability, weighed down by anthropocentrism, is a global one. Chakrabarty, *Climate of History*, 81–85, with quote from 83.

104. See Langmuir and Broecker, *How to Build*, 595. Their one-sentence account of fossil fuel usage brilliantly elucidates how our modern lives rely on past life: "We take the organic carbon stored over hundreds of millions of years of photosynthesis, and combine it with the oxygenated atmosphere developed by the billions of years of planetary evolution, reversing photosynthesis and releasing the stored energy." Langmuir and Broecker, *How to Build*, 575.

105. Chakrabarty, *Climate of History*, 86–87. To gain traction on entities that are so beyond human-scaled, Morton uses the term *hyperobjects* to describe "things that are massively distributed in time and space relative to humans." Timothy Morton, *Hyperobjects: Philosophy and Ecology after the End of the World* (Minneapolis: University of Minnesota Press, 2013), 1. For a brief, nontechnical discussion of some of the math involved in such large scales, see Langmuir and Broecker, *How to Build*, 2–4.

106. For a discussion of the outer and inner boundaries of the Earth system, see Lenton, *Earth System Science*, 14–17.

107. For example, Will Steffen et al., "Trajectories of the Earth System in the Anthropocene," *Proceedings of the National Academy of Sciences* 115, no. 33 (August 2018): 8252–59.

108. Stephen Jay Gould, *Time's Arrow, Time's Cycle: Myth and Metaphor in the Discovery of Geological Time* (Cambridge, MA: Harvard University Press, 1987).

109. Lisa Messeri, *Placing Outer Space: An Earthly Ethnography of Other Worlds* (Durham, NC: Duke University Press, 2016), 11.

110. Chakrabarty, *Climate of History*, 203.

111. The ability to interfere with planetary processes, however, does not mean that humans can control them. Accounting for human involvement is not the same as accounting for human mastery. Planetary issues are all affected by human action, yet our impact is often unintentional, and we do not always possess the capability to command its direction. Nevertheless, our concern in this book is for those planetary processes and conditions for which there is a human factor. The argument for planetary governance that we develop in this book is rooted in an understanding that humans cannot aspire to Promethean mastery. The vision of planetary governance that we offer is something more like kayaking down a river rapid: you don't seek to tame and master the river, but rather paddle hard in order to control and enjoy your own passage through it.

112. See, for example, S. Witman, "More Earthquakes May Be the Result of Fracking Than We Thought," *Eos*, February 8, 2018, https://eos.org/research-spotlights/more-earthquakes-may-be-the-result-of-fracking-than-we-thought.

113. Anna Lowenhaupt Tsing, Andrew S. Mathews, and Nils Bubandt, "Patchy Anthropocene: Landscape Structure, Multispecies History, and the Retooling of Anthropology: An Introduction to Supplement 20," *Current Anthropology* 60, no. S20 (August 2019): S186–S197.

114. Messeri, *Placing Outer Space*, 10.

Chapter 4

1. David Mitrany, *A Working Peace System: An Argument for the Functional Development of International Organization* (London: Royal Institute for International Affairs, 1943), 31. For Mitrany's background and thought, see Dorothy Anderson, "David Mitrany (1888–1975): An Appreciation of His Life and Work," *Review of International Studies* 24, no. 4 (October 1998): 577–92; and Or Rosenboim, *The Emergence of Globalism: Visions of World Order in Britain and the United States, 1939–1950* (Princeton, NJ: Princeton University Press, 2017), 24–55.

2. Mitrany, *Working Peace System*, 15.

3. Indeed, multitiered polities (*multitiered governance* refers to the larger umbrella concept, which multilevel and multiscalar exist within)

date back to early recorded history: ancient Sumerians were governed by a network of city-states, which were each composed of villages, which were each composed of hamlets. See Daniel Treisman, *The Architecture of Government: Rethinking Political Decentralization* (New York: Cambridge University Press, 2007), 7.

4. Our usage of *scale* and *level* differs from that of scholars like Gibson, Ostrom, and Ahn, who use *scale* to mean the dimension of a problem (spatial, temporal, analytical, etc.) and *level* to mean the units arrayed along each scale. But our usage does reflect our reading of the "scale debates" among geographers: we understand scales as socially and politically constructed, reflecting the contested, power-laden processes by which they are established and work in the world. Clark C. Gibson, Elinor Ostrom, and T. K. Ahn, "The Concept of Scale and the Human Dimensions of Global Change: A Survey," *Ecological Economics* 32, no. 2 (February 2000): 217–39; see also David W. Cash et al., "Scale and Cross-scale Dynamics: Governance and Information in a Multilevel World," *Ecology and Society* 11, no. 2 (December 2006), http://www.ecologyandsociety.org/vol11/iss2/art8/. For the debate in geography, see Neil Brenner, "The Limits to Scale? Methodological Reflections on Scalar Structuration," *Progress in Human Geography* 25, no. 4 (December 2001): 591–614; and Sallie A. Marston, John Paul Jones III, and Keith Woodward, "Human Geography without Scale," *Transactions of the Institute of British Geographers* 30, no. 4 (December 2005): 416–32.

5. "The League of Nations and now the United Nations, as their names imply, rest upon national separateness," observed Mitrany, only three years into the UN's existence. David Mitrany, "The Functional Approach to World Organization," *International Affairs* 24, no. 3 (July 1948): 351.

6. Samuel Moyn, *Not Enough: Human Rights in an Unequal World* (Cambridge, MA: Belknap Press of Harvard University Press, 2018); Samuel Moyn, "Fantasies of Federalism," *Dissent*, Winter 2015, https://www.dissentmagazine.org/article/fantasies-of-federalism/.

7. As Elinor Ostrom argues, we must move beyond "the contemporary presumption by some scholars that only the global scale is relevant for policies related to global public goods." Her research, and that of others, offers evidence that effective governance requires large-scale units *and* medium- and small-scale units. "An important lesson," she explains, "is that simply recommending a single governance unit to solve global collective-action problems—because of global impacts—needs to be seriously rethought."

Elinor Ostrom, "Polycentric Systems for Coping with Collective Action and Global Environmental Change," *Global Environmental Change* 20, no. 4 (October 2010): 552.

8. See Elinor Ostrom, "Decentralization and Development: The New Panacea," in *Challenges to Democracy: Ideas, Involvement and Institutions*, ed. Keith Dowding, James Hughes, and Helen Margetts (New York: Palgrave, 2001), 253.

9. Mitrany, *Working Peace System*, 20.

10. Mitrany, *Working Peace System*, 38. We explain this argument further in chapter 6.

11. Ernst B. Haas, *The Uniting of Europe: Political, Social, and Economic Forces, 1950–1957* (Stanford, CA: Stanford University Press, 1958), xiii.

12. Mitrany, "Functional Approach," 360.

13. We are not the first to suggest a multiscalar design for the governance of planetary issues. In climate change governance, for instance, multiscalar approaches are commonly prescribed. Polycentric governance, promoted by Ostrom and others, and "global experimentalist governance," recommended by Sabel and Victor, to take two prominent models, are both explicitly multiscalar in design. Rockström and colleagues' notion of "planetary stewardship" entails innovation at the global and local levels, which is meant to be interlinked and cooperative. More generally, Habermas suggests a multiscalar system to govern the "pluralist world society." On polycentric governance, see Ostrom, "Polycentric Systems for Coping"; and Andrew Jordan et al., eds., *Governing Climate Change: Polycentricity in Action?* (Cambridge: Cambridge University Press, 2018). On experimentalist governance, see Charles F. Sabel and David G. Victor, *Fixing the Climate: Strategies for an Uncertain World* (Princeton, NJ: Princeton University Press, 2022). On planetary stewardship, see Johan Rockström and Mattias Klum, *Big World, Small Planet: Abundance within Planetary Boundaries* (New Haven, CT: Yale University Press, 2015); Will Steffen et al., "The Anthropocene: From Global Change to Planetary Stewardship," *Ambio* 40, no. 7 (November 2011): 739–61. Jürgen Habermas, "A Political Constitution for the Pluralist World Society?," *Journal of Chinese Philosophy* 40, no. S1 (December 2013): 226–38.

14. For background on Althusius and political thought in his time, see Frederick S. Carney, introduction to *The Politics of Johannes Althusius: An Abridged Translation of the Third Edition of "Politica Methodice Digesta, Atque Exemplis Sacris,"* trans. Frederick S. Carney (Boston: Beacon, 1964),

xiii–xxxvii; Andreas Føllesdal, "Survey Article: Subsidiarity," *Journal of Political Philosophy* 6, no. 2 (June 1998): 200–203; and Nadia Urbanati, "Subsidiarity and the Challenge to the Sovereign State," in *Forms of Pluralism and Democratic Constitutionalism*, ed. Jean Cohen, Andrew Arato, and Astrid von Busekist (New York: Columbia University Press, 2018), 197–98.

15. Johannes Althusius, "Preface to the Third Edition (1614)," in *Politics of Johannes Althusius*, 10.

16. Johannes Althusius, *Politics Methodically Set Forth*, in *Politics of Johannes Althusius*, 43 and 68.

17. Althusius, *Politics of Johannes Althusius*, 116.

18. Althusius, *Politics of Johannes Althusius*, 68; and Althusius as quoted in Thomas O. Hueglin, *Early Modern Concepts for a Late Modern World: Althusius on Community and Federalism* (Waterloo, Ontario: Wilfrid Laurier University Press, 1999), 42.

19. Ketteler quoted in Martin O'Malley, "Currents in Nineteenth-Century German Law, and Subsidiarity's Emergence as a Social Principle in the Writings of Wilhelm Ketteler," *Journal of Law, Philosophy and Culture* 2, no. 1 (Spring 2008): 51.

20. Ketteler quoted in O'Malley, "Currents in Nineteenth-Century German Law," 49–50. Ketteler took this principle very seriously: following it "to its last consequence," he demanded that both Protestants and Catholics "have the right to educate their children as Protestants and Catholics" and even defended "the awful right of the unbeliever to educate his children in ignorance of religion."

21. Otto von Gierke, *The Development of Political Theory*, trans. Bernard Freyd (New York: Norton, 1939), 11. The book's original title was *Johannes Althusius and the Development of Natural Rights Based Political Theory*.

22. Gierke, *Development of Political Theory*, 257.

23. Gierke, *Development of Political Theory*, 331.

24. Leo XIII, *Rerum novarum*, May 15, 1891, no. 1, https://www.vatican.va/content/leo-xiii/en/encyclicals/documents/hf_l-xiii_enc_15051891_rerum-novarum.html. For background, see Joseph Boyle, "*Rerum novarum* (1891)," in *Catholic Social Teaching: A Volume of Scholarly Essays*, ed. Gerard V. Bradley and E. Christian Brugger (New York: Cambridge University Press, 2019), 69–89; and Urbanati, "Subsidiarity and the Challenge," 199.

25. Leo XIII quoted in M. C. Mirow, "*Rerum Novarum*: New Things and Recent Paradigms of Property Law," *University of the Pacific Law Review* 47, no. 2 (January 2016): 191.

26. Leo XIII, *Rerum novarum*, no. 14.

27. Leo XIII, *Rerum novarum*, no. 30.

28. Pius XI, *Quadragesimo anno*, May 15, 1931, no. 80, https://www
.vatican.va/content/pius-xi/en/encyclicals/documents/hf_p-xi_enc_
19310515_quadragesimo-anno.html. The term *subsidiarity* comes from
the Latin for "to assist," *subsidium*. As Gregg points out, the word's literal
meaning feeds into the concept: "Assistance means precisely that: to *help*
a person or a group rather than take over his or the group's activities by
making the choices that fulfill the duties remote from the person or group
to whom those responsibilities properly belong." Samuel Gregg, "*Quadragesimo anno* (1931)," in Bradley and Brugger, *Catholic Social Teaching*, 100.

29. Pius XI, *Quadragesimo anno*, no. 79.

30. Pius XI, *Quadragesimo anno*, no. 78.

31. Pius XI, *Quadragesimo anno,* no. 80.

32. Our interpretation of *Quadragesimo anno* draws from Gregg,
"*Quadragesimo anno* (1931)"; and Urbanati, "Subsidiarity and the Challenge," 199–201.

33. Urbanati, "Subsidiarity and the Challenge," 199. It is no surprise
that the three leading figures in the European Community's founding—
Germany's Konrad Adenauer, Italy's Alcide De Gasperi, and France's
Robert Schuman—were all Catholics and Christian Democrats. Moreover,
they self-consciously understood the projects of European integration and
Christian Democracy as linked. As Adenauer wrote to Schuman in 1951: "I
hold it as a particularly favorable and perhaps even providential sign that
all the weight of the tasks to accomplish falls on the shoulders of men who,
like you, our common friend President De Gasperi and myself, are pene-
trated by the desire to establish the European edifice on Christian foundations." Quoted in Carlo Invernizzi Accetti, *What Is Christian Democracy?
Politics, Religion and Ideology* (New York: Cambridge University Press,
2019), 135. See also Jan-Werner Müller, *Contesting Democracy: Political Ideas
in Twentieth-Century Europe* (New Haven, CT: Yale University Press, 2011),
141.

34. Dahrendorf quoted in Ken Endo, "The Principle of Subsidiarity:
From Johannes Althusius to Jacques Delors," *Hokkaido Law Review* 44, no.
6 (March 1994): 2019, https://eprints.lib.hokudai.ac.jp/dspace/bitstream/
2115/15558/1/44(6)_p652-553.pdf.

35. Mark Mazower, *Governing the World: The History of an Idea, 1815 to the
Present* (New York: Penguin, 2013), 406–9. The motivation behind Spinel-

li's support for including subsidiarity in EC proposals for further European integration, some suspect, was to mollify skeptics' fears of centralization while actually pursuing increased centralization. The conjecture is that subsidiarity was intended as a fig leaf of limits on some European powers within a broader project of increasing the proposed EU's overall authority. Endo, "Principle of Subsidiarity," 2016n19 and 2009.

36. Delors's awareness of subsidiarity may have come from his French Catholic upbringing or from the advice of his advisers. (See Endo, "Principle of Subsidiarity," 2007n56; and Michael Burgess, *Federalism and the European Union: The Building of Europe, 1950–2000* [London: Routledge, 2000], 231.) Either way, the principle fit well with both his political and his religious commitments, rooted in the Catholic tradition of personalism. "Subsidiarity," according to Delors, "is not simply a limit to intervention by a higher authority *vis-a-vis* a person or community in a position to act itself, it is also an obligation for this authority to act *vis-a-vis* this person or this group to see that it is given the means to achieve its ends." The "essential objective" for him was "the development of each individual." Delors quoted in Endo, "Principle of Subsidiarity," 2003–2002 (pagination backwards because this English article is in a Japanese journal).

37. Endo, "Principle of Subsidiarity," 2005–2004.

38. Treaty on European Union (Maastricht Treaty), February 7, 1992, *Official Journal of the European Communities* C 191/1 (1992), preamble and art. 3b.

39. John Major quoted in Robert Frederick Jonasson, "The Political Uses of Subsidiarity: From Thomas Aquinas to Thomas Courchene" (PhD diss., University of Western Ontario, 2000), 153. See the general discussion on these divergent interpretations in Jonasson, "Political Uses of Subsidiarity," 151–54.

40. Jonasson, "Political Uses of Subsidiarity," 143.

41. Jonasson, "Political Uses of Subsidiarity," 140–42.

42. Alexander Mackenzie Stuart quoted in Jonasson, "Political Uses of Subsidiarity," 141.

43. Treaty of Amsterdam Amending the Treaty on European Union, the Treaties Establishing the European Communities and Certain Related Acts, October 2, 1997, *Official Journal of the European Communities* C 340 (1997), Protocol on the Application of the Principles of Subsidiarity and Proportionality, para. 5.

44. Treaty of Amsterdam, Protocol on the Application of the Principles of Subsidiarity and Proportionality, para. 3.

45. Treaty of Lisbon Amending the Treaty on European Union and the Treaty Establishing the European Community, December 13, 2007, *Official Journal of the European Union* C 306 (2007), art. 3b (our italics).

46. Nevertheless, an objection from a national parliament doesn't necessarily stop legislation from moving forward. See Philipp Kiiver, "The Treaty of Lisbon, the National Parliaments and the Principle of Subsidiarity," *Maastricht Journal of European and Comparative Law* 15, no. 1 (March 2007): 77–83.

47. One 2019 poll found that of all the negative characteristics that the survey asked about, such as intrusiveness and inefficiency, more respondents stated that the EU was out of touch and doesn't understand the needs of its citizens (62 percent) than anything else. Richard Wike, Janell Fetterolf, and Moira Fagan, "Europeans Credit EU with Promoting Peace and Prosperity, but Say Brussels Is Out of Touch with Its Citizens," Pew Research Center, March 19, 2019, https://www.pewresearch.org/global/2019/03/19/europeans-credit-eu-with-promoting-peace-and-prosperity-but-say-brussels-is-out-of-touch-with-its-citizens/.

48. To one critic, the EU is "an anti-subsidiarity machine." Dominic Burbidge, "The Inherently Political Nature of Subsidiarity," *American Journal of Jurisprudence* 62, no. 2 (December 2017): 153.

49. In other words, we must understand how subsidiarity, in Gareth Davies's searing terms, came to serve "primarily as a masking principle, presenting a centralizing polity in a decentralizing light." Gareth Davies, "Subsidiarity: The Wrong Idea, in the Wrong Place, at the Wrong Time," *Common Market Law Review* 43, no. 1 (February 2006): 77.

50. See Deborah Z. Cass, "The Word That Saves Maastricht? The Principle of Subsidiarity and the Division of Powers within the European Community," *Common Market Law Review* 29, no. 6 (December 1992): 1107–36.

51. Davies, "Subsidiarity," 67–68.

52. This assumption might work in the Catholic Church, but it does not travel to other complex organizations. See Davies, "Subsidiarity," 78; Accetti, *What Is Christian Democracy?*, 127–28.

53. Treaty on European Union, art. 5(3).

54. Markus Jachtenfuchs and Nico Krisch, "Subsidiarity in Global Governance," *Law and Contemporary Problems* 79, no. 2 (2016): 13.

55. As Davies, "Subsidiarity," 72, points out, EU competences are defined by objectives, not activities to be regulated.

56. Jachtenfuchs and Krisch, "Subsidiarity in Global Governance," 8.

57. Davies, "Subsidiarity," 64. No surprise, then, that the Court of Justice has never found the EU in violation of the principle of subsidiarity. Burbidge, "Inherently Political Nature," 152.

58. More charitably, some argue that the European centralizers hoped that the process of centralization would itself *create* consensus and a shared European identity—a sort of "fake it till you make it" theory of governance and legitimacy. Adrian Pabst, "The Concept of New Democratic Legitimacy and the Future of the European Union," *Outlines of Global Transformations: Politics, Economics, Law* 10, no. 1 (2017): 13–32.

59. Mitrany, "Functional Approach," 357.

60. See Trevor Latimer, "The Principle of Subsidiarity: A Democratic Reinterpretation," *Constellations* 25, no. 4 (December 2018): 586–601.

61. Burbidge, "Inherently Political Nature," 154; and N. W. Barber, "The Limited Modesty of Subsidiarity," *European Law Journal* 11, no. 3 (May 2005): 318.

62. See Jachtenfuchs and Krisch, "Subsidiarity in Global Governance," 21.

63. In this way, we build on a central insight from functionalist theory—that the form of authority should follow the function it is tasked with governing—without embracing its teleological baggage (the idea that integration will inevitably lead to more integration).

64. Cash et al., "Scale and Cross-scale Dynamics."

65. Jachtenfuchs and Krisch, "Subsidiarity in Global Governance," esp. 8 and 24.

66. John XXIII, *Pacem in Terris*, April 11, 1963, para. 137, quoted in Accetti, *What Is Christian Democracy?*, 132.

67. See Accetti, *What Is Christian Democracy?*, 131–38, esp. 137.

68. Matching political boundaries to "natural" boundaries is not a new idea. In the late nineteenth century, John Wesley Powell, the famed explorer and second director of the US Geological Survey, recommended that the borders of states in the American West should follow the shape of watersheds. See Korena Di Roma Howley, "Green and Grand: John Wesley Powell and the West That Wasn't," *Eos*, May 23, 2019, https://doi.org/10.1029/2019EO124111. Yet for an argument that even scales as seemingly natural as watersheds are socially and political constructed, see Alice

Cohen, "Rescaling Environmental Governance: Watersheds as Boundary Objects at the Intersection of Science, Neoliberalism, and Participation," *Environment and Planning A: Economy and Space* 44, no. 9 (September 2012): 2207–24.

69. Adriana Erthal Abdenur, *What Can Global Governance Do for Forests? Cooperation and Sovereignty in the Amazon* (New York: United Nations University, 2022), 19; and Paul Martin et al., "Governance and Metagovernance Systems for the Amazon," *Review of European, Comparative and International Environmental Law* 31, no. 1 (April 2022): 126–39.

70. Determining the boundaries of such a unit, however, is no simple thing. Should it be defined by hydrographical criteria? Ecological criteria? Biogeographical criteria? Moreover, a planetary perspective reveals the importance of intertwined systems in maintaining life and the conditions for life in specific environments. In the case of the Amazon, for example, the luxuriant plant life is fertilized by nutrient-rich dust that travels thousands of miles by wind from the Sahara Desert in North Africa. Should Saharan dust be a subject of Amazonian governance? Developing governance units that can manage such spatial and temporal complexity is a major challenge. H. D. Eva and O. Huber, eds., *A Proposal for Defining the Geographical Boundaries of Amazonia* (Luxembourg: Office for Official Publications of the European Communities, 2005); J. Besl, "Africa's Earth, Wind, and Fire Keep the Amazon Green," *Eos*, March 23, 2022, https://doi.org/10.1029/2022EO220151.

71. Subsidiarity, as our history traced, is especially salient during periods of institutional transformation. See also Føllesdal, "Survey Article," 191.

72. Paolo G. Carozza, "The Problematic Applicability of Subsidiarity to International Law and Institutions," *American Journal of Jurisprudence* 61, no. 1 (June 2016): 53.

73. The term *subsidiarity assembly* and many of our ideas for it come from Latimer, "Principle of Subsidiarity," 594–98. Units should also be able to voluntarily transfer decision rights to other scales, but we suspect that an adjudication body will still be necessary.

74. Michael Zürn, *A Theory of Global Governance: Authority, Legitimacy, and Contestation* (New York: Oxford University Press, 2018), identifies the current global governance system's lack of a meta-authority as a source of its legitimation problem.

75. Ihnji Jon, "Scales of Political Action in the Anthropocene: Gaia,

Networks, and Cities as Frontiers of Doing Earthly Politics," *Global Society* 34, no. 2 (October 2019): 167.

76. In place of an assembly, we could imagine a court serving as the meta-authority for subsidiarity, but we favor an assembly specifically because it is more political. On participatory and deliberative democracy, see James S. Fishkin, *When the People Speak: Deliberative Democracy and Public Consultation* (New York: Oxford University Press, 2009); John S. Dryzek, *Foundations and Frontiers of Deliberative Governance* (New York: Oxford University Press, 2010); and Hélène Landemore, *Open Democracy: Reinventing Popular Rule for the Twenty-First Century* (Princeton, NJ: Princeton University Press, 2020).

77. A point made well by Amartya Sen, *The Idea of Justice* (Cambridge, MA: Harvard University Press, 2009).

78. See Sabel and Victor, *Fixing the Climate*.

79. Sarah Dry, *Waters of the World: The Story of the Scientists Who Unraveled the Mysteries of Our Oceans, Atmosphere, and Ice Sheets and Made the Planet Whole* (Chicago: University of Chicago Press, 2019), 253, discusses the invention of global average temperature as a metric.

80. Liesbet Hooghe and Gary Marks, *Multi-level Governance and European Integration* (Oxford: Rowman and Littlefield, 2001), 5.

81. This does not mean that we think, following the international relations theorist Alexander Wendt, that a world state is inevitable. The logic of shifting authority could lead in numerous directions, not just a unitary world state. See Alexander Wendt, "Why a World State Is Inevitable," *European Journal of International Relations* 9, no. 4 (December 2003): 491–542.

82. John B. Goodman, "The Politics of Central Bank Independence," *Comparative Politics* 23, no. 3 (April 1991): 329–49.

83. A formulation we draw from Liesbet Hooghe and Gary Marks, *Community, Scale, and Regional Governance: A Postfunctionalist Theory of Governance*, vol. 2 (New York: Oxford University Press, 2016), 1.

84. See Andreas Wimmer, "Worlds without Nation-States: Five Scenarios for the Very Long Term," *Nations and Nationalism* 27, no. 2 (April 2021): 309–24. Classic studies on the relationship between nationalism and social, economic, cultural, political, and technological conditions include Benedict Anderson, *Imagined Communities: Reflections on the Origin and Spread of Nationalism*, rev. ed. (London: Verso, 1991); and Eugen Weber, *Peasants into Frenchmen: The Modernization of Rural France, 1870–1914* (Stanford, CA: Stanford University Press, 1976). We make these claims

fully aware of nationalism's endurance over the past centuries. Prior predictions of nationalism's obsolescence—like the wildly mistaken assessment by leading scholar of the ideology Hans Kohn in 1937 (!) that nationalism "seems today at the climax of its historical development"—have thus far been proven wrong, but we remain convinced that over the *longue durée* it will surely be replaced. Hans Kohn, "The Twilight of Nationalism?," *American Scholar* 6, no. 3 (Summer 1937): 266.

85. Erving Goffman, *The Presentation of Self in Everyday Life* (New York: Anchor Books, 1959).

86. For example, Daniel N. Posner, *Institutions and Ethnic Politics in Africa* (New York: Cambridge University Press, 2005).

87. David Mitrany, *The Progress of International Government* (London: Allen and Unwin, 1933), 140.

88. There are numerous available ratings and rankings, each of them flawed but still offering a heuristic. For example, Freedom House currently rates 43 percent of states as "Free," while the Economist Intelligence Unit judges that 43 percent of states (home to 45 percent of the world population) are full or flawed democracies. See Yana Gorokhovskaia, Adrian Shahbaz, and Amy Slipowitz, *Freedom in the World 2023: Marking 50 Years in the Struggle for Democracy* (Washington, DC: Freedom House, 2023), 1, https://freedomhouse.org/sites/default/files/2023-03/FIW_World_2023 _DigtalPDF.pdf; and Economist Intelligence Unit, *Democracy Index 2022: Frontline Democracy and the Battle for Ukraine* (London: Economist Intelligence), 3, https://pages.eiu.com/rs/753-RIQ-438/images/DI-final-version -report.pdf.

Chapter 5

1. Gemma Holliani Cahya, "Climate Change Cause of Greater Jakarta Floods, BMKG Says," *Jakarta Post*, February 26, 2020, https://www.the jakartapost.com/news/2020/02/26/climate-change-behind-2020-floods -that-displaced-thousands-in-jakarta-agency-says.html.

2. It's unclear whether this plan will succeed. See Faris Mokhtar, "Ambitious Plans to Build Indonesia a Brand New Capital City Are Falling Apart," *Bloomberg*, December 4, 2022, https://www.bloomberg.com/news/features /2022-12-05/indonesia-s-new-rainforest-city-president-jokowi-s-nusantara -plans-face-trouble#xj4y7vzkg.

3. Richard Forster, "Jakarta and Rotterdam to Cooperate on Flood Management," *Cities Today*, January 11, 2013, https://cities-today.com/ja

karta-and-rotterdam-to-cooperate-on-flood-management/. See also Patrick J. Ward et al., "Governance of Flood Risk Management in a Time of Climate Change: The Cases of Jakarta and Rotterdam," *Environmental Politics* 22, no. 3 (May 2013): 518–36.

4. On the Connecting Delta Cities Network, see Piet Dircke, Jeroen C. J. H. Aerts, and Arnoud Molenaar, eds., *Connecting Delta Cities: Sharing Knowledge and Working on Adaptation to Climate Change* (Rotterdam: Connecting Delta Cities, 2010); and Kian Goh, "Flows in Formation: The Global-Urban Networks of Climate Change Adaptation," *Urban Studies* 57, no. 11 (August 2020): 2222–40.

5. See Olivia Tasevski, "The Dutch Are Uncomfortable with Being History's Villains, Not Victims," *Foreign Policy*, August 10, 2020, https://foreignpolicy.com/2020/08/10/dutch-colonial-history-indonesia-villains-victims/. Only in 2022 did the Dutch prime minister offer "deep apologies to the people of Indonesia today on behalf of the Dutch government." John McBeth, "Dutch Finally Admit 'Shameful Acts' in Colonial Indonesia," *Asia Times*, February 22, 2022, https://asiatimes.com/2022/02/dutch-finally-admit-shameful-acts-in-colonial-indonesia/. Concerning the implications of colonial history for water management, see Lauren Yapp, "Familiar Waters: Jakarta's Floods as Colonial Inheritance, Dutch Interventions as Postcolonial Challenge," *Explorations* 14 (Spring 2018): 5–17; and Simon Richter, "The Translation of Polder: Water Management in the Netherlands and Indonesia," in *The Oxford Handbook of Translation and Social Practices*, ed. Sara Laviosa and Meng Ji (Oxford: Oxford University Press, 2020), 222–42.

6. Molly Quell, "The Netherlands Is Sinking and Here's Why," *Mother Jones Magazine*, January 19, 2020, https://www.motherjones.com/environment/2020/01/the-netherlands-is-sinking-and-heres-why/; Associated Press, "Indonesia's Capital Is Rapidly Sinking into the Sea," NPR, January 26, 2022, https://www.npr.org/2022/01/26/1075720551/jakarta-indonesia-sinking-into-java-sea-new-capital?t=1646835929551.

7. "Jakarta, Rotterdam to Develop Jakarta Bay," *Tempo*, June 14, 2017, https://en.tempo.co/read/884315/jakarta-rotterdam-to-develop-jakarta-bay.

8. On Jakarta real estate development, see Nashin Mahtani, "Torrential Urbanism and the Future Subjunctive," *e-flux*, September 2020, https://www.e-flux.com/architecture/accumulation/345108/torrential-urbanism-and-the-future-subjunctive/.

9. Ahmed Aboutaleb, "Rotterdam Partners with More Than 100 Companies and Social Organisations to Halve CO₂ Emissions by 2030," C40 News and Insights, January 9, 2020, https://www.c40.org/news/rotterdam-partners-with-more-than-100-companies-and-social-organizations-to-halve-co2-emissions-by-2030/.

10. Trevor Latimer, *Small Isn't Beautiful: The Case against Localism* (Washington, DC: Brookings Institution Press, 2023).

11. Liesbet Hooghe and Gary Marks, "Unraveling the Central State, but How? Types of Multi-level Governance," *American Political Science Review* 97, no. 2 (May 2003): 233–43.

12. By *cities*, we really mean metropolitan areas, which "generally encompass cities together with their adjacent communities that have a high degree of economic and social integration with the city. These adjacent communities represent a commuter belt that generates a daily flow of people into the city and back." The OECD also refers to metropolitan areas as "functional urban areas," a concept that captures the sense in which it functions as a single integrated unit on many dimensions, regardless of formal jurisdictional boundaries. See Lewis Dijkstra, Hugo Poelman, and Paolo Veneri, "The EU-OECD Definition of a Functional Urban Area," OECD Regional Development Working Paper No. 2019/11, July 2019, 22–23. For another approach to a functional definition of cities, see UN Habitat, *What Is a City?* (Nairobi: UN Habitat, 2020), https://unhabitat.org/sites/default/files/2020/06/city_definition_what_is_a_city.pdf.

13. "68% of the World Population Projected to Live in Urban Areas by 2050, Says UN," UN Department of Economic and Social Affairs News, May 16, 2018, https://www.un.org/development/desa/en/news/population/2018-revision-of-world-urbanization-prospects.html.

14. European Commission Joint Research Centre, *Atlas of the Human Planet 2019—A Compendium of Urbanisation Dynamics in 239 Countries* (Luxembourg: European Commission, 2020), 43, https://doi.org/10.2760/014159.

15. Though difficult to calculate precisely, the IPCC estimates that cities produce 71 to 76 percent of global CO₂ emissions from energy use. Karen C. Seto et al. "Human Settlements, Infrastructure and Spatial Planning," in *Climate Change 2014: Mitigation of Climate Change. Contribution of Working Group III to the Fifth Assessment Report of the Intergovernmental Panel on Climate Change*, ed. O. Edenhofer et al. (New York: Cambridge University Press, 2014), 923–1000. On pandemics, see Diego Santiago-Alarcon and

Ian MacGregor-Fors, "Cities and Pandemics: Urban Areas Are Ground Zero for the Transmission of Emerging Human Infectious Diseases," *Journal of Urban Ecology* 6, no. 1 (June 2020): juaa012.

16. Different, yes, but not necessarily harmonious. Inevitably there will be conflicts between the different scales and units. An example of this is now playing out in the Southwest of the United States, where a diminishing Colorado River has set the stage for difficult decisions that must be made, pitting local officials interested in building more housing (where future residents will need water) against watershed managers concerned with availability of water for all parties. The debate is highly acrimonious. See Christopher Flavelle, "A Breakthrough Deal to Keep the Colorado River from Going Dry, for Now," *New York Times*, May 22, 2023, https://www.nytimes.com/2023/05/22/climate/colorado-river-deal.html.

17. On "task-specific, intersecting, and flexible jurisdictions," see Hooghe and Marks, "Unraveling the Central State."

18. One consequence of a functional and dynamic approach to local governance is that existing city boundaries must be reevaluated. Our willingness to break institutions into smaller parts is now apparent. But in the case of urban areas, jurisdictions often need to be made *larger*. Many current institutions for local-scale governance are too geographically constrained, and metropolitan areas are frequently institutionally fragmented. For some issues, the boundaries of local institutions should even extend beyond the geographic limits of urban development, to include the suburbs, exurbs, urban peripheries, and surrounding rural regions and wilderness. See Benjamin Barber, *If Mayors Ruled the World: Dysfunctional Nations, Rising Cities* (New Haven, CT: Yale University Press, 2013), 345. The need to rethink local institutions is especially important in urban areas that span international borders. Transnational metropolises, like El Paso-Juarez and San Diego-Tijuana, are particularly difficult sites to manage, since what is really one functional unit falls in multiple sovereign jurisdictions. They are micro-level manifestations of one of the key problems diagnosed in this book: the mismatch between the scale of challenges and the scale of governance institutions, made worse by negative sovereignty.

19. Paulina Ochoa Espejo, *On Borders: Territories, Legitimacy, and the Rights of Place* (New York: Oxford University Press, 2020), 174.

20. Espejo, *On Borders*, 19.

21. This is even true of local officials in authoritarian systems like China, which regularly dismisses local-level leaders who anger their constituents.

See Yongshun Cai and Lin Zhu, "Disciplining Local Officials in China: The Case of Conflict Management," *China Journal* 70 (July 2013): 98–119.

22. Local experimentation and diffusion are core features of "experimentalist governance." See Gráinne De Búrca, Robert O. Keohane, and Charles Sabel, "Global Experimentalist Governance," *British Journal of Political Science* 44, no. 3 (July 2014): 477–86; and Charles F. Sabel and David G. Victor, *Fixing the Climate: Strategies for an Uncertain World* (Princeton, NJ: Princeton University Press, 2022).

23. Mikael Granberg et al., "Can Regional-Scale Governance and Planning Support Transformative Adaptation? A Study of Two Places," *Sustainability* 11, no. 24 (December 2019): 1–17.

24. See Alex Schafran, Matthew Noah Smith, and Stephen Hall, *The Spatial Contract: A New Politics of Provision for an Urbanized Planet* (Manchester: Manchester University Press, 2020). For a vivid account of the local politics of clean energy, see the ethnography of a Spanish village surrounded by wind turbines in David McDermott Hughes, *Who Owns the Wind? Climate Crisis and the Hope of Renewable Energy* (London: Verso, 2021).

25. Jack Ewing, "A City Where Cars Are Not Welcome," *New York Times*, February 28, 2021, https://www.nytimes.com/2021/02/28/business/heidelberg-cars-environment.html.

26. Liz Koslov, "The Case for Retreat," *Public Culture* 28, no. 2 (May 2016): 359–87.

27. Michele Acuto and Benjamin Leffel, "Understanding the Global Ecosystem of City Networks," *Urban Studies* 58, no. 9 (July 2021): 1758–74.

28. Parag Khanna, "The End of the Nation-State?," *New York Times,* October 14, 2013.

29. Barber, *If Mayors Ruled the World*, 336.

30. Kathryn Davidson, Lars Coenen, and Brendan Gleeson, "A Decade of C40: Research Insights and Agendas for City Networks," *Global Policy* 10, no. 4 (December 2019): 697–708.

31. C40 Cities, *Annual Report* (London: C40 Cities, 2020), 4, https://www.c40.org/wp-content/uploads/2021/11/C40_Annual_Report_2020_vMay2021_lightfile.pdf.

32. Davidson, Coenen, and Gleeson, "Decade of C40," 698; Michele Acuto, "Give Cities a Seat at the Top Table," *Nature* 537, no. 7622 (September 2016): 612.

33. Emelia Smeds and Michele Acuto, "Networking Cities after Paris:

Weighing the Ambition of Urban Climate Change Experimentation," *Global Policy* 9, no. 4 (November 2018): 549–59.

34. Davidson, Coenen, and Gleeson, "Decade of C40," 699.

35. C40 Cities, *The C40 Cities Finance Facility* (London: C40 Cities, 2021), https://cff-prod.s3.amazonaws.com/storage/files/XcWwW0cFyIeI h7O9BKLdq1pYDU5yGFsHgn1w2Q4D.pdf.

36. David J. Gordon and Craig A. Johnson, "City-Networks, Global Climate Governance, and the Road to 1.5C," *Current Opinion in Environmental Sustainability* 30 (February 2018): 35–41.

37. "407 US Climate Mayors Commit to Adopt, Honor and Uphold Paris Climate Agreement Goals," Medium, June 1, 2017, https://medium.com/ @ClimateMayors/climate-mayors-commit-to-adopt-honor-and-uphold -paris-climate-agreement-goals-ba566e260097; "One Year after Trump Decision to Withdraw from Paris Agreement, U.S. Cities Carry Climate Action Forward," C40 News and Insights, June 1, 2018, https://www.c40 .org/news/one-year-after-trump-decision-to-withdraw-from-paris-agree ment-u-s-cities-carry-climate-action-forward/.

38. Fearless Cities, "About," accessed June 30, 2023, https://www.fear lesscities.com/en/about.

39. Fearless Cities, "Map," accessed June 30, 2023, https://www.fearless cities.com/en/map?field_region_tid=All&field_mov_status_tid=All.

40. Matthew Thompson, "What's So New about New Municipalism?," *Progress in Human Geography* 45, no. 2 (April 2021): 321.

41. Gerardo Pisarello, introduction to *Fearless Cities: A Guide to the Global Municipalist Movement*, ed. Barcelona en Comú (Oxford: New Internationalist, 2019), 9.

42. Barber, *If Mayors Ruled the World*, 336–37.

43. Barber, *If Mayors Ruled the World*, xviii.

44. Global Parliament of Mayors, "About Us," https://globalparliament ofmayors.org/.

45. Acuto, "Give Cities a Seat," 612.

46. C40 quoted in Davidson, Coenen, and Gleeson, "Decade of C40," 701.

47. Mike Scott, "Hard-Hit by Climate Change, Winemakers Turn to Sustainability to Ride the Storms," Reuters, September 14, 2022, https:/ /www.reuters.com/business/sustainable-business/hard-hit-by-climate -change-winemakers-turn-sustainability-ride-storms-2022-09-14/.

48. Ulla Ovaska et al., "Network Governance Arrangements and Rural-Urban Synergy," *Sustainability* 13, no. 5 (March 2021): 2952.

49. Scott M. Moore, "The Dilemma of Autonomy: Decentralization and Water Politics at the Subnational Level," *Water International* 42, no. 2 (January 2017): 222–39.

50. Daniel Treisman, *The Architecture of Government: Rethinking Political Decentralization* (Cambridge: Cambridge University Press, 2007), 5.

51. Elinor Ostrom, "Decentralization and Development: The New Panacea," in *Challenges to Democracy: Ideas, Involvement, and Institutions*, ed. Keith Dowding, James Hughes, and Helen Margetts (New York: Palgrave, 2001), 237–56.

52. Treisman, *Architecture of Government*, 6.

53. Ostrom, "Decentralization and Development," 253.

Chapter 6

1. Will Steffen et al., "Planetary Boundaries: Guiding Human Development on a Changing Planet," *Science* 347, no. 6223 (February 2015): 1259855; Linn Persson et al., "Outside the Safe Operating Space of the Planetary Boundary for Novel Entities," *Environmental Science and Technology* 56, no. 3 (February 2022): 1510–21; Lan Wang-Erlandsson et al., "A Planetary Boundary for Green Water," *Nature Reviews Earth and Environment* 3, no. 6 (June 2022): 380–92. Novel entities are "new substances, new forms of existing substances, and modified life forms that have the potential for unwanted geophysical and/or biological effects." Steffen et al, "Planetary Boundaries," 1259855-7.

2. Erman refers to a similar notion as "sufficient stateness." Eva Erman, "Does Global Democracy Require a World State?" *Philosophical Papers* 48, no. 1 (May 2019): 123–53.

3. Our vision for institutional restraint echoes the light-touch global institutions imagined by Christian Democratic theorists in mid-twentieth-century Europe, discussed in chapter 4. More recently, Jonas Tallberg et al., *Global Governance: Fit for Purpose?* (Stockholm: SNS Democracy Council, 2023), 15, 174–75, similarly recommend the creation of "new fully empowered institutions" of global governance, with each focused on a specific issue.

4. The IPCC isn't an ideal model for a planetary institution since it's expressly intergovernmental in name and constitution. Although the governments of the member states do not play a role in editing the IPCC's Assessment Reports, the IPCC's Summaries for Policymakers, produced for each Assessment Report, are edited line-by-line by government rep-

resentatives before approval. Mark Vardy et al., "The Intergovernmental Panel on Climate Change: Challenges and Opportunities," *Annual Review of Environment and Resources* 42 (October 2017): 58–59.

5. See Mike Hulme, "Problems with Making and Governing Global Kinds of Knowledge," *Global Environmental Change* 20, no. 4 (October 2010): 558–64.

6. The IPCC, however, doesn't conduct its own original research. Its mandate, rather, is to reach, assess, and communicate consensus on the state of the art in climate science. See Vardy et al., "Intergovernmental Panel."

7. There are a number of new initiatives beginning to do just this. The nonprofit coalition Climate TRACE, for example, uses "satellite imagery and other forms of remote sensing, artificial intelligence, and collective data science expertise to track human-caused GHG emissions with unprecedented detail and speed." Climate journalist David Wallace-Wells describes this work as part of the "development of a sort of global carbon surveillance state"—a term he doesn't mean pejoratively. We agree with him, though we call it planetary sapience. See "About Climate TRACE," Climate TRACE, accessed June 30, 2023, https://climatetrace.org/about; and David Wallace-Wells, "The Global Carbon Surveillance State Is Coming," *New York Times*, November 16, 2022, https://www.nytimes.com/2022/11/16/opinion/environment/surveillance-state-climate-change.html.

8. Louise H. Taylor, Sophia M. Latham, and Mark E. J. Woolhouse, "Risk Factors for Human Disease Emergence," *Philosophical Transactions of the Royal Society B* 356, no. 1422 (July 2001): 983–89; Kate E. Jones et al., "Global Trends in Emerging Infectious Diseases," *Nature* 451, no. 7181 (February 2008): 990–93.

9. Amesh A. Adalja et al., "Characteristics of Microbes Most Likely to Cause Pandemics and Global Catastrophes," in *Global Catastrophic Biological Risks*, ed. Thomas V. Inglesby and Amesh A. Adalja (Cham, Switzerland: Springer, 2019), 1–20; Stephen S. Morse et al., "Prediction and Prevention of the Next Pandemic Zoonosis," *The Lancet* 380, no. 9857 (December 2012): 1956–65.

10. Taylor, Latham, and Woolhouse, "Risk Factors"; Jones et al., "Global Trends"; Mark Woolhouse et al., "Human Viruses: Discovery and Emergence," *Philosophical Transactions of the Royal Society B* 367, no. 1604 (October 2012): 2864–71; William B. Karesh et al., "Ecology of Zoonoses:

Natural and Unnatural Histories," *The Lancet* 380, no. 9857 (December 2012): 1936–45.

11. Nathan D. Wolfe, Claire Panosian Dunavan, and Jared Diamond, "Origins of Major Human Infectious Diseases," *Nature* 447, no. 7142 (May 2007): 279–83; Jones et al., "Global Trends."

12. Feng Gao et al., "Origin of HIV-1 in the Chimpanzee *Pan troglodytes troglodytes*," *Nature* 397, no. 6718 (February 1999): 436–41; Ignacio Mena et al., "Origins of the 2009 H1N1 Influenza Pandemic in Swine in Mexico," *eLife* 5 (June 2016): e16777, https://doi.org/10.7554/eLife.16777.

13. Andrew P. Dobson et al., "Ecology and Economics for Pandemic Prevention," *Science* 369, no. 6502 (July 2020): 379–81.

14. Jones et al., "Global Trends," 991.

15. Review on Antimicrobial Resistance, *Tackling Drug-Resistant Infections Globally: Final Report and Recommendations*, May 2016, https://amr-review.org/sites/default/files/160518_Final%20paper_with%20cover.pdf; Interagency Coordination Group on Antimicrobial Resistance, *No Time to Wait: Securing the Future from Drug-Resistant Infections*, report to the Secretary-General of the United Nations, April 2019, https://www.who.int/publications/i/item/no-time-to-wait-securing-the-future-from-drug-resistant-infections.

16. Dobson et al., "Ecology and Economics"; Aaron S. Bernstein et al., "The Costs and Benefits of Primary Prevention of Zoonotic Pandemics," *Science Advances* 8, no. 5 (February 2022): eabl4183.

17. Dobson et al., "Ecology and Economics," 380. Further demonstrating the general lack of attention to the capacity of governing institutions to carry out their objectives, Dobson et al. (p. 379) comment that reducing tropical deforestation would "require national motivation and political will," ignoring the necessity of state capacity.

18. Holistic approaches to health include Planetary Health, One Health, and EcoHealth. For a discussion of the similarities and differences between these, see Henrik Lerner and Charlotte Berg, "A Comparison of Three Holistic Approaches to Health: One Health, EcoHealth, and Planetary Health," *Frontiers in Veterinary Science* 4 (2017). See also E. Paul J. Gibbs, "The Evolution of One Health: A Decade of Progress and Challenges for the Future," *Veterinary Record* 174, no. 4 (January 2014): 85–91; Sarah Whitmee et al., "Safeguarding Human Health in the Anthropocene Epoch: Report of the Rockefeller Foundation-*Lancet* Commission on Plan-

etary Health," *The Lancet* 386 (November 14, 2015): 1973–2028; and Samuel Myers and Howard Frumkin, eds., *Planetary Health: Protecting Nature to Protect Ourselves* (Washington, DC: Island Press, 2020). For an analysis of the global health approach that guides the WHO and most other big world health actors, see Andrew Lakoff, "Two Regimes of Global Health," *Humanity* 1, no. 1 (Fall 2010): 59–79.

19. Quote is from Kim Gruetzmacher et al., "The Berlin Principles on One Health—Bridging Global Health and Conservation," *Science of the Total Environment* 764 (April 2021): 142919.

20. As Larry Brilliant, who, among many other things, was a leader the WHO Smallpox Eradication Program, and colleagues put it: "Spillover and outbreaks are inevitable, but pandemics are not." Larry Brilliant et al., "Inevitable Outbreaks: How to Stop an Age of Spillovers From Becoming an Age of Pandemics," *Foreign Affairs* 102, no. 1 (January/February 2023), https://www.foreignaffairs.com/world/inevitable-outbreaks-spillovers-pandemics.

21. For use of "Disease X," see, for instance, "WHO to Identify Pathogens That Could Cause Future Outbreaks and Pandemics," World Health Organization, November 21, 2022, https://www.who.int/news/item/21-11-2022-who-to-identify-pathogens-that-could-cause-future-outbreaks-and-pandemics.

22. Jones et al., "Global Trends"; Katherine F. Smith et al., "Global Rise in Human Infectious Disease Outbreaks," *Journal of the Royal Society Interface* 11, no. 101 (December 2014): 20140950. It is difficult to know, however, whether these findings pointing to an increase in new diseases over time reflect an actual trend or increased monitoring and detection.

23. Jacques Pepin, *The Origins of AIDS* (Cambridge: Cambridge University Press, 2011).

24. To their credit, the founders of the WHO also made gaining knowledge about disease a central mission of the organization. The problem was that they also enshrined state sovereignty in the WHO constitution. Moreover, they assumed that their science-based mission to improve global health transcended politics. The structure of the WHO thus undermined its own pursuit of knowledge by ignoring the politics involved and giving member states an effective veto over information about diseases within their borders. This design problem was compounded by the 2005 revisions to the International Health Regulations, which further restricted the WHO's authority to act autonomously and reasserted the inviolability

of state sovereignty. See Eyal Benvenisti, "The WHO—Destined to Fail? Political Cooperation and the COVID-19 Pandemic," *American Journal of International Law* 114, no. 4 (October 2020): 588–97.

25. For a similar recommendation, see Andy Haines, Craig Hanson, and Janet Ranganathan, "Planetary Health Watch: Integrated Monitoring in the Anthropocene Epoch," *The Lancet: Planetary Health* 2, no. 4 (April 2018): e141–e143; and Bing Lin et al., "A Better Classification of Wet Markets Is Key to Safeguarding Human Health and Biodiversity," *The Lancet: Planetary Health* 5, no. 6 (June 2021): e386–e394.

26. Dobson et al., "Ecology and Economics," 380.

27. To ease data aggregation, the PPA should also promote data standards so that it—and national states—can share data and a framework for sifting signals from noise. For examples of the use of remote sensing to predict and detect disease outbreaks, see Assaf Anyamba et al., "Prediction of a Rift Valley Fever Outbreak," *Proceedings of the National Academy of Science* 106, no. 3 (January 2009): 955–59; Timothy E. Ford et al., "Using Satellite Images of Environmental Changes to Predict Infectious Disease Outbreaks," *Emerging Infectious Diseases* 15, no. 9 (September 2009): 1341–46; and Kasha Patel, "Of Mosquitoes and Models: Tracking Disease by Satellite," NASA Earth Observatory, July 9, 2020, https://earthobservatory.nasa.gov/features/disease-vector.

28. Filippa Lentzos and Gregory D. Koblentz, "Fifty-Nine Labs around World Handle the Deadliest Pathogens—Only a Quarter Score High on Safety," *The Conversation*, June 14, 2021, https://theconversation.com/fifty-nine-labs-around-world-handle-the-deadliest-pathogens-only-a-quarter-score-high-on-safety-161777; Alex de Waal, "Lab Leaks," *London Review of Books* 43, no. 22 (December 2021): 28.

29. The contrast with the development and distribution of the COVID-19 vaccines is instructive. The rapid invention of the COVID-19 vaccines was nothing short of extraordinary. The system of medical innovation worked better than was imagined possible. The problems emerged with vaccine distribution. As of June 13, 2023, 13.42 billion doses have been administered, and 70 percent of the world population has received at least one vaccine dose. These impressive figures, however, mask colossal (and unjust) disparities. Many wealthy countries have large majorities of their populations fully vaccinated. But despite the work of COVAX to address this inequality, people living in poor countries, especially in Africa, have almost no access to the vaccines, with only 30 percent of the residents of

low-income countries having received at least one shot. The consequences of unequal vaccine distribution aren't only an affront to human justice but also an active problem for disease containment. Vaccine nationalism, in short, has prolonged and deepened the pandemic in the very countries that hoarded the vaccine. While the multilateral, voluntary WHO was unable to distribute the COVID-19 vaccines globally, the PPA must be empowered to do so. "Coronavirus (COVID-19) Vaccinations," Our World in Data, accessed June 30, 2023, https://ourworldindata.org/covid-vaccinations? country=OWID_WRL. Highlighting the rapid global development and distribution of COVID vaccines as well as the neglect of the world's poor is Amanda Glassman, Charles Kenny, and George Yang, "COVID-19 Vaccine Development and Rollout in Historical Perspective," CGD Working Paper 607, Center for Global Development, 2022, https:// www.cgdev .org/publication/covid-19-vaccine-development-and-rollout-historical -perspective. For an approach to blunting vaccine nationalism in the existing international system, see Prabhat Jha et al., "A Global Compact to Counter Vaccine Nationalism," *The Lancet* 397, no. 10289 (May 2021): 2046–47.

30. See Tingyang Zhao, *All under Heaven: The Tianxia System for a Possible World Order*, trans. Joseph E. Harroff (Oakland: University of California Press, 2021), esp. 22 and 183. Establishing planetwide units is a key feature of planetary governance, and one that distinguishes it from other approaches that aim to manage planetary issues with new institutions based on cooperation among a small number of national states (for instance, economist William Nordhaus's climate clubs, historian Adam Tooze's G-40 for climate, and philosopher Roberto Unger's coalitions of the willing). In the near term, these proposals are certainly more likely to be built than our idea for planetary institutions, and if they can reduce harm to the planet, we'd support their construction. However, they still fail to face the condition of planetarity and therefore don't create the politics or governing structures at the scale required for the long-term flourishing of humans and the biosphere. William Nordhaus, "Climate Clubs: Overcoming Free-Riding in International Climate Policy," *American Economic Review* 105, no. 4 (April 2015): 1339–70; Adam Tooze, "Welcome to the Final Battle for the Climate," *Foreign Policy*, October 17, 2020, https://foreignpolicy.com /2020/10/17/great-power-competition-climate-china-europe-japan/; Roberto Mangabeira Unger, *Governing the World without World Government* (London: Verso, 2022).

31. As an example of the practical impacts of thinking in terms of the Planetary, Pongsiri et al. argue how the concept of "planetary health can move consideration of multiple benefits, trade-offs, and unintended consequences beyond national boundaries." They observe how US policymakers—not using a planetary lens—tried to reduce domestic greenhouse gas emissions by supporting biofuels, which led Indonesian palm oil producers to clear rainforests for palm cultivation to meet the new demand. This deforestation was detrimental to the human health in the region and released stored carbon into the atmosphere—thus undermining American officials' goal. "A planetary health understanding," the authors conclude, "could have informed early development of [US] mitigation actions and strategies for evaluating policy implementation with a focus on communities most vulnerable and least resilient to the adverse effects on health and wellbeing." Montira J. Pongsiri et al., "Planetary Health: From Concept to Decisive Action," *The Lancet: Planetary Health* 3, no. 10 (October 2019): e403.

32. On UNEP, see Maria Ivanova, *The Untold Story of the World's Leading Environmental Institution: UNEP at Fifty* (Cambridge, MA: MIT Press, 2021). Since the 1990s, scholars and activists have floated various proposals to upgrade and strengthen UNEP by forming a World Environmental Organization. Where our proposed planetary institutions come embedded within a larger structural transformation establishing a general governance architecture principle, namely planetary subsidiarity, the WEO would sit within the existing UN system. See Frank Biermann and Steffen Bauer, eds., *A World Environment Organization: Solution or Threat for International Environmental Governance?* (Aldershot, UK: Ashgate, 2005).

33. The phrase "epistemic operating system" is drawn from Jonathan Rauch, *The Constitution of Knowledge: A Defense of Truth* (Washington, DC: Brookings Institution Press, 2021).

34. James C. Scott, *Seeing Like a State: How Certain Schemes to Improve the Human Condition Have Failed* (New Haven, CT: Yale University Press, 1998).

35. Dr. Suess, *The Lorax* (New York: Random House, 1971), which is yet another product of the early 1970s environmental and planetary moment discussed in chapter 3.

36. One potential way to square the necessity of expertise in planetary governance with the demands for democratic values is found in philosopher Anne Jeffrey's proposal for "limited epistocracy," "rule by a certain kind of

organized body of experts . . . with the political power to make decisions and issue commands in the area of their expertise." Anne Jeffrey, "Limited Epistocracy and Political Inclusion," *Episteme* 15, no. 4 (December 2018): 412–32 (quote from p. 413). Jason Brennan, *Against Democracy* (Princeton, NJ: Princeton University Press, 2016), makes the general case for "epistocracy." For analysis of broad approaches to organizing the relationship between democratic publics and experts, see Alfred Moore, "Three Models of Democratic Expertise," *Perspectives on Politics* 19, no. 2 (June 2021): 553–63.

37. There are, of course, many other forms of knowledge besides the Western scientific one that we emphasize here for use in planetary institutions. Many of these forms of knowledge are necessary for other institutional scales of planetary subsidiarity, especially the local institutions, to function well and legitimately. Local, circumstantial, and experiential knowledges, including ones that emerge from entirely different epistemologies, must inform the governance of smaller scales. But for the governance of the planetary scale, systemic knowledge that can be gained only from certain ways of knowing the world is required. Different forms of knowledge are appropriate for different scales of governance. See Ortwin Renn, *Risk Governance: Coping with Uncertainty in a Complex World* (London: Earthscan, 2008), 281. Scott, *Seeing Like a State*, makes a powerful case for practical knowledge (*metis*) in contrast to technical knowledge (*techne*); while *techne* is invaluable, Scott is doubtless correct that techno-modernity has undervalued *metis*.

38. See Thomas Nagel, "What Is It Like to Be a Bat?," *Philosophical Review* 83, no. 4 (October 1974): 435–50.

39. Andreas Duit and Victor Galaz, "Governance and Complexity—Emerging Issues for Governance Theory," *Governance* 21, no. 3 (July 2008): 311–35.

40. Hanna Fenichel Pitkin, *The Concept of Representation* (Berkeley: University of California Press, 1967), 8–9.

41. Joel Wainwright and Geoff Mann, *Climate Leviathan: A Political Theory of Our Planetary Future* (London: Verso Books, 2018), 29. Where Wainwright and Mann see this prospect as generally menacing, we see it as a positive way forward.

42. See the classic account in Eugen Weber, *Peasants into Frenchmen: The Modernization of Rural France, 1870–1914* (Stanford, CA: Stanford University Press, 1976).

43. Zhao, *All under Heaven*, 9.

44. Zhao, *All under Heaven*, 186.

45. Lorenzo Marsili, *Planetary Politics: A Manifesto* (Cambridge: Polity Press, 2021), 55.

46. It was almost otherwise. As the UN Charter was being drafted in San Francisco in 1945, "it was widely anticipated that individuals, and not just states, would be able to petition the new organization, and even to claim representation within its ranks." Glenda Sluga, *Internationalism in the Age of Nationalism* (Philadelphia: University of Pennsylvania Press, 2013), 89.

47. Margaret E. Keck and Kathryn Sikkink, *Activists beyond Borders: Advocacy Networks in International Politics* (Ithaca, NY: Cornell University Press, 1998).

48. Christopher D. Stone, "Should Trees Have Standing? Toward Legal Rights for Natural Objects," *Southern California Law Review* 45, no. 2 (Spring 1972): 450–501. Stone's article, yet another product of the protean moment of the early 1970s, was promptly picked up and deployed by US Supreme Court Justice William O. Douglas in his remarkable dissent in Sierra Club v. Morton, 405 U.S. 727, 741 (1972). In the years since, a number of legal systems have granted nonhumans not just standing but rights. Enhancing and extending the "rights of nature" is a rapidly evolving aspect of law around the world. In 2008, for instance, Ecuador became the first national state to grant rights to "Nature, or *Pacha Mama*," in its constitution. Constitution of Ecuador, 2008, Art. 71, https://www.constituteproject.org/constitution/Ecuador_2021?lang=en. For more on the Rights of Nature, see Craig M. Kauffman and Pamela L. Martin, *The Politics of Rights of Nature: Strategies for Building a More Sustainable Future* (Cambridge, MA: MIT Press, 2021); Mihnea Tanasescu, *Understanding the Rights of Nature: A Critical Introduction* (Bielefeld: transcript Verlag, 2022); and Elizabeth Kolbert, "Testing the Waters," *New Yorker*, April 18, 2022, 16–20.

49. Bruno Latour, *We Have Never Been Modern*, trans. Catherine Porter (Cambridge, MA: Harvard University Press, 1993), 142–45 (quote is from p. 144). See also https://theparliamentofthings.org/ for proposed operationalizations of Latour's idea. Other important contributions to the question of extending political representation to nonhumans include Robyn Eckersley, "Representing Nature," in *The Future of Representative Democracy*, ed. Sonia Alonso, John Keane, and Wolfgang Merkel (New York: Cambridge University Press, 2011), 98–113; Mihnea Tanasescu, "Rethinking Representation: The Challenge of Non-humans," *Australian Journal of Political*

Science 49, no. 1 (2014): 40–53; and Anthony Burke and Stefanie Fishel, "Across Species and Borders: Political Representation, Ecological Democracy and the Non-human," in *Non-human Nature in World Politics: Theory and Practice*, ed. Joana Castro Pereira and André Saramago (Cham, Switzerland: Springer, 2020), 33–52.

50. Karen Bakker's lively book documents the richness of nonhuman lives and the technologies that have revealed the new level of human understanding. Karen Bakker, *The Sounds of Life: How Digital Technology Is Bringing Us Closer to the Worlds of Animals and Plants* (Princeton, NJ: Princeton University Press, 2022).

51. Frans de Waal, *Chimpanzee Politics: Power and Sex among Apes* (New York: Harper and Row, 1982), 212.

52. Of interest here are also initiatives to represent future generations in governance, such as the Future Generations Commissioner for Wales, which is mandated to advise and assist Welsh government bodies to consider the long-term impacts of their policies. See "Future Generations Commissioner for Wales," accessed June 30, 2023, https://www.futuregenerations.wales/.

53. There is, of course, the extraplanetary realm—stars, other planets, and the space between them—but, as of now, it isn't yet a political arena. If anything, the extraplanetary realm is a place where humans project their political hopes and fears. See Claire Webb, "Worlds beyond Ours," *Noema* magazine, February 18, 2021. One day it might become one (if, for instance, we encounter extraterrestrial intelligent life), but today, planetary politics stops at the High Earth orbit's edge. See Daniel Deudney, *Dark Skies: Space Expansionism, Planetary Geopolitics, and the Ends of Humanity* (New York: Oxford University Press, 2020).

54. Scheuerman argues that many proponents of global democracy are so opposed to the idea of a world state that they fail to notice that their proposals often are quite state-like but under a different name. Perhaps he would say the same of us. William E. Scheuerman, "Cosmopolitanism and the World State," *Review of International Studies* 40, no. 3 (July 2014): 419–41.

55. John Rawls quoted in Scheuerman, "Cosmopolitanism and the World State," 421. Kant's eighteenth-century concerns, moreover, may not carry well to the twenty-first century. As Craig points out, when Kant wrote, the threat of war did not come close to global nuclear annihilation, and planetary problems like climate change were unknown. Thus the status quo of eighteenth-century international politics—namely, the occasional war,

some of which were still rather destructive—was not nearly as dangerous as ours is now. Campbell Craig, "The Resurgent Idea of World Government," *Ethics and International Affairs* 22, no. 2 (June 2008): 141.

56. "It is of the essence of sovereignty," observes Alexander Wendt, "that power and violence can be exercised against non-members without any accountability. Is not *that* 'despotism'? Whether justified or not, to whom is the United States accountable for its recent killing of thousands of civilians in Kosovo, Afghanistan and Iraq? Whatever the accountability problems in a world state might be, they seem far less than those in anarchy." Alexander Wendt, "Why a World State Is Inevitable," *European Journal of International Relations* 9, no. 4 (December 2003): 526.

57. Robert O. Keohane, Stephen Macedo, and Andrew Moravcsik, "Democracy-Enhancing Multilateralism," *International Organization* 63, no. 1 (January 2009): 1–31. More generally, scholars of constitutionalism argue that binding oneself to rules is a mechanism for enhancing, not diminishing, freedom and democracy. Constitution writing, observes Gargarella, is a "purely rational act to ensure future freedom" because constitutions are "the means we use to keep our freedoms intact by preventing the abuses that tempt anyone—ourselves included—with power." Roberto Gargarella, *The Law as a Conversation among Equals* (New York: Cambridge University Press, 2022), 233.

58. Michael Mann, *The Sources of Social Power*, vol. 2, *The Rise of Classes and Nation-States, 1760–1914* (Cambridge: Cambridge University Press, 1993), 55. See Scheuerman, "Cosmopolitanism and the World State," 429; and Erman, "Does Global Democracy Require a World State?," 144–45.

59. On the case for redundancy, see Peter M. Haas, "Addressing the Global Governance Deficit," *Global Environmental Politics* 4, no. 4 (November 2004): 3.

60. There is always a risk that antiplanetary forces take power in planetary institutions, but we can't account for every possibility. The structure of planetary subsidiarity matters here, however. No matter what happens to the politics of planetary institutions, they have only limited authority.

61. For an interesting argument about how technocracy and popular politics have combined forces (though not by political actors we generally endorse), see Christopher J. Bickerton and Carlo Invernizzi Accetti, *Technopopulism: The New Logic of Democratic Politics* (New York: Oxford University Press, 2021).

62. National Research Council, *Public Participation in Environmental Assessment and Decision Making* (Washington, DC: National Academies Press, 2008). See also the treatment of the "transparent" or "inclusive" governance model (which features deliberation and coproduction by representatives from government, business, academia/science, and civil society in framing a problem, producing response options, assessing options, and agreeing on a conclusion) in Renn, *Risk Governance*, esp. 273–83.

63. On citizens' assemblies, see, for example, Hélène Landemore, *Open Democracy: Reinventing Popular Rule for the Twenty-First Century* (Princeton, NJ: Princeton University Press, 2020). Proposals for global citizens' assemblies have been put forward by John S. Dryzek, André Bächtiger, and Karolina Milewicz, "Toward a Deliberative Global Citizens' Assembly," *Global Policy* 2, no. 1 (January 2011): 33–42; and John S. Dryzek et al., "Global Citizen Deliberation on Genome Editing," *Science* 369, no. 6510 (September 2020): 1435–37. Efforts to convene a Global Citizens' Assembly on Genome Editing are underway; see https://www.globalca.org/. And a virtual global assembly on climate change was held in 2021 and presented the results of its deliberations to COP26; see https://globalassembly.org/.

64. Zhao, *All under Heaven*, 253.

65. Paul C. Stern, "Design Principles for Global Commons," *International Journal of the Commons* 5, no. 2 (August 2011): 222.

Conclusion

1. W. H. Auden, "New Year Letter," in *Collected Poems*, ed. Edward Mendelson (New York: Vintage, 1991), 226, 207, 199.

2. Auden, "New Year Letter," 207–8.

3. On "New Year Letter," see Edward Mendelson, *Early Auden, Later Auden: A Critical Biography* (Princeton, NJ: Princeton University Press, 2017), 427–54.

4. Charles H. Langmuir and Wally Broecker, *How to Build a Habitable Planet: The Story of Earth from the Big Bang to Humankind*, 2nd ed. (Princeton, NJ: Princeton University Press, 2012), 593–94.

5. Achille Mbembe, "How to Develop a Planetary Consciousness," *Noema* magazine, January 11, 2023, https://www.noemamag.com/how-to-develop-a-planetary-consciousness/.

6. Adam Frank, David Grinspoon, and Sara Walker, "Intelligence as a Planetary Scale Process," *International Journal of Astrobiology* 21, no. 2

(April 2022): 12. See also Timothy M. Lenton and Bruno Latour, "Gaia 2.0," *Science* 361, no. 6407 (September 2018): 1066–68; and Benjamin H. Bratton, *The Terraforming* (Moscow: Strelka Press, 2019).

7. On the role of education in making national citizens, see, for instance, Eugen Weber, *Peasants into Frenchmen: The Modernization of Rural France, 1870–1914* (Stanford, CA: Stanford University Press, 1976).

8. Sharon L. Deem, Kelly E. Lane-deGraaf, and Elizabeth A. Rayhel, *Introduction to One Health: An Interdisciplinary Approach to Planetary Health* (Hoboken, NJ: John Wiley and Sons, 2019).

9. Similarly, Büscher and Fletcher call for "deeper, more numerous and more radical connections between the sciences, particularly those natural and social sciences dedicated to the big environmental questions of our time.... We want to ... [focus] in particular on generating engaged and effective *political* alliances." Bram Büscher and Robert Fletcher, *The Conservation Revolution: Radical Ideas for Saving Nature beyond the Anthropocene* (London: Verso, 2020), 133 (italics in original).

10. Michael Cabanatuan, "BART-to-SFO Work Delayed / Squashed Endangered Garter Snake Quashes Progress on Extension," May 11, 2002, https://www.sfgate.com/bayarea/article/BART-to-SFO-work-delayed-Squashed-endangered-2838759.php; Andrew Lakoff, "The Zone of Entrainment," *Limn* 7 (July 2016), https://limn.it/articles/the-zone-of-entrainment/.

11. C40 Cities, "Funders & Partners," https://www.c40.org/funders-partners/.

12. See, for example, Nadia Urbanati, "Subsidiarity and the Challenge to the Sovereign State," in *Forms of Pluralism and Democratic Constitutionalism*, ed. Jean Cohen, Andrew Arato, and Astrid von Busekist (New York: Columbia University Press, 2018), 187–210.

13. Declaration of the Rights of Man and of the Citizen of 1789, https://www.elysee.fr/en/french-presidency/the-declaration-of-the-rights-of-man-and-of-the-citizen.

14. Quoted in Benedict Anderson, *Imagined Communities: Reflections on the Origin and Spread of Nationalism*, rev. ed. (London: Verso, 1991), 20.

15. Stephen D. Krasner, *Sovereignty: Organized Hypocrisy* (Princeton, NJ: Princeton University Press, 1999).

16. Abram Chayes and Antonia Handler Chayes, *The New Sovereignty: Compliance with International Regulatory Agreements* (Cambridge, MA: Harvard University Press, 1995), 26–27. See also Slaughter's conception

of sovereignty as "relational . . . , in the sense that it describes a capacity to engage rather than a right to resist," in Anne-Marie Slaughter, *A New World Order* (Princeton, NJ: Princeton University Press, 2004), 268.

17. Tingyang Zhao, *All under Heaven: The Tianxia System for a Possible World Order*, trans. Joseph E. Harroff (Oakland: University of California Press, 2021), 22.

18. Daniel Deudney, "Global Village Sovereignty: Intergenerational Sovereign Publics, Federal-Republican Earth Constitutions, and Planetary Identities," in *The Greening of Sovereignty in World Politics*, ed. Karen T. Liftin (Cambridge, MA: MIT Press, 1998), 303, 312. See, also, the other essays in Liftin, *Greening of Sovereignty*; and Robyn Eckersley, *The Green State: Rethinking Democracy and Sovereignty* (Cambridge, MA: MIT Press, 2004), esp. 203–40. Deudney's conception of sovereignty leads him to endorse a "federal-republican Earth constitution," which is different from our view of planetary institutions but similarly avoids the creating of a world state. "An Earth constitution," he argues, "would not require and would not be consistent with a centralized and hierarchical world state or government, because such an entity would amplify the power of one group of the living members of the sovereign intergenerational public not only against future members of the sovereign entity, but against living ones as well." Deudney, "Global Village Sovereignty," 312.

19. Isaiah Berlin, "Two Concepts of Liberty," in *Liberty*, ed. Henry Hardy (New York: Oxford University Press, 2002), 177, 169.

20. Berlin, "Two Concepts of Liberty," 169.

21. For example, Michael Walzer, "The Moral Standing of States: A Response to Four Critics," *Philosophy and Public Affairs* 9, no. 3 (Spring 1980): 209–29; and Thomas Nagel, "The Problem of Global Justice," *Philosophy and Public Affairs* 33, no. 2 (Spring 2005): 113–47.

22. Hannah Arendt, *The Origins of Totalitarianism* (New York: Harcourt, 1966), 295, 296.

23. A number of analysts conclude, specifically with regard to climate change, that there can be no abatement without the serious reform if not complete dismantlement of global capitalism. That may be the case, but it is not the question posed by our book. See, for example, Naomi Klein, *This Changes Everything: Capitalism vs. the Climate* (New York: Simon and Schuster, 2014); Andreas Malm, *Fossil Capital: The Rise of Steam Power and the Roots of Global Warming* (London: Verso, 2016); and Kim Stanley Robinson, *New York 2140* (London: Orbit Books, 2017).

24. Stewart M. Patrick, *The Sovereignty Wars: Reconciling America with the World* (Washington, DC: Brookings Institution Press, 2017).

25. Joel Wainwright and Geoff Mann, *Climate Leviathan: A Political Theory of Our Planetary Future* (London: Verso Books, 2018); Ross Mittiga, "Political Legitimacy, Authoritarianism, and Climate Change," *American Political Science Review* 116, no. 3 (August 2022): 998–1011.

26. For recommendations for "upgrading interstate cooperation," see Jonas Tallberg et al., *Global Governance: Fit for Purpose?* (Stockholm: SNS Democracy Council, 2023), 171–72. On technological Hail Maries, see Holly Jean Buck, *After Geoengineering: Climate Tragedy, Repair, and Restoration* (London: Verso Books, 2019); and Jonathan S. Blake, "A Messiah Won't Save Us," *Noema* magazine, May 17, 2022, https://www.noemamag .com/a-messiah-wont-save-us/.

27. Milton Friedman, *Capitalism and Freedom* (Chicago: University of Chicago Press, 1982), ix. Of course, the policy alternatives that Friedman nurtured only made many of the planetary challenges more difficult to manage, but his insight is powerful nonetheless.

28. Kim Stanley Robinson, *The Ministry for the Future* (London: Orbit Books, 2020).

29. Much of this exploration is taking place in fictional rather than analytical accounts. See Alexandra Alter, "'We've Already Survived an Apocalypse': Indigenous Writers Are Changing Sci-Fi," *New York Times*, August 14, 2020, https://www.nytimes.com/2020/08/14/books/indigenous-native -american-sci-fi-horror.html. For an important scholarly analysis, see Kyle P. Whyte, "Indigenous Science (Fiction) for the Anthropocene: Ancestral Dystopias and Fantasies of Climate Change Crises," *Environment and Planning E: Nature and Space* 1, nos. 1–2 (March-June 2018): 224–42.

30. Carl Sagan, *Pale Blue Dot: A Vision of the Human Future in Space* (New York: Random House, 1994), 6, 2.

31. Sagan, *Pale Blue Dot*, 6–7.

32. For critiques of such a view, see Émile P. Torres, "Against Longtermism," *Aeon*, October 19, 2021, https://aeon.co/essays/why-longtermism -is-the-worlds-most-dangerous-secular-credo; Alexander Zaitchik, "The Heavy Price of Longtermism," *New Republic*, October 24, 2022, https://new republic.com/article/168047/longtermism-future-humanity-william-mac askill.

Index